Praise for *Spiritual Care First Aid*

"Many people attend church dreaming about the redemptive care they will receive from Jesus one day in the future, while unconsciously diminishing their very own caring potential for others in the here and now. In this book, Cody Sanders offers an easy-to-follow blueprint for a scaffold of communal care by and for congregants that can reinvigorate the weariest church community and beyond."

—**Pamela Ayo Yetunde**, pastoral counselor and author of *Casting Indra's Net: Fostering Spiritual Kinship and Community*

"From a wise pastor and scholar deeply acquainted with current literature in his field and with the human condition comes this thoughtful and practical guide to providing spiritual care. Whether a layperson or ordained minister, a reader will find astute insight for their practices of care for those who need companionship through their suffering and journey toward healing. I commend this as a textbook for seminarians, pastors, and lay ministers. Its reflection on hearing the other is especially well crafted, identifying where a person's story becomes a key resource in the movement toward wholeness."

—**Molly T. Marshall**, president, United Theological Seminary of the Twin Cities

"You may know how to pack a medical first-aid kit, but do you know how to pack a spiritual first-aid kit? Cody Sanders gets specific: words, phrases, beautiful questions, practices to use, and avoiding things done with good intention that often make matters worse. Focusing on strengths and stories, Sanders prepares individuals and teams to hear difficult things, to help immediately while professionals are on the way, and to support healing around life's deep difficulties. *Spiritual Care First Aid* equips us to be the trusted (often untrained) first responders to address the spiritual-care situations that will most certainly come our way. Full of example scripts and practice exercises, *Spiritual Care First Aid* is easily adaptable for classrooms and care teams. The world needs confident and capable people who, with the help of this book, carry spiritually grounded basic skills through this

messy, beautiful world, more prepared to meet those unexpected moments when spiritual first aid is needed *now*."

—**Mindy McGarrah Sharp**, associate professor of practical theology and pastoral care, Columbia Theological Seminary, and author of *Misunderstanding Stories: Toward a Postcolonial Pastoral Theology* and *Creating Resistances: Pastoral Care in a Postcolonial World*

"Cody Sanders is a gifted teacher, pastor, and caregiver, and in this highly useful and lovingly written book, he shares his gifts with us. *Spiritual Care First Aid* exemplifies all the patience, attention, and compassion it explains. It offers practical advice to its readers, along with profound and essential pastoral grounding and orientation. It will be an indispensable pastoral and practical resource for anyone—lay or ordained, novice or expert, in almost any caregiving context—who hopes to care for others in need."

—**Matthew Ichihashi Potts**, Plummer Professor of Christian Morals and Pusey Minister in the Memorial Church, Harvard University

Spiritual Care First Aid

Spiritual Care FIRST AID

An **All-Hands** Approach for Church and Community

Cody J. Sanders

FORTRESS PRESS
MINNEAPOLIS

SPIRITUAL CARE FIRST AID
An All-Hands Approach for Church and Community

30 29 28 27 26 25 3 4 5 6 7 8 9

Library of Congress Control Number: 2024946979 (print)

Cover design: Kristin Miller
Cover illustration: *The Mothers*, woodcut print, Käthe Kollwitz (MET, 62.695.135), sourced from Metropolitan Museum of Art/Wikimedia Commons

Print ISBN: 979-8-8898-3400-7
eBook ISBN: 979-8-8898-3401-4

Dedicated to the congregation of Old Cambridge Baptist Church,
who trusted me to be their pastor for eight wonderful years,
and to my colleagues among the chaplains of Harvard University,
who trusted me to serve as their president.

Serving alongside these compassionate communities
was my great privilege.

CONTENTS

Appendices

ACKNOWLEDGMENTS

So many individuals and communities helped me to hone the insights and practices that eventually became this book. The Unitarian Universalist Church of Davis, California, brought me on staff to help do exactly what this book sets out to do—cultivate a community of care within the congregation in which every member plays a vital part. UUCD was a living laboratory in which we experimented with better and better ways of cultivating caring community together. Old Cambridge Baptist Church of Cambridge, Massachusetts, then called me to be their pastor. I shared eight years with this congregation, where many of the ideas of the book were worked out even further. OCBC exemplifies a church where care and justice are held together in inextricable mutuality. I am grateful to both congregations for their trust in me and for the many ways that insights in this book were shaped and honed by these communities.

I had the great privilege of serving for several years in higher-education chaplaincy simultaneously at Harvard University and at the Massachusetts Institute of Technology. These communities were very much unlike a congregation in the ways caring community was cultivated. What I learned alongside my chaplaincy colleagues and the staff, faculty, and students we served in those institutions helped to shape this book in a way that could prove useful to communities beyond the church. These are communities where people show up bringing the fullness of themselves into connection with one another, sharing both joys and sorrows. And they are communities where a small cadre of professionals cannot possibly provide for all the spiritual care that is needed, where an all-hands approach to caring community is necessary. I'm grateful for all I learned in these institutions that helped to shape this text.

Several institutions have entrusted me to teach pastoral care, counseling, and chaplaincy studies to their students over the years, where many practices in this book were honed in the classroom with incredible groups of students: Andover Newton Theological School; Brite Divinity School; Chicago Theological Seminary; Fordham University; the Center for Chaplaincy Studies and its several partner schools; Columbia Theological Seminary; and my current academic home, Luther Seminary, where I have been warmly embraced into the role of forming students in the theology and praxis of congregational and community care leadership.

Many individuals read and provided feedback on various parts of this book throughout the writing process: Lanny Peters, Jennifer Stuart, C. J. Fowler, Isaac Horwedel, Keith Menhinick, Staci Stought, Zachary Moon, Hollie Holt-Woehl, Brent Newberry, Kelsey Stillwell, and, finally, Meg Hess, who read nearly the entire manuscript in draft form and provided invaluable feedback.

My editor at Fortress Press, Yvonne D. Hawkins, deserves immense thanks for the many ways she expertly guided the publication process and for helping to make this a better book than it otherwise would have been. I am grateful for the ways she immediately saw the usefulness of this text for faith communities and for her encouragement and support along the process of writing and publication.

A special thanks to my partner, Cody VanWinkle, for his support of my work through the years and to our two dogs, who provided constant companionship through many hours of writing: Suzie, my longtime companion and Buddy, who died during the writing of this book. The multispecies home we cultivate makes all my work possible.

INTRODUCTION

We all provide care to others throughout our lives. It is part of the human experience. Likewise, every spiritual community and congregation striving to become a place of compassion and belonging needs people who take the responsibility of caring for others as a serious call, a sacred responsibility. Care is a vital practice of spiritual community.

Care, at its most basic, is concern for another. When we talk about *practicing* care, we are attempting to *operationalize* that concern we feel for the life and well-being of another—to put that caring concern into action. Our caring action can be performed with varying degrees of competence and skill. The aim of this book is to increase your ability to practice care. Practicing *spiritual* care means attending to the fullness of another's life and being—body, mind, and spirit. This involves being interested in the ways that each of those aspects of our lived human experience comprise an integrated whole, each one affecting and informing the other. Being able to practice skillful spiritual care also means honing our skills in attending to the depths of human experience—our grounding connections to the sacred, the holy, the Divine, or God. While not all expressions of spiritual care practice will explicitly attend to this sacred dimension of experience, it is always within the purview of a spiritual caregiver, who pays careful attention to a careseeker's connection to the sacred however it may show up and in whatever religious, spiritual, or philosophical language it appears.

While many forms of care require various levels of professional training and experience to responsibly practice, everyone can become equipped with first aid skills. We should all receive some basic training in giving CPR to someone in cardiac arrest, mouth-to-mouth resuscitation for someone who has stopped breathing, applying pressure to a wound to stop blood flow, or performing the Heimlich maneuver for someone chocking. A person in any of these circumstances may need the care of paramedics, doctors and nurses in an emergency room, and perhaps even surgical intervention in their long-term care. But even in these extreme situations that require sophisticated intervention, being able to provide the basics of first aid can save a life. At other times, all that is needed is the ability to clean a small wound and apply a bandage to stave off infection and let the body's healing work begin. Whether the wound is big or small, the person best positioned to provide first aid is the one who is there with basic skills at the time aid is needed.

Similarly, there are many needs that arise in our lives affecting our spiritual, emotional, and relational well-being. Some of the concerns affecting our integrated spiritual-emotional-physical health may call for the care of a minister with training in theological higher education. Or we may find ourselves in a hospital being cared for by a chaplain with extensive training in clinical pastoral education. Some concerns may be well addressed by a spiritual director, others by a spiritually integrated psychotherapist. But often, before we reach out to any of these spiritual care professionals, we turn to a friend, a family member, a person we know from a book club or Bible study, maybe even a stranger we're sitting next to on a plane—the person who is there when we need help. That's where spiritual care first aid becomes integral in cultivating caring communities

I first encountered the term *spiritual first aid* as developed by Unitarian Universalist minister and Air National Guard chaplain Rev. Julie Taylor.[1] While Taylor develops this framework for helping within the context of disaster and crisis response, I am expanding the concept to describe the ways we can address everyday situations that call for spiritual care. Spiritual care first aid is the accompaniment of someone in need of care at an opportune time using enough skillfulness to be helpful in the immediate term and enough knowledge to direct a person to caring professionals if further support is needed. Spiritual care first aid is frontline, short-term, and employs caring skills that every minister should know and every layperson can learn.

Everyday situations offer several contexts for spiritual care first aid. In a crisis or disaster, spiritual care first aid may provide a one-time, immediate conversation that helps a person become more stable or grounded, companioning them through an initial stage of difficulty, while a professional such as a counselor or physician will pick up the longer-term support. In less crisis-oriented situations, spiritual care first aid might offer accompaniment to someone discerning an important turning point in their life and support them with skills to listen deeply, ask helpful questions, and help them clarify their most important values and aspirations. No more caring support may be needed beyond a conversation or two that helps the careseeker take the next step in their discernment process. Or perhaps a referral to a spiritual director or spiritually integrated life coach may help further the exploration. Spiritual care first aid also may be offered when a mental health concern, abuse, or violence shows up in a community. A spiritual care first aid responder ideally knows enough to recognize the signs that something important needs attention, acts skillfully to support the person in seeking the assistance they need, and is aware of the directions to point that person toward quality care.

Spiritual care first aid is a caring practice that nearly anyone can be trained to perform, and it can be lifesaving. Yet we are not always trained by the ambient lessons of our society and culture to care for others in intentional ways. When someone turns to us for care, we may feel we come up short, not knowing how to provide the basics of caring presence to others. This is true even in many churches. Communities of faith are vibrant and busy places with so much calling for our faithful attention: acting with compassion and justice, creating inspiring beauty in worship, sustaining ministries that enact faith and hope and love within our towns and cities. Cultivating competence in care for one another can continually get pushed down the agenda of the spiritual community's list of concerns.

There are several ways we cultivate a sense of confidence and skill in practicing care with others in our lives and in the faith communities to which we belong. Sometimes we watch others who are especially good at embodying care, and we try to emulate them, learning by example. We may sign up for a workshop on grief or attend a seminar on mental health or read a pamphlet on depression, learning by cobbling together bits of knowledge and skill where and when we can find them. But the art of practicing care within a community of faith is too important to leave to the chance good fortune of having a stellar example to learn from or to haphazard development in a piecemeal fashion. Care within communities of faith is vital, and it is everyone's responsibility—not just the ordained or those called into specialized roles of ministry.

We are all already caregivers in ways we may not even recognize. Think of the people in your life who come to you when they have a problem they want to talk through, or the ones who call you for help fulfilling a need, or those who lean on you for support after experiencing an especially hard time in their life. They may be your parents, children, or siblings. They may be your friends, neighbors, or fellow congregants. You are a caregiver to someone already. We all are. But we exercise our caregiving roles with varying degrees of confidence and competence. This book aims to increase your confidence in embodying the practice of spiritual care and to provide you with a usable toolbox of caregiving skills that you will need along the way.

The book is formed around three components of compassion and care that make up the basic skills of spiritual care first aid: the art of hearing, the skills of helping, and sources of healing. Hearing, helping, and healing are resources of compassion and care that are at once both simple and profound, easy to understand and challenging to practice, already available to us while also inviting us to stretch ourselves toward further growth.

HEARING

Compassionate care cannot be practiced outside of a relationship formed around the practice of deeply hearing another person. This is *the* essential resource for the practice of care. Seems deceptively simple, doesn't it? But how well we listen will determine what we hear. And the breadth of listening tools and techniques we have to draw on will shape how much we are able to hear.

For example, when we listen to another, what are we listening for? Do we listen in order to hear a person's feelings or the content of a story they're sharing? Do we listen most attentively for the problems they're sharing, or do we stay alert for unexpected possibilities to emerge in the story? Are we capable of listening to hear how the presence of the Divine is made palpable in a person's life? Do we listen only for words spoken, or can we hear what silence can say or how the language of a body speaks? And when we commit to listening to another person, how do we communicate that we are really hearing what the person is communicating to us? How do we know we've heard what most needs hearing?

All of these questions should alert us to the fact that listening is both an art and a skill. You know good listening when you experience it, even if you can't always put your finger on what contributes to its quality. This book will help you identify those markers of compassionate listening and careful hearing. No matter your current level of artistry at listening, there are skills that you can improve on to hone your hearing abilities.

HELPING

Every time I train students or congregations in caregiving practices, there is always a restlessness to get beyond the skills of listening and hearing in order to move on to skills useful for actually helping people. Let me assure you up front that deeply hearing people communicate the multiple layers of meaning in their lives *is* helping them. In fact, you cannot really help anyone without the ability to really hear their hurts, their needs, and their longings. Hearing and helping, as well as healing, are all interlocking resources in spiritual care first aid.

And yet I know what students mean when they express an eagerness to get to the helping skills. There are situations that call for care in which a person needs some specific form of help: help working through a problem or reaching a goal, help in the form of material assistance from a faith community, help to move through a particular crisis, or help finding the necessary resources to deal with a tough situation or cope with a crisis.

I invite you to consider the helping practices in this book as resources you can draw on to companion people in gaining stability as they move through shaky ground, to find their footing when the life becomes precarious. Helping is not always synonymous with problem-solving or fixing a situation. Many problems you will encounter with others in caregiving ministry will not have a solution, and profound and meaningful questions will often go unanswered. But that doesn't mean you aren't helping others in those situations.

Yet there are resources for helping in situations that call for care that are important for competent and compassionate caregiving. Having these helping skills available to you can even be lifesaving at times. And as important as they are, the helping skills covered in this book are fairly simple to use. They just take a bit of time and thoughtfulness to develop before you get into a situation in which they are called for. There are also exercises for practicing each skill at the end of every chapter.

HEALING

Healing is a foundational commitment for communities of faith. Healing is fundamental to the practice of spiritual care. And healing is complicated.

Who defines what healing means and for whom? How do we discern when healing has taken place? Which sources of healing are appropriate for a situation that calls for a caring response: meditation or medication, prayer or psychotherapy, soup or surgery, or some combination of multiple sources of healing? What do we do when healing doesn't happen or doesn't happen in the ways we hoped it might?

As a caregiver for and with others, you are an agent of healing. If you are a representative of your congregation as a lay caregiver, you serve as an extension of your church's healing ministry. If you are a pastor or chaplain, you are part of a profession bound up with the healing resources of religious and spiritual traditions. In a theological sense, when your caregiving is rooted in the Christian tradition, you are an incarnational representation of Christ's healing presence with others as well.

Healing will come in multiple forms throughout your caregiving ministry—some anticipated and others a complete surprise. Your role as a caregiver is to become familiar with multiple sources of healing that you can help others draw on when the time is right. You cannot control whether or not healing occurs, but you can prepare to serve as a conduit of care and compassion through which healing comes about in the lives of others.

HOW TO USE THIS BOOK

We are all capable of care. We are all called to care. We will all have the opportunity to practice care with others in our lives. The lessons and practice exercises in this book aim to help you live more fully into your call as a caregiver and to hone your caring capacities in community with others who are on this journey alongside you. At many points in your life, you'll be the one who is there when help is needed. *Spiritual Care First Aid* aims to help you develop the basic skills of care needed to become a helpful and healing presence in the lives of those who need it.

You may be reading this book on your own to develop or hone your caring skills so that you can be more fully present in a healing way to friends, family, and members of your community who look to you in times of trouble. If that is the case, you should find the material in this book helpful. You may wish to move back and forth between chapters to address various skills and situations of pressing interest to you. As you move through the book, keep in mind the complexities of the larger community in which you are embedded—whether a church, friendship network, or community organization of which you are a part. While individual care responders can be of extraordinary assistance in situations that call for spiritual care first aid, care is always practiced within community. Sometimes that community will be an important resource in healing, at other times that community can be a source of harm, and many times it is both. This book will invite you to see yourself as a part of a larger whole and understand how to help others seek the care they need within a network of care.

Others may be reading this book as a part of a community of caring practice—perhaps your church's care team, or volunteers at a shelter or food assistance program, or student leaders in a campus ministry, or lay leaders in a congregation. This book is well suited for group study, and many of the practice exercises you'll find throughout the text will ask you to turn to some of the others who are along on this journey with you to practice the skills you are learning together. The book's layout is amenable to study one chapter at a time over the course of fifteen weeks or so (about the length of a semester). Chapters can also be broken down into smaller parts for use over an even longer stretch of time. Facilitators of spiritual care first aid training groups may assign reading a chapter prior to the group meeting, go over the content of that chapter with the group for the first part of your meeting, and then spend ample time together practicing the skills you are learning together with feedback from more advanced practitioners of those skills.

In whatever ways you use this book, cultivating the vibrant communities of compassion and belonging that we all need and desire requires an all-hands approach to care. That means you! So let your spiritual care first aid journey begin.

NOTES

1 Julie Taylor, “Spiritual First Aid,” in *Disaster Spiritual Care: Practical Clergy Responses to Community, Regional and National Tragedy*, 2nd ed., ed. Willard W. C. Ashley Sr. and Stephen B. Roberts (Nashville: Skylight Paths, 2017), 128–141.

PART ONE

THE ART OF HEARING

1

HEARING WITH COMPASSIONATE PRESENCE AND ATTENTIVE LISTENING

You are currently sitting with the most helpful resource for caregiving that you will ever know. This invaluable resource is you. Your compassionate and caring presence can be a gift to those in the midst of pain, uncertainty, or crisis. A ministry of presence sounds simple, but its effects can be profound for one who is seeking care.

There are many situations that call for our caring response that have no easy (or even complex) solution. There's no problem to solve and no fix we can offer for the painful situation. In conversation with me about the ministry of presence, UCC minister and therapist Jennifer Stuart said, "In times of trauma, research has shown that having someone with you (be it in acute circumstances or chronic)—just the presence of another—can help mitigate the symptoms of PTSD or decrease the damage of terrible life happenings. Truly . . . love can make all the difference—even if it means simply going forward one day at a time."[1]

Even in less traumatic and difficult situations, when we are lonely, feeling sad, experiencing the pain of grief or even just the mundane listlessness that emerges in life, having someone whose presence we can count on as steady and less anxious is a gift. This is what my colleague and pastoral psychotherapist Meg Hess calls *less-reactive functioning*. While our anxiety will inevitably arise at times, the question becomes: How can I best work with it in a way that helps me stay in my own skin and keeps my focus on the other person? We can notice our own anxiety rising without being reactive to it. When we feel our anxiety rising, our listening and attentive presence don't have to be driven by that anxiety. Hess says the questions caregivers can attend to in preparing for those times are these:

- How can I tolerate my own helplessness in the face of such heartache and suffering that I cannot necessarily fix?
- What is my role here that will help me stay in the difficult place of holding the space as I tolerate my own anxiety?
- Is my own drive or desire to be helpful getting in the way of my ability simply to be present with the other in the midst of their pain?[2]

In so many of the situations that call for care in the day-to-day life of a community, this less anxious and reactive ministry of presence is what is most called for. As an educator of leadership, spirituality, and social change, Parker Palmer advises, "No fixing, no saving, no advising, no setting each other straight."[3] As simple as it may sound, it is often difficult to tolerate our own anxiety and put the brakes on our drive to be helpful so that we aren't led into offering quick fixes and easy solutions to situations that require our steady presence with another in the midst of pain. This is the essential foundation for spiritual care first aid.

The power of loving presence is even portrayed in the biblical text in ways we sometimes overlook. Acts 14:19–20 read, "Then they stoned Paul and dragged him out of the city, supposing that he was dead. But when the disciples surrounded him, he got up and went into the city." What is most remarkable about this text is that the factor the author most palpably portrays as serving a healing function for Paul is the surrounding love and concern of the disciples who witnessed his pain and suffering. Lovingly witnessing the suffering of others—even when we can do nothing to fix it or salve their wounds—is a gift. But it takes our own careful self-work to be fully present with another without letting our anxiety push us into trying to fix situations that cannot be fixed or rush toward solutions when what is needed is caring companionship.

Consider this exquisite description of the ministry of presence (and what gets in our way of enacting it) from the great Catholic spiritual teacher Henri Nouwen:

> More and more, the desire grows in me simply to walk around, greet people, enter their homes, sit on their doorsteps, play ball,

> throw water, and be known as someone who wants to live with them. It is a privilege to have the time to practice this simple ministry of presence. Still, it is not as simple as it seems. My own desire to be useful, to do something significant, or to be part of some impressive project is so strong that soon my time is taken up by meetings, conferences, study groups, and workshops that prevent me from walking the streets. It is difficult not to have plans, not to organize people around an urgent cause, and not to feel that you are working directly for social progress. But I wonder more and more if the first thing shouldn't be to know people by name, to eat and drink with them, to listen to their stories and tell your own, and to let them know with words, handshakes, and hugs that you do not simply like them, but truly love them.[4]

In the majority of situations that call for care in a congregation or community of faith, the caring response most called for will be a ministry of presence. Good listening skills can help. But being lovingly present with another in the fullness of their experience without anxiously trying to fix their situation or provide solutions to their problems is a gift that should not be undervalued in the ministry of care.

People may forget what you say to them in a caring conversation. They may completely misquote the eloquent prayer you prayed over them when they recount it to others later on. They may not recall what delicious food you brought to comfort them. But people rarely forget that you were there for them—present with them—in their time of need. This is the ministry of healing presence.

Practice Exercise: Compassionate Presence

How do you experience yourself being invited into other roles (fixer of problems, organizer of solutions) when you are trying to provide a steady, less anxious presence with others? Is it the voice of anxiety that whispers, "You're not being very helpful to this person! Why don't you do something useful?" Perhaps the sadness you sense in the other person's life compels you to try to brighten their day or cheer them up. Or maybe the situation they're dealing with is similar to something you've experienced, and you just want to jump into a problem-solving mode with them to teach them what you did in that situation.

Schedule some time to spend with someone who could use your caring presence—perhaps an elderly person in your congregation who doesn't leave the house much or who is in a nursing home. Try entering that time with them without an agenda, with just a willingness to be present and attentive to that person for an hour or so. While you spend time with them, be attentive to the voices that arise within you, inviting you into other roles like problem-solving or advice-giving or cheerleading.

Just notice these voices and pressures that you experience. Try not to judge yourself for having them. Try not to react to them, either by accepting their invitations or by trying to force them out of your awareness. Acknowledge their presence and then simply turn back toward a ministry of presence with the person in front of you. Simply noticing with awareness how these voices and pressures arise for you in the moment will help you decline their invitation and cultivate your capacity for practicing healing presence with others.

HEARING THROUGH ATTENTIVE LISTENING

Attentive listening, sometimes called *active* listening, *deep* listening, or *reflective* listening, is foundational to compassionate care. It builds on your healing presence by helping to communicate your close attention to the situation a careseeker is living or the story they are trying to tell you. Until you can compassionately listen to and accurately hear what the careseeker is hoping to share with you, the caring relationship will not develop toward helping and healing. In many instances, being fully present with another while actively, attentively, and compassionately listening to what they need to say will be the primary source of healing in the life of the careseeker. I've had experiences in my spiritual care practice in which I've listened carefully to someone for a half hour when they suddenly say, "Oh, I've finally realized what I really wanted to say. Thank you for listening; it helped to clarify what I needed to express." Without an attentive listening presence, they may not have discovered what they most needed to say. The importance of your ability to listen well and to communicate your care and compassion through the act of hearing another cannot be overstated.

Experience-Near Listening

Sometimes when we listen to the story of another person we can listen from an unintentionally self-centered place, filtering their experience through our own personal lens. "Ahh yes, I recognize this story. It's like the time I experienced a very similar circumstance." We can even hold the mistaken idea that we know where the story is going or what a person thinks or feels about a situation that is similar to one we've encountered. It is very important that you practice listening (yes, it requires a lot of practice!) in a way that centers the experience of the careseeker. That is, listening that remains near to the experience of the careseeker.

What we, as compassionate caregivers, are interested in when listening attentively to another is how the careseeker is experiencing *their* life at this time so that we can better understand the situation that led them to reach out for caring companionship. This part of the caring relationship cannot be rushed. We often have the tendency to want to move quickly toward problem-solving or even advice-giving (as unadvisable as that usually is). We must put aside our desire to be seen as wise or skillful and even our yearnings to help solve another's problem. If we can do this, listening in an attentive and reflective way invites the fullness of a person into the caring relationship. Without that crucial step, the relationship is not likely to develop characteristics of compassion and care that can lead toward helping and healing.

As a caring companion to another, you must decenter yourself and bracket your interpretations and opinions, no matter how helpful you believe they may be. Then you will be better able to center the other by deeply listening to the contours and nuances of their particular experience.

Reflective Responses

We almost never listen to another in absolute silence. Our facial expressions (such as the raising of our eyebrows at a surprising turn or mirroring on our face an expression of pain we notice in the other), our body's posture (such as leaning in a bit), and our movement (such as gentle nodding) all communicate that we are attending to another. The small sounds and verbalizations—*ah*, *oh!*, *mmm*—communicate that we're with another in their story. Beyond these microcommunications of face and body and vocalization, our deep and attentive listening to another can be expressed in short statements of reflection on what we are hearing from another.

Importantly, these statements are not interjections of your opinion or wisdom or advice. They are brief, gentle, and tentative reflections on exactly what you are hearing from the other, with ample room to be corrected if the other is hoping for you to hear something different from what you believe you heard. We are aiming for description, not diagnosis. We are leaning into the mystery of another's experience, not developing knowledgeable mastery over their life or their problem. Every reflective statement should be in service to better hearing a person's story.

It can be helpful to practice several ways of opening space for your reflective responses as you listen to another. You might find it helpful at times to ask for a little space to reflect on what you've heard thus far: "I wonder if we could pause for a moment and let me reflect back to you what I'm hearing so that I'm sure I'm paying attention to what you most want to communicate." This can be very helpful when you need to open a little space for reflection so that you can remember the details in a very lengthy narrative that someone is sharing with you.

At other times, these openings for reflective responses come naturally during a conversation, and you may preface your reflective response in a way that communicates that you're about to let the other know what you're hearing from them. For example, "It sounds like what you're saying is . . ." communicates to the other person that this is what you're hearing but also leaves room for them to say more or to correct your understanding of their story.

It is very important that you try to stay close to the language that the other person is using. You don't have to repeat back to them verbatim what you've heard them saying; this can be tedious. But you should strive to use the precise words they are using to describe important aspects of the story: what is happening, how they are feeling, and what they are desiring. Stick close to the careseeker's language rather than paraphrasing important content in your own language. Using the same words or ones that are closely synonymous for the important pieces of the story you are hearing avoids subtly interjecting your own interpretations and misconstruing what is really being said by the careseeker.

Some helpful reflective responses to the story of a careseeker *respond to the content* of what we are hearing in their story. This is perhaps the easiest of the reflective responses we can make to another because it is simply recalling pertinent details in the other's story. The purpose behind these responses is to be sure you're hearing the important details of their story well and communicating that you're with them in the narrative they're developing: "What I'm hearing you say is that there are several ways you are experiencing stress in your life right now: the hectic pace of your work during this season, trying to care for your father through his illness, and supporting your children in their school and extracurricular activities." These responses can stand on their own as a way of tracking the details of a person's story and ensuring that what you're hearing is what the other is intending to communicate. They stick to the facts of the story without developing any interpretations you have about those facts.

Other reflective responses can *respond to the emotions* we are hearing expressed as a careseeker communicates their story or discusses a situation that calls for care: "I hear you when you say that you've been feeling sad and lonely lately. That sounds important, and I want to be sure not to gloss over that experience." Remember to stick close to the careseeker's own language. If they say they feel *sad*, don't reflect back to them that you hear them say they feel *depressed*. These words may mean two very different things to them. If they say, "I'm pretty happy about" don't then reflect back to them, "I hear you say you're feeling overjoyed about." The important purpose of attentive listening is that you communicate what you are hearing from the other, not your interpretations of what you're hearing. Being attentive to the language a careseeker uses is vital in that process.

Still further, we can reflectively *respond to the longings and desires* we hear expressed in another's story: "As you've been telling me this story, you've said a few times that while you have a hard time keeping up with everything going on in your life right now, you'd really like to develop some ways of responding to these stressors in ways that feel more effective to you. Did I hear that right?" These responses reflect what you are hearing in the person's story about the movements they wish to make in their life, the ways they may want something to change about their situation, or the desires they hold for their life or situation being discussed. It is very important to hear exactly what they are desiring or longing for so that you don't unintentionally replace their desires with projections of your own desires onto their story.

In a caring conversation, you may move among responses to the story's content, responses that reflect the emotions people experience about the situation they are describing, and responses that communicate that you are really hearing what they most desire in relation to the situation they are describing. In your practice caregiving conversations, however, it can be helpful to focus on just one of these types of responses at a time and really get good at each of them. Reflectively responding to another as you are deeply listening to their story is harder than it seems and requires our focused and compassionate attention. While we aren't often taught to listen to others in this way in our daily lives, these skills can be practiced and honed over time.

In every reflective response you make as you listen to another, open room for the other to alter or amend or add to what you've reflected back to them. "Did I hear this correctly?" can be a very helpful question to add to your regular caring vocabulary. Always invite the careseeker to correct what you are reflecting if there are nuances you may have missed in their story or if there are ways that you're hearing some parts of their story but not the parts they most want to focus on.

A helpful metaphor once offered by a ministerial student of mine, C. J. Fowler, is that of the caring listener's responses acting like a spotlight on stage, shining a light on what is taking place in the drama of the careseeker's story. Or, alternatively, like being in a sound booth, turning up the volume a bit on some parts of the story by reflecting those back to the careseeker. As you spotlight certain details of a story or emotions you are hearing expressed, always allow the careseeker to direct you toward other parts of the story you may be missing at the time or to ask you to turn up the volume on other parts of the story that you didn't realize were important but that the careseeker wants to be sure you heard.

ATTENDING TO POSSIBILITIES, NOT JUST PROBLEMS

It may not seem like it at first, but even the ways we attend to and reflect on certain parts of a person's story and not others can direct a conversation.

We must be very careful not to spotlight only the things we want to attend to in our reflective responses. Try to place the spotlight on things that you're picking up as important from the careseeker. For example, it can be tempting for a caregiver to attend only to the problems we hear in the story of another and ignore the gifts, strengths, and possibilities we hear expressed alongside those problems. As you are reflecting back what you hear from a careseeker, be attentive to both the problems you hear expressed and the possibilities you pick up on. For example, "You've said a few times how anxious these various sources of stress are for you in your life right now, and they have you feeling like you're all on your own. And I also noticed you say at one point that you're really proud of yourself for how well you've dealt with these concerns while caring for your family, and that has helped you to keep going. Did I catch what you were saying accurately there?"

A person's life is never totally defined by the problem they are facing at the moment. Your attentive, reflective listening should help a careseeker hear reflected back to them that while their problems are very important to attend to, there is also more to their story that you're hearing come through. That type of deep listening to both problems and possibilities will be a gift to those with whom you practice care.

Practice Exercise: Reflective Listening

Find a willing partner—perhaps another person who is also working on developing caring skills—and ask if you can listen to them for a half hour or more in order to practice being a good listener. During this time, practice your skills at responding to what you are hearing without the use of any questions, just attentive listening skills. Practice reflectively responding to what you are hearing, naming the issues and concerns that might arise in the story in the language of the other person, reflecting the emotions you hear the other express about the situation, naming the longings and desires you are picking up, and, of course, using micro-responses like *ah* and *um-hum* to communicate that you are with the person in the story.

After the practice conversation, engage in some reflection on how the other person felt being listened to. Which statements and expressions did they find affirming and validating? Which statements and expressions did they find less helpful? What did they enjoy about the conversation when someone was listening in an attentive and validating way?

FURTHER READING

Miller, James E. *The Art of Listening in a Healing Way*. Fort Wayne, IN: Willowgreen, 2003.

Miller, James E., and Susan Cutshall. *The Art of Being a Healing Presence: A Guide for Those in Caring Relationships*. Fort Wayne, IN: Willowgreen, 2001.

NOTES

1 Jennifer Stuart, email message to author, June 8, 2020.

2 Meg Hess, email message to author, July 19, 2023.

3 Parker Palmer, *A Hidden Wholeness: The Journey toward an Undivided Life* (San Francisco: Jossey-Bass, 2004), 115.

4 Henri J. M. Nouwen, *Gracias* (New York: Harper & Row, 1983), 147–148.

2

HEARING WITH QUESTIONS, ANSWERS, AND SILENCE

Questions can be a cornerstone of spiritual care if a caregiver treats them like an artist's tool. Beautifully formed questions can invite the picture of a careseeker's life to develop gradually over time, with deeper tones and richer texture. Questions can bring forth greater clarity about the careseeker's life, the problem they may be facing, and their hoped-for future. Drawing on the power of questions in this way takes intention and practice.

Questions can also be a hindrance to good spiritual care if a caregiver uses them haphazardly or with no sense of purpose. Careseekers can feel interrogated with rapid-fire questions. Some questions can seem inappropriate. Others can simply feel misplaced or without real purpose. Questions can aid our process of dialogue and understanding, but too many questions, or questions that do not communicate that we're really hearing a careseeker, can be a hindrance rather than a help.

When asking questions in caregiving conversations, it is important to be attentive to whether you are asking them out of nervousness and uncertainty about how to proceed or out of compassionate curiosity to further develop the conversation. Whenever one is at a loss for how to proceed in a caregiving conversation, the fallback conversational move should always be to more attentive, reflective listening, not asking more and more questions.

While questions may seem like an entirely different skillset from that of active, attentive listening, they should only emerge from this listening posture. Form your questions from what you've been hearing from a careseeker's concerns and not from a template you have in your mind about which types of questions should be asked. You are always asking questions that build on what you are hearing from the careseeker, sticking close to the story they are developing in conversation with you. Remember, you are aiming for richer description, not diagnosis. Ask questions that help a story to be richly told.

Sometimes we need to know more from a careseeker about a situation that calls for our caring response. Other times, we want to invite a person to say more about the concern they are dealing with. This is when helpful questions can be useful caring tools, adding to our skills in active listening. Asking questions should not be an entirely separate skill from listening but should develop as a component of our listening, caring presence with another.

CURIOUS QUESTIONS, NOT LEADING QUESTIONS

It is not true that there are no bad questions. There are. Here's one type: questions to which you already know the answer. Here's another: questions that are thinly veiled attempts to lead a person in a certain direction. And one more: questions that communicate scrutiny or judgment and invite shame. Not everyone is already good at asking questions, but everyone can learn to ask better ones. So put aside the notion that any question is as good as the next and take the necessary time to learn the art of asking beautiful questions and then practice! Practice a lot.

Curiosity is a vital resource for caring, not curiosity for the sake of the caregiver but a compassionately engaged curiosity that is focused on the life and experience of the careseeker for their sake. Curiosity about a person's life, a person's perspective, a person's experience of a problem, a person's relationships and their joys—all of these can fill a caregiving relationship with the richness that is necessary to invite a careseeker's story into speech, developing over time into a fuller, richer picture of that person's life in the world.

Some types of questions are inherently more compassionately curious than others. Closed questions usually invite yes-or-no responses, while leading questions communicate the answer in the question itself. Neither of these is typically respectful of or receptive to the complexity and beauty of a careseeker's life and experience. Closed questions can be helpful in soliciting some needed information (Do you have a means of transportation to get to the doctor? Are there ways the church can be helpful to you in this crisis? Are you comfortable taking a walk while we chat?). Use these types of questions sparingly and only when you really need the information. When closed questions become leading questions, they are really suggestions disguised as questions (Don't you think it would be better if . . .? But wouldn't you feel happier doing . . .?), and that is typically quite unhelpful! Strike these phrases from your interrogative vocabulary.

Open and curious questions leave room for the careseeker to respond in a wide variety of ways—ways that can surprise you. They open avenues for exploration and dialogue and possibility. They leave room for wonder and uncertainty. They aren't questions you already know the answer to. Curious questions embody the value of not knowing and place the careseeker in the expert position in their own life and narrative. Here are a few examples:

> *What else would be important for you to tell me about this situation?*
>
> *What would be some signs that the situation was starting to take a turn for the better?*
>
> *Have you experienced a situation like this in the past that has taught you anything about how you might respond in the situation you face now?*
>
> *I wonder when you first noticed anxiety showing up in your life around this situation.*

Notice in that last question that questions don't necessarily need to be phrased as a question if the intent to invite a response is clear. *I wonder* or *I'm curious about* are helpful phrases to play with when practicing your ability to invite careseekers to say more about their life or situation.

Leading questions close off possibilities and direct the careseeker where you want them to go, not where they may need or desire to go. Curious questions open possibilities for the caregiving conversation that can move in spirals and branch off in new directions that the careseeker determines in response to your caring questions. Practice curiosity and compassion in your question-asking.

STRENGTHS-BASED QUESTIONS, NOT DEFICIT-FOCUSED QUESTIONS

We aren't trained to ask questions about people's strengths. In fact, when it comes to caregiving, we're often prone to only ask questions about people's deficits, their problems, their adverse experiences, and the like. While all of those things are important to consider in the developing story of a person seeking compassionate conversation with you, it is helpful to also invite stories of strength and pride if we are going to attend to the fullness of a person's life and narrative.

When a careseeker comes to you to talk about a problem, you definitely need to spend time in conversation with the person in order to understand the problem story. However, the person you are sitting with is more than their problem, no matter how big the problem is.[1] They have a sense of identity and purpose, goals and desires, and a spiritual life that isn't totalized by the problem they are inviting you to face with them. Spend time in each caring encounter getting to know the person outside of the ways the problem is currently shaping their life. When other aspects of a person's life are invited into the conversation—their strengths, prides, joys—these can also become helpful in addressing the problem they face later on. You can consider questions and invitations like:

> *Tell me a bit about your life, who you are, what you're proud of. I'd love to get to know you a bit more fully before we delve into some of the reasons you reached out to me.*

> *What are you appreciating about your life right now? What is bringing you a sense of joy, or fulfillment, or purpose?*

These questions aren't ways of avoiding the difficult conversation about the person's concerns. In fact, communicate your intention to get to those concerns. These are simply invitations for the person to become a fuller, more textured, and more nuanced human being in your presence and a reminder that the problem they're facing is not the whole story of this person's life.

Another way of developing strengths-based questions, even in relation to the problem itself, is to ask questions about experiences when the person got a leg up on the problem in some form or fashion. For example, after a careseeker has described the problem they are facing in some detail and, through attentive listening, you've developed a good picture of what's going on, you might ask something like,

> *Are there times when you've responded differently to this situation that have given you some influence over the problem?*
>
> *How have you noticed yourself responding to the situation in ways you're proud of?*
>
> *Have you thought of any good experiments you could try in relation to the concern?*

Note that I'm using the term *the problem* or *the situation* in these questions, but recall that you should be using the language that the careseeker uses to describe the issue or concern they face. What should be clear here is that even when asking questions about the problem situation, you can ask questions that invite a careseeker to reflect on their strengths and ingenuity in facing the problem.[2]

One practice I have kept for years now is keeping a notebook full of beautiful questions. Whenever I read or overhear a well-articulated question communicating compassion and curiosity, I write it down. I have pages full of questions on so many different topics. Periodically, I read over these questions just to fuel my imagination for the possibilities that questions can open. You might give this a try if it sounds like a helpful practice to you.

Finally, it can be helpful to avoid questions that start with the word *why*. Why questions often invite us into a defensive posture, even if the question isn't asked in a judgmental or scrutinizing way. Try replacing why questions with other ways of asking the same question differently. For example, "Why did you make that choice?" immediately sounds a bit disapproving, as though maybe we shouldn't have made that choice. Instead, you can say, "Tell me a little more about what went into that decision for you." Immediately you can probably see how the anxiety of judgment washes away with this rephrasing, even though you are asking the same basic thing. Likewise, for example, "Why did you respond that way to your boss?" can be reshaped into "What were some of the reasons you had for responding in the way you did?" "Why?" is a perfectly fine type of question to ask in many other areas of life—scientific inquiry, teaching, journalism, and on and on. But in a caring conversation, try to avoid why questions as much as possible so that you avoid unintentionally communicating a deficit in the careseeker's actions.

Practice Exercise: Beautiful Questions

Find a partner who is willing to share a story with you. It doesn't have to be a story about a problem or a situation that calls for care, but it can be. It could also be a story of a recent experience of joy. Either way, ask them if they'll just start telling you about an experience and allow you to get curious with them about that experience and practice asking beautiful questions. (You can also mix in reflective, attentive listening skills throughout the conversation.)

Then after the conversation has gone on for a half hour or so, ask the person to reflect with you on the questions they found most helpful. Which questions caused them to think in new directions about their story? Which questions issued an invitation to explore their experience in ways they hadn't thought of before? Which questions caused them to feel like you didn't quite get what they were trying to share? Which questions opened possibilities in the person's exploration, and which foreclosed potential pathways? There's no shame in a conversation like this. It is explicitly for the purpose of helping you become adept at asking more beautiful questions. And that can take a lot of practice!

HEARING WITH OUR ANSWERS

There are situations in which a careseeker may really press you for an answer to their problem. They might say something like "I just want to know what you think," "I really want to hear what you would do in this situation," or "I know you're listening to me and care for me, but what should I do?"

For a variety of reasons, you may not be able to provide the answer the person is looking for. For example, you may think that giving advice is premature or altogether inappropriate. You may want to know more about the situation before giving an opinion. You may believe your opinion isn't really what the person needs to hear and listening in a caring way is much more important. Or you may have no idea what answer to provide. In any of these situations, it's okay to say something like "I hear you saying that you'd really like me to give you an answer for the situation you're facing. I really wish I could. Right now, I don't think I have any helpful advice to give. But I'd really like to keep this conversation going with you so that we might be able to figure something out together."

In many instances—perhaps most—you are not going to be in a position to give advice in many situations that call for your caring presence. For the most part, providing care in the context of communities isn't about advice-giving anyway. Advice is often one of the least helpful responses to a situation that calls for care. So let yourself off the hook for always being in the know about the best advice to give on any particular situation. Your solicitous care is a more important gift than your sagely advice.

QUESTIONING QUESTIONS

Sometimes it can be helpful to ask a compassionately curious question about a careseeker's quest for answers. For example, you may be asked by a careseeker for advice on a subject that you aren't able to provide: Should I leave my job? Is it right for me to withdraw care from my mother if the doctors say she isn't going to recover? How do you think God sees my decision to seek a divorce?

In addition to the gentle and caring way you may acknowledge and affirm a person's deep desire for answers despite your inability to provide one, you may get curious about the questions behind their questions in order to help them move toward some clarity without sliding into an advice-giving stance. In situations like these, when a question seems to be pointing to a larger consideration that the careseeker is trying to address, you might try a question like:

That seems like an important question for you. I'm curious to hear more about what leaving your job might mean to you in your life right now?

It sounds like you have a big decision to make, and you need some help talking through that question so you don't have to answer it alone. Can we talk a little more about what questions you're wrestling with regarding your mother's continued care?

How God sees this decision seems like an important consideration to you. Tell me a little more about how you came to understand God's perspective on relationships? How did you develop the theological values you hold about partnership, marriage, and divorce?

Very often, behind each of these really big questions, there are myriad smaller questions that may help break the situation down into more approachable considerations. In helping the careseeker talk down the big questions into their component parts, the caring conversation can also move them toward the clarity they desire without your assuming the role of advice-giver. Helping the other come to a decision or answer that is congruent with their most deeply cherished values will be a much more important gift to them than any answer you can provide from your own perspective.

HELPFUL ANSWERS

At times, the answer a careseeker desires is information about resources they may be able to draw on in the situation they are facing: Where can I go to get the services I need to address x, y, or z? How do I access assistance with this need I am experiencing? Which professional would be appropriate to reach out to for help with this situation? If a mother comes to you for care and is asking about where she can find food assistance for her family, there isn't a lot of need to try to discern what is behind that question. The need is clear and apparent: the need to feed her family.

These are the types of answers you may very well be able to provide. If you don't know right off hand how to point a careseeker to the resources they are seeking, it's okay to say something like "I'm not entirely sure, but I know there's an answer out there, and I'm glad to help find the information you need." Appendix II is one resource to begin building your network of resources and referrals. Ministers in your congregation or service providers in your community may be another place you turn to help a careseeker find the resources they're searching for in a time of crisis or special need. If you believe a referral to another caregiver is what is most needed, see the "Helpful Introductions" section in chapter 6.

Practice Exercise: Avoiding Premature Answers
It can be difficult to refuse to directly answer someone's question while continuing to feel like you are communicating compassion and care toward another. To hone this skill with a partner, practice asking one another some really big questions that call for something more than a simple answer. (You can make them up. They don't need to be questions you're really wrestling with.)

Practice the skills above being very attentive to both (1) affirming the importance of the question and the desire for an answer despite your inability to provide one and (2) helping the other talk through the big question in ways that illuminate the values, considerations, and smaller questions that may be hiding just behind the really big question. After you've practiced these skills, talk through with your partner what you found helpful and most difficult about the exercise.

HEARING SILENCE

One of the most difficult things for most people who want to be helpful is knowing when to speak and when not to speak. Sometimes we speak because of our own anxiety about a situation we are facing in a helping relationship, so we treat our anxiety with words. Occasionally we talk unnecessarily because a situation seems beyond our ability to control, and talking at least gives us the illusion of having a handle on the situation. Other times we speak because being in silence with another makes us nervous. Or as a care responder, we feel like we should be saying something, so we do . . . even if we don't really have anything meaningful to say.

There's an acronym I've see floating around in various circles the past few years that could be helpful to care responders to assess our own need to speak. It is WAIT, which stands for the question, *Why am I talking?* There are times when our reason to talk is clear: we are actively listening to another; responding to the content, feelings, and longings we are hearing them express; tracking their speech with our own to ensure clarity on our part and to communicate our listening and understanding to the careseeker. At other times, we are asking helpful questions that are drawing more of the story needing to be told into the conversation, inviting the careseeker into further speech.

There are also times when we may find ourselves talking yet simultaneously searching for what to say. Or talking and suddenly realizing that we aren't really saying anything. Or talking when we realize that the careseeker seems to have drifted off because perhaps what we're saying isn't really connecting. Those are the times when we need to ask ourselves: Why am I talking? Am I nervously filling what otherwise might be a welcomed and needed silence? Am I trying to fix something with my words that simply can't be fixed with speech? Am I trying to control a situation that seems chaotic?

There are helpful reasons to allow, or even invite, some silence in a caring conversation. Silence can invite a time for reflection during a particularly intense conversation. A bit of silence can honor an especially difficult story that has just been shared that needs to sink in for a moment before the conversation moves forward. Silence can help us invite the presence of the Spirit into a caring conversation, provoking a sense of the profundity of the moment being shared.

Sometimes the silence just comes naturally, punctuating a conversation with brief periods of speechlessness. When this doesn't happen and you feel that some silence could be useful, it can feel a little unnerving to impose silence on a conversation. So practice a few ways of inviting that silence between you and the careseeker. For example, "I'm sitting with the importance of what you've just shared with me and trying to let it sink in a bit. Would it be okay with you if we just held a moment or two of silence to honor what you've said before we move the conversation further?"

Or during an especially difficult conversation when you sense that the anxiety level is pretty high, you may suggest pausing the conversation to suggest some silence paired with a spiritual practice. For example, you might offer, "What we're discussing is a difficult matter, and I wonder if it would be helpful to just take a little break to hold some silence and attend to our breathing for a minute or two?" If a careseeker is amenable to this suggestion, you can offer some simple instructions on how to use one's breath to calm the body and mind: "If it's comfortable for you, let's just sit in silence and let our minds focus on our breath. When your mind wanders and thoughts come, as they will, simply return your attention to your breath—each breath in and each breath out. If it helps, you can put a short mantra to your breath like 'Breathing in grace. Breathing out anxiety.'" Then simply resume the conversation after it seems that the silence has settled you both a bit.

On some occasions, our fear of saying the wrong thing causes us to hold back words that are needed from us. We may experience bodily or mental fatigue, or our own minds wandering during a conversation, and lose track of the conversation. When we find ourselves *not* talking, we can augment the WAIT acronym a bit to help us ask, "Why *aren't* I talking?" If there is purpose to your silence, or the moment seems to call for it, then that could be a very good reason not to say anything. But if you are silent due to your own anxiety about the situation, or because you are having difficulty paying enough attention to know what to say, or because you feel stuck in the caring encounter, then there may be something for you to address in order to more effectively engage in the conversation.

Attending to your own bodily needs—eating, sleeping, exercising your body before a caring encounter—may help you be more alert and present. Draw on your own spiritual practices so that you can stay grounded in a situation that invites anxiety for you. And if you are simply at a loss for what to say next, you can always return to your foundational caring practices of attentive, reflective listening and let that get the caring conversation going again if you feel stuck.

Practice Exercise: Sitting with Silence

Our world is filled with noise. Our society leaves little room for silence. One of the most helpful ways to cultivate a sense of the sacredness of silence in our helping relationships and caring conversations is to become more comfortable with silence in our own lives. This exercise comes in two parts: one in solitude and one with a partner or partners.

When you are by yourself, set aside ten minutes to sit in silence. Not while you read or knit or perform any activity. Let the silence be your only activity. Pay attention to your mind as you sit in silence. Is it racing with thoughts? Jittery with anxiety and the desire to do something? If you can calm your mind—perhaps with the use of a spiritual practice like the breath practice described above—pay even more careful attention to the silence. What can you hear that you would have missed if it were covered by talking or music or television or your internal monologue?

Now solicit the help of a willing partner who will sit with you for ten minutes in silence. You don't need to do anything specific other than be together in the same room and commit to keeping silence together for a short stretch of time. Let this simple exercise strengthen your ability to sustain silence in the presence of others when it is called for in a caregiving situation.

FURTHER READING

Denborough, David. *Retelling the Stories of Our Lives: Everyday Narrative Therapy to Draw Inspiration and Transform Experience*. New York: W. W. Norton, 2014.

Justes, Emma J. *Hearing beyond the Words: How to Become a Listening Pastor*. Nashville: Abingdon, 2006.

NOTES

1 In the now famous words of narrative therapist Michael White, "The person is not the problem, the problem is the problem." See Michael White, *Maps of Narrative Practice* (New York: Norton, 2007).

2 Many of the suggestions in this chapter, like getting to know the person outside of the problem's influence and asking questions about how a person is already getting a leg up on the problem, come from the narrative therapeutic tradition. To learn more about narrative therapy and community practice, see the recommended reading at the end of this chapter or visit dulwichcentre.com.au.

3

HEARING STORIES AND SPIRITUAL NARRATIVES

We cannot understand who we are without stories. Say anything about yourself—who you are, what is important to you, what you love and care about—and there is guaranteed to be a story behind each of those claims. Our entire sense of self, our most important identities, our deepest held values, our best hopes, and looming fears are all shaped by stories. We cannot understand who we are in relation to God, Divine Presence, the Sacred, the Holy without stories. And when there's a situation in our life that calls for care, there's a story behind that too. Your role as a caregiver inviting forth stories from those with whom you practice care is to simultaneously embody compassionate curiosity about the stories that need telling, show deep respect for the storied lives of those for whom you care, and pose skillful questions that invite careseekers to engage story's capacity to shape their lives in preferred directions.

INVITING STORIES OF STRENGTH, PRIDE, AND GOODNESS

A person's narrative is like their home. They are the hosts; you are the guest. We must treat their stories and preferred directions with respect—reverence, even. At the same time, the questions we choose to ask inevitably exert a profound influence on the stories that develop in the conversation between caregivers and careseekers. When we only ask questions about the problem or concern that a person brings to us, that invites more of that problem story to be told, making it ever stronger in the telling and retelling. The more a story gets told—told by us, told about us, or imposed on us to tell—the stronger it grows in its power to shape our lives.

While the problem story is important to understand and hear with compassion, it is not the only story that is possible to tell. There are other stories residing in a careseeker's living narrative library that, if invited, can help them live into their most deeply held values and most hoped-for directions. It is your privilege as a caregiver who asks rich and beautiful questions to hear when those stories are trying to emerge and to ask questions that invite those stories into the room.

Recall that at the start of a caregiving relationship, it can be important to invite stories of success and pride before stories about problems become the focus. For example, you might start a caring conversation with someone by asking them to tell you a bit about what's going well in their lives right now:

> As we get started in the conversation, I would really love to hear something about what's bringing you joy or connecting you to goodness in your life right now.
>
> I know you wanted to talk about a specific problem you're facing, but before we get to that, I wonder if you could share with me something that's going on in your life right now that you're proud of or excited about?
>
> If we were meeting for the first time, what would you most want me to know about you and your life that would help me get who you are?

These stories may not become the focus of the caring conversation, but these types of questions set the stage for the stories to come by inviting careseekers to situate themselves in the caregiving relationship from a place of ability and pride before entering the vulnerable space of discussing the problems that they bring.

HEARING PROBLEM STORIES WITHOUT STRENGTHENING THE PROBLEM

In inviting stories from careseekers, we are not simply trying to get the person to talk, nor even trying to gain information. We are inviting into the room the material out of which their lives are stitched together. In this process, we become attentive to the ways that certain stories—often stories about problems—are defining a person's sense of self, sense of worth, sense of purpose, sense of agency or competency, and so forth. But our lives are multistoried. No single story defines us. The problem story is just one story among many that is possible to tell about a careseeker's life. Nevertheless, the problem story is an important story and likely the reason they reached out to you for caring conversation.

Once we get to stories of the problem that a person is facing—and inviting you to face as a caring ally alongside them—there are ways of attending to the language we use in relation to these problems that help people tell the story of the problem without strengthening that story. One simple technique that narrative practitioners often call *externalizing* the problem helps separate the person from the problem so that the person doesn't become the problem in the story that is being told.[1]

One simple way of creating a little breathing room between the person and the problem is to talk about the problem as a noun rather than an adjective. For example, a caregiver's statement "I'm just a very anxious person" can be met with a question that puts a little distance between anxiety and the careseeker: "Tell me a little about how anxiety visits you in the course of your daily life?" The difference is subtle, but the effect can be profound. What was an identity claim in relation to the problem, "I am an anxious person," becomes a curiosity about how a person's relationship with anxiety is taking shape.

When asking questions to gain a better sense of the person's relationship with the problem they are facing, be sure to use the language that they use to describe the problem rather than imposing your own. But get creative with the ways you allow that problem to exist outside of the person's identity, letting the life of the problem exist alongside (not inside) the life of the person. Let's look at two examples of conversations.

Example 1

Careseeker: *Lately, I've just been feeling really sad every time I think about my relationship to my partner and the troubles we're having.*

Caregiver: *It sounds like sadness has been a frequent visitor in your life lately. What does sadness say to you when it comes knocking on the door?*

Careseeker: *Oh, I think the main thing sadness says is, "Things aren't going to get any better for you. Might as well give up and call it quits."*

Caregiver: ***Ah, so sadness is trying to convince you that you might as well not even try to work things out. When sadness enters the room, it says, "Time to give up!" Is that right?***

Example 2

Careseeker: *When I leave work after days like this, I just feel so incompetent. I just have this feeling that I can't do anything right.*

Caregiver: ***This can't-do-anything-right feeling seems to be really strong for you on workdays like this. What experiences or circumstances do you think open the door for can't-do-anything-right to get into your life on these occasions?***

Careseeker: *Well, definitely when I make mistakes in my work and especially when my boss or coworkers are the ones who notice it and have to correct them. I mean, I hardly ever make big blunders, but when I do, I just feel like such a failure. Then I have a hard time getting back into the groove of my job.*

Caregiver: ***So it sounds like the can't-do-anything-right feeling is right there beside you, looking over your shoulder at the desk. And when you make a mistake and others take notice, it starts to suggest you're a failure and gets you off track for the day.***

Do you see the way that speaking of the problem as a noun rather than an adjective puts a little distance between the person and the problem they are trying to address? It's not necessary to force this externalized language on a caregiver. However, using it consistently in your contributions to the conversation is an invitation for the other person to also see the problem as separate from who they are as a person—a problem with which they have a particular relationship. And relationships with problems can change.

Finally, it is important to ask a simple question about a person's preference in relation to the problem they are facing to help them take the kind of stand they are wishing to take. Continuing with the two examples begun above:

> **Example 1 Continued**
> **Caregiver:** ***It sounds like you don't really want to believe sadness when it shows up and starts to try to convince you that you might as well give up, like sadness is trying to get you to give up on something you really believe. Is that the case?***
>
> Careseeker: *Oh, yes. I don't think I need to give up on the relationship. There's so much I love about being with my partner. It's just hard to keep working on things when sadness is speaking so loudly in my ear. It's exhausting. But I definitely don't want to listen to sadness—not yet anyway.*
>
> **Example 2 Continued**
> **Caregiver:** ***So if I'm hearing you correctly, there are plenty of times when this can't-do-anything-right feeling is pretty silent, and you get through the workday feeling okay about things. But when it does show up with its messages of failure and giving up, trying to get you off track for the rest of the day, what would you rather be able to do in those moments?***
>
> Careseeker: *I think I'd rather just be able to accept that mistakes happen, and they don't define who I am as an employee. There's more to my worth than the feeling is giving me credit for.*

Questions like these allow you and the careseeker to be on the same page about what story is preferred and why so that you can stand together in solidarity in diminishing the power of the problem story and increasing the possibilities for living into preferred narratives. You enter into solidarity as allies against the problem.

INVITING STORIES OF POTENTIAL TO COME OUT FROM UNDERNEATH THE PROBLEM STORY

If we only ask questions about the problem story, that is likely the only story that will be told, and it will become thicker and stronger the more it becomes the focus of our questions. In our attentive listening, we must be on the lookout for other stories that are attempting to break through the thick layer of the problem story. These other stories are indicated by what many in the tradition of narrative practice call *unique outcomes* that signal to us the fact that another story is already present—times when the problem isn't as much of a problem.

Yet careseekers may not even notice when the problem isn't present because they've been paying so much attention to the problem story. These other stories of possibility beyond the problem simply need some attention so that the thick layer of the problem story's sediment doesn't become concretized, and people can move in more preferable directions, exercising skill and agency in relation to the problem.

In the process of hearing stories of problems, you may very well hear hints of other stories trying to break through. Specifically, there is typically always another story of a person's relationship to the problem that exists in the careseeker's narrative library but isn't being told and likely isn't being noticed. Importantly, this isn't an attempt to make up new stories but a careful way of listening that picks up on the possibilities already present in the person's story. Sometimes helpful questions can be used to bring those stories to the surface for examination.

Example 1 Continued

Caregiver: ***Are there times when you feel like the volume is turned down on the voice of sadness, and you're able to lean into this desire you expressed to work things out with your partner?***

Careseeker: *Oh, sure. I'd say about 20 percent of the time I'm able to have really meaningful conversations with my partner about our relationship and feel fine about how things are developing between us.*

Caregiver: ***Wow, that's very interesting. It sounds like you've been able to get out from under the shadows of sadness fairly often. What do you think is different about that 20 percent of your time when you're able to turn the volume down on sadness's messages and talk with your partner about the things that are important to you? What feels different about those times?***

Careseeker: *Well, I've never thought about what is different about those times. But I guess if I think about one time last week when that was true, it was a day when I had kind of prepared myself for the conversation by doing something relaxing beforehand. I remember I had just gone on a long walk in the woods, listening to some music I really enjoy, and then later, over dinner, I had a very helpful and serious conversation with my partner about things without feeling exhausted or like giving up.*

Caregiver: ***Ah, so doing some things that help you feel relaxed like walking in the woods and listening to music helped to turn down the volume on sadness long enough for you to have the conversation you wanted to have that evening. Is that right?***

Other times, the suggestion of the alternative story is already there in what the careseeker has said and just needs to be picked up on and held up to the light so you can both wonder about its significance.

Example 2 Continued

Careseeker: *I remember the other day I made a huge mistake—really, really big—on an account I was working on. And a couple of hours later, I had a feeling that I needed to double check my work and went back and caught it and just laughed at how ridiculous that would have been if I had let it slip.*

Caregiver: ***So when you made that mistake the other day, you were actually able to laugh at yourself and fix it without can't-do-anything-right feelings making an appearance at all? What do you make of that?***

Careseeker: *Oh, that's interesting. Yeah, I didn't come home feeling like a failure that day. Just fixed the error and moved on with my day.*

Caregiver: ***How did you manage that? Was there something different about what you were doing that day that kept failure from looming over you?***

Careseeker: *You know, I think it was just that I was able to laugh at the situation and say to myself, "Life's too short to let this ruin your day." And I felt really proud of having realized the mistake anyway, even if I was the one who made it.*

Caregiver: ***Ah, you were able to insert your own message about the blunder before can't-do-anything-right was able to show up and start its speech to you about it.***

Listening to stories of people's strengths and the ways they are getting the upper hand over the problem creates openings for further exploration of their competencies and skills. When you hear one of these stories start to emerge from the problem story, it is an invitation to stop and wonder about these stories of possibility.

People will tell you about the problem no matter what. What they won't necessarily tell you about are their strengths and points of pride and places of resilience unless you invite those stories. You must always attentively listen for these alternative stories so that you can help a careseeker see the significance of these times when the problem story wasn't reigning supreme. Then you can invite them to decide what these stories suggest about the kind of person they are and the preferences they have for their lives. These stories may also contain the seeds of how the person is already handling the problem in constructive ways that they may not have even noted as significant. Through some careful attention and questions, you can help the careseeker nurture these seeds into full-grown strategies to move in their preferred direction in relation to the problem.

Example 1 Continued

Caregiver: *You seem to have a repertoire of strategies that help you feel relaxed enough to enter into these conversations you want to have. You named walking in the woods and listening to music you enjoy. Are there other things you've found that help you relax into that conversational posture you want to adopt?*

Example 2 Continued

Caregiver: *When can't-do-anything-right doesn't get the first word in, you have some of your own messages you carry about what it means to make mistakes at work, like "Life's too short for this to ruin my day."*

> *What else have you found yourself saying that interrupts can't-do-anything-right's ability to get a word in?*

None of these is a trick or technique for fixing problems or looking on the bright side. They are simply ways of being intentional about how we talk about problems and possibilities and how we invite stories from those with whom we practice care. If our lives are made of stories, it matters how we talk about those stories, which stories we invite and which we overlook, and the language we use to narrate our storied lives.

A NOTE ON NOTETAKING

For the most part, spiritual care first aid is not a caregiving response that requires notetaking, with a few exceptions. If, for example, you are engaged in your faith community's care team and you know that after your initial response, you are going to be engaged in caring conversation with a person over the course of three or four conversations, each separated by a week or more, it could be helpful to take a few notes about the situation so that you can review them to refresh your memory about the person and their situation before your next conversation. I have also encountered situations in training care responders in which a particular cognitive processing or neurological concern means that a very adept care responder has trouble tracking the details of a conversation without taking notes as they listen. Thus, taking notes was vital to their caregiving, even within a single conversation. If you decide that notes are necessary, here are a few things to keep in mind.

Always ask permission of the careseeker before you take notes during your conversation. If they find it a distraction or it makes them nervous to see you writing down their words, then forgo the notetaking. Notes will not be as important as your attentive presence with them. Trust that you will remember what you need to remember and can be reminded of what you might forget.

Always offer to give the person a copy of your notes or let them take a photograph of the notes with their phone at the end of the conversation if they wish. This is their story, even if you've written parts of it down to help you remember it. They own the rights to it, so to speak. Nothing in your notes is a secret from them.

Finally, keep any notes you take during a caregiving conversation in a safe and secure place (e.g., locked in a desk drawer or filing cabinet). Ideally, only refer to the careseeker with initials and not with their full name just in case the notes are ever lost. Only keep the notes for as long as they are useful for the immediate caregiving relationship. When a caregiving relationship has ended and a person is no longer visiting with you for conversation, shred the notes you've taken during prior conversations.

However, there are a multitude of situations in which notetaking simply will not be helpful or appropriate: most hospital visits, attending to someone during a crisis, impromptu caring conversations, and so forth. In situations like these in which you may need to follow up with a careseeker, you may need to jot a note down about a next step in providing care. But write down only what is helpful in following up in a caring way with the careseeker.

Practice Exercise: Separating People from Problems

You can practice this with a partner, or you can practice on your own. Either way, try talking with someone else about a problem (real or made up) or with your own internal monologue about a problem you personally face, using language that puts a little distance between you and the problem. Use nouns rather than adjectives, giving the problem some legs by looking at how it shows up and operates, asking how one would prefer to relate to this problem. Then start to notice times when the problem didn't have the upper hand, even in very small ways. Get curious about those times using some of the above skills. This way of talking may not feel very natural at first. But over time, talking about problems and possibilities differently may open up space for you to enter into different relationships with the problems you face and facilitate your invitation of stories from those with whom you practice care.

HEARING SPIRITUAL STORIES

In the practice of spiritual care first aid, many of the stories we hear will have spiritual, religious, or theological themes—ways that a person is making meaning of a situation drawing on their most cherished religious beliefs or spiritual frameworks. The spiritual or theological nature of a caring relationship doesn't depend on whether God is a topic of conversation. A caring relationship can become spiritual care when the fullness of a person's meaning-making is invited into the space between careseeker and care responder. You don't need to be a theologian to engage in caring conversation about a careseeker's spiritual life. Nor does the careseeker need to identify with any particular religious tradition in order to have a spiritual life. Atheist or Christian, Buddhist or Baptist, we all have the capacity for making meaning of life experiences in ways that could be described as *spiritual*.

For caregivers, some of the most essential ingredients for providing helpful spiritually focused care are humble curiosity, respectful listening, and an openness to awe and wonder. For careseekers, spiritual stories can emerge in caring conversations for many reasons: a search for meaning amid difficult circumstances, discomfort with received theological frameworks, the need for practices that help connect a person to realities beyond their individual life, a desire for a sense of spiritual mooring during turbulent times.

Spiritual stories and theological narratives are about the ways people make sense of their lives within an ultimate context. Sometimes we call that ultimate context *God*, while other times we are oriented to this context with language that places love or ethics or deep connection to others at the point of ultimacy in our lives. Spiritual stories can be about the narratives and practices that connect us to the goodness, gifts, and graces we experience in life. They can be stories of how we are tethered in relationship to God or how we feel ourselves coming untethered. Spiritual stories can even iterate how we experience our kinship with a larger web of life that enfolds us in an earth community that transcends our humanness.

Sometimes these stories will be woven with the language that we often think of as inherently spiritual—for example, the language of Spirit, God, calling, and conviction or with references to passages from Scripture, experiences of Divine presence, or teaching of a religious tradition. But at other times, spiritual stories can be shaped by language that doesn't necessarily sound spiritual or theological on the surface but points toward a person's deepest sense of meaning-making in the world and how they see their lives within a context of ultimate concern—for example, questions about what is most important in life and where one should place one's time and energy, concerns over ethical ways of living life in relation to others or ecological contexts, and engaged searches for how one should live one's life in relation to family, vocation, intimate relationship, and so forth.

Don't be surprised if you get deep into a conversation about someone's spiritual narrative before you realize that you're even talking about something spiritual.

ATTENDING TO LAYERS OF SPIRITUAL STORY

It can be helpful to listen to the various layers of a person's spiritual story that display both the theological and spiritual teachings one has inherited and those that a person is more deliberately thinking through and developing anew. Embedded theology is the theology we pick up in our faith practices throughout life: the theology we've heard from the pulpit over time, sing in our hymns, learn in prayers that we repeat from a young age, receive in the creeds and confessions of our tradition. Deliberative theology comes through reflection—careful, critical, deliberate thoughtfulness and practice about our spiritual and religious life.[2] Each of these layers of theological and spiritual material exists in our lives simultaneously. There are times when certain embedded theological narratives get called into question through our lived experience.

For example, an embedded theological notion about God's goodness and care for us can be called into question by an experience of personal or familial tragedy. A careseeker may, for the first time, wonder, "Where is God amid the suffering that I am facing?" This type of question—called *theodicy* in the Christian theological tradition—is one that nearly everyone practicing a faith tradition that teaches the goodness of God must address if we are to live life with our eyes open to suffering and violence in the world around us, whether it directly touches our personal life or not. At times, holding two opposing notions at once—a loving God and a suffering world—can create the tension that brings an embedded theological narrative to the light of deliberative inquiry. This can also be distressing to a careseeker if the opposing notions are difficult or impossible to resolve yet rest at the crux of one's theological world

This tension can occur on larger scales too. Confronted by a situation of social injustice, an embedded theological belief in the essentially just nature of the society in which we live can be ruptured by coming face to face with an extreme injustice like the killing of unarmed Black people by the police or discovering the truth about our religious tradition's involvement in violence against Native and Indigenous people. One's embedded theological assumptions about justice may be formed around privileged racial or gender or cultural identities and embodiments. The theological assumptions formed around those identities and embodiments, however, may never have been questioned until encountering the lived experience of another with different embodiments and identities.

On a planetary scale, an embedded theological teaching about God's intentionality behind all that takes place in the world—that is, everything happens for a reason as a part of God's plan—can be brought into critical reflection when large-scale natural disasters occur, causing devastation to people who may already be living amid precarious economic circumstances. Witnessing this experience and really paying attention to the experience of others may lift an embedded theological assumption into deliberative light so that a person can explore questions of God's involvement in the world with more careful and critical questions.

In each of these situations, embedded theologies passed down to us through sermons and liturgy and church teachings may be called into question. This questioning of long-held theological assumptions alone can cause some discomfort or distress, as our theological worlds are often presumed to be the steadiest and sturdiest components of our lives. But theological reflection with a compassionate caregiver can help by providing a safe relational context into which a person can speak about their theological queries and spiritual explorations without fear of judgment or correction. Questions are at the heart of the spiritual journey, and openness to address these questions with careseekers will be a gift that will serve to support their spiritual maturation and growth.

CARE AMID SPIRITUAL STRUGGLES

We should also remember that the stories of questioning and struggle in sacred texts like the Bible are the struggles of the faithful—those who become the prophets and leaders of communities in the text. However, recognizing the centrality of questions and struggle at the heart of the major figures of our religious tradition shouldn't diminish the recognition of the pain these struggles can cause when they occur in life. At times, spiritual struggles can create an extremely disorienting feeling for careseekers who are trying to make meaning out of some of the most painful experiences of suffering, tragedy, and injustice in life.

Spiritual struggles can also arise in the lives of careseekers over moral or ethical questions, questions related to the meaning of life, doubts about long-held religious beliefs, and conflict that arises within one's religious or spiritual community. Kenneth Pargament and Julie Exline, researchers in the psychology of spiritual struggle, are helpful in reminding care responders that "spiritual struggles are not signs of weakness, pathology, immaturity, or weak faith."[3] In fact, spiritual struggles are often signs that people are "striving to find and realize their most important goals and purposes," and they play a key role in a person's development, even offering the opportunity for growth to occur.[4]

We must recognize the seriousness of pain and distress that spiritual struggles can create in a person's life while also holding out hope for the possibilities that working through the struggles with a compassionate care provider can result in growth and spiritual development, even if the shape of one's spiritual life or theological world shifts dramatically. We cannot meet profound questions and spiritual struggle with trite answers and simple solutions. This takes disciplined patience on the part of the care responder to sit with struggle and pain with humble curiosity and a commitment to a less anxious presence.

SPIRITUAL HUMILITY

As previously mentioned, the essential ingredients for providing helpful spiritually focused care are humble curiosity, respectful listening, and an openness to awe and wonder. Respectful and active listening skills are the subject of other chapters, as is the role of wonder in the spiritual life. But a further word on humble curiosity is important when engaging spiritual narratives.

Exploring the spiritual stories of others within caring conversation isn't a time for teaching doctrine or instructing in religious experience.

Sometimes a careseeker may want to know what the Bible or a particular religious tradition teaches about x, y, or z topic. While it is okay to help them explore what you know about the subject from the teachings of a tradition or the contents of Scripture, it is far more helpful to preface that conversation with a careseeker to discern how this question has arisen in their life. You might ask, "That sounds like a question that's very important to you. I wonder how that came up for you and what makes it especially meaningful for you to explore at this point in time?"

You don't need to have all the answers to careseekers' religious, spiritual, and theological questions. In fact, sometimes your answers are not the most helpful responses to spiritual questions when they arise. A posture of humble curiosity will allow you to lean in when life gets difficult and questions about God, faith, ethics, or spiritual practice become especially profound. Those are times when caring spiritual companionship is most needed. Below are further questions that may help you become a humble and curious spiritual care responder to those seeking your companionship.

The writer of the Gospel of John said at the end of the Gospel account, "But there are also many other things that Jesus did; if every one of them were written down, I suppose that the world itself could not contain the books that would be written" (John 21:25 NRSVue). It is striking that the writer of one of the greatest spiritual/theological narratives of all time humbly states his own inability to capture the fullness of the life and meaning of Jesus, the cornerstone of Christian faith—one religion among a multitude of rich religious and spiritual traditions. This should help us all to enter the sacred ground of another's spiritual narrative with a sense of humility.

Know that there is always much you don't know about the spiritual lives of others. And there's even more you don't know about the theological possibilities that exist for making meaning from the rich tapestry of human experience, much less of the excess of meaning that can be made of the transcendent ultimate contexts for which we have many names. Enter spiritual conversations with humility, willing to be surprised by what you discover. Here are a few examples of questions that can be helpful in exploring a careseeker's spirituality:

How are you experiencing the sacred in your life right now? or How have you experienced the sacred in your life in the past?

Are there beliefs, teachings, or practices that you find grounding, intimately connecting you to something that is larger than yourself?[5]

Are there beliefs, teachings, or practices that you've inherited? Are there times when you've found those meaningful at certain points in your life?

Are there any beliefs, teachings, or practices that currently aren't working as well to connect you to goodness or sustain you spiritually? What do you imagine has changed to bring that shift about?

Which practices are you finding helpful right now in sustaining yourself emotionally and spiritually?

Which places feel especially sacred to you right now? What is it like for you to inhabit those spaces?

Are there people with whom you engage in spiritual practice or religious life? What holds you together as a spiritual community?

Are there verses or stories within sacred texts (e.g., the Bible) that feel especially important to you right now? Passages or stories that you return to in times of difficulty or in times of joy?

Where do you see God / the Holy / Spirit at work in your life or in the world today?

Practice Exercise: Attending to Spiritual Struggle

Think of a time in your past when something important in your spiritual or religious life became a point of questioning or concern. Perhaps your identity as a Christian amid the troublesome rise of white Christian nationalism. Perhaps a key doctrine or teaching in your faith tradition that a personal experience has called into question. Perhaps some harm or failure you've experienced in spiritual community that called that community's theological framework into question for you.

Attempt to trace the trajectory of this spiritual struggle or theological deliberation in your life. How did it begin? What did it raise for you emotionally? Where did you feel the struggle in your body? With whom were you able to bring the questions that arose into conversation? How did talking through them with another feel to you? Where are you now in that trajectory? If there has been something that feels like a resolution to the questions or struggle, how did that come about? How did your spiritual practice or life of faith or theological beliefs shift during this period?

If you know others who are working on these skills alongside you, consider having a mutual conversation with someone else about these issues and practice your ability to sit with one another in humble curiosity and ask more beautiful questions about the spiritual stories of another.

FURTHER READING

Coyle, Suzanne M. *Uncovering Spiritual Narratives: Using Story in Pastoral Care and Ministry*. Minneapolis: Fortress, 2014.

Marshall, Joretta L., and Christie Cozad Neuger. *Lay Pastoral Care: A Narrative Approach*. Minneapolis: Fortress, 2022.

NOTES

1 For more on this technique beyond what this chapter offers, see the further reading recommended at the end of this chapter.

2 To learn more about embedded and deliberate theology and the ways we can engage in theological reflection, see Howard W. Stone and James O. Duke, *How to Think Theologically*, 4th ed. (Minneapolis: Fortress, 2023).

3 Kenneth I. Pargament and Julie J. Exline, *Working with Spiritual Struggles in Psychotherapy: From Research to Practice* (New York: Guilford, 2022), 17.

4 Pargament and Exline, *Working with Spiritual Struggles in Psychotherapy*, 17.

5 You might use the term *God* for the something larger than yourself if that is language for *ultimacy* that the careseeker normally uses.

4

HEARING FEELINGS AND THE BODY

Our feelings are a powerful source for our decision-making, our ways of relating to others, and our spiritual lives. We don't often talk about what a *feeling* is, though I imagine we all think we have some idea. Likely, when we talk about feelings, we usually mean one of several things: emotions, moods, or temperaments.

Emotions are the feelings stimulated by something in our immediate context and usually only last a few seconds. You're cut off in traffic and feel an immediate rush of anger. Once you get to your destination, however, that emotion is probably long gone. Emotions are an important part of our embodiment and assist us in responding to our environment in ways that help us survive. They provide important information about our surroundings and move us to action.

Emotions that last more than a few seconds can be described as a *mood*, which may last for days or weeks. Our moods form at the intersection of our immediate emotional experience and our larger history and life situation. For example, persistent experiences that invite emotions of sadness can build on one another and result in longer-lasting moods of sadness. Our moods—whether angry, sad, happy, or so forth—shape our thinking and our behavior and our ways of relating to others over longer periods of time.

Over time, our emotions and moods can become elongated into something more like a *temperament* or a pervasive outlook on life. For example, a constant diet of social media and virtual engagement with others over contentious and anger-inducing topics can develop well beyond emotions and even moods into long-lasting ways of experiencing life from an oppositional or angry place. Anger, or any other feeling, can come to color the way we see the world in its entirety. Learning to address specific experiences of sadness, anger, fear, anxiety, wonder, gratitude, and grief will help us think through how to appreciate emotions for the information they convey to us about our experience; it can also help us avoid developing some of those emotions into longer-lasting temperaments that may cause us harm while we intentionally cultivate other emotions that we may wish to exert more influence in our lives. For now, let us focus on how to work with feelings more generally in our caregiving practice.

NOTICING YOUR FEELINGS

It is helpful to become attentive to your own feelings, treating that awareness as vital information about how you're experiencing your immediate surroundings. When left unattended, our emotions and moods can shape our decisions, actions, and relationships in powerful ways that remain outside of our ability to regulate.

It will not be unusual for you to bring the feelings of your day with you into your caregiving practice in ways of which you are unaware if you aren't careful to attend to your own emotional experience before entering a conversation with another. Take a few minutes to perform a brief body scan before entering a caregiving conversation or making a visit to a careseeker. Sit comfortably. Start at the top of your head, very slowing moving your attention, inch by inch, down your body. Alternatively, you could start at the soles of your feet and the sensation of them resting on the floor and move progressively up your legs and the rest of your body.

Spend at least 20–30 seconds on each small segment of your body, paying attention to how that part of your body feels—as in your body's *sensations*, not your emotions. Perhaps your jaw is clenched tight. Maybe you notice you are taking rather shallow breaths. You may notice that your stomach is grumbling. Don't judge yourself for any of these sensations. Simply notice them with a gentle statement in your mind such as "My jaw is clenched. My leg muscles are restless."

Next, ask compassionate questions about the sensations you notice: "My jaw is clenched. What could this mean? Is there anxiety or stress from the day that I'm holding with me? Is there a message my body is holding that I need to pay attention to?" Let your attention rest on each bodily sensation that you noticed and compassionately consider the message it may be holding.

Finally, return your focus to some of those parts of your body that seemed to hold a message about a strong emotion that may be present in your body and spend just a minute or so on each area that needs some tender attention. If you've noticed tension in your muscles someplace in your body—your forehead, your shoulders, your legs—take a moment to work those muscles a bit so they start to relax. If your breathing is shallow, spend some time breathing deeply, attending to each inhale and exhale until you are breathing more comfortably.

You may not be able to do anything about a particular emotion you've noticed just before entering a caregiving conversation. But having an awareness that you're holding that emotion in your body and that you need to direct some compassionate attention to it later in the day—especially when it is a difficult or discomforting emotion—can help keep the emotion or mood from directing your caregiving encounter outside of your awareness. The point is being in a relationship with our feelings so that you are not being involuntarily directed by them.

NOTICING OTHERS' FEELINGS

A body scan may also be a helpful exercise to use with careseekers who may need help attending to the ways we hold emotions in our bodies. At other times, we may pick up on some emotion that is presenting itself in a person's face or body language that needs to be noted in conversation. Perhaps emotions are palpable in the room yet unspoken. For example, you might say something like "I'm noticing as you describe your relationship with your child that a big smile spread over your face. Can you tell me about that?"; "I'm noting how your posture shifts when you describe that experience. What do you make of that?"; or "From the look on your face, it seems like this is a difficult subject for you to talk about. Is that accurate?" Each of these simple statements of observation, offered tentatively and not as pronouncements, allows an unspoken emotion to be brought more clearly into the conversation if the careseeker so desires.

One of the most obvious nonverbal expressions of emotion is tears. Tears are a very normal part of many caregiving conversations. Tears are a signal that something important is happening. It is vital that you increase your own comfort with the tears of others. Subtle cues of our own discomfort with the emotions of others can easily shift a conversation away from important areas of exploration. If a careseeker simply needs a moment to shed tears before continuing the conversation or if they begin to apologize for crying, it can be helpful to simply say something like "It's perfectly fine to cry here. I'm glad to just sit with the tears a moment."

It is almost instinctual to hand a person a tissue when they begin to cry. But sometimes handing a person a tissue can inadvertently communicate the message that you would rather they not be crying. Instead, if you are meeting in a space you've set up, you can have tissues close to the chair of the careseeker so that they can access them when needed. Tears are normal, and crying is okay. Make tissue available but don't force them on another.

It is also important to note that when we are providing care to others in difficult situations, we may also feel tears welling up. It is perfectly okay to experience our own tears when dealing with a difficult situation in the life of a careseeker. However, you and your tears should not become the center of the caregiving relationship in that moment. Tears shared in a mutual emotional experience in caring conversation can be quite validating. Falling apart emotionally so that the careseeker must comfort *you* is an inappropriate shift in focus of the caring conversation.

ASKING QUESTIONS ABOUT FEELINGS

"How does that make you feel?" We've all heard that question posed by someone trying to be caring. It is the quintessential caricature of a therapeutic inquiry we see on television and in film. Given that, it is also a bit worn out. So try to ask more beautiful and compassionately curious questions about feelings so that you can leave that tired old question behind.

There's a lot that we take for granted about another person's feeling based on our own experience. Don't assume you know how a feeling feels to another person. Get curious with them about the feelings they bring up in relation to the stories they are telling and the situations they are facing. Here are a few types of feeling-oriented questions you might practice to see how they help promote caring conversations:

- Body-focused questions like "When you say you feel dread, what does that feel like in your body? How do you first notice the dread coming on?" These kinds of questions can help a person begin noticing how feelings show up in their body sooner than they may be registering in their conscious thought.
- Relationship-focused questions like "When anxiety shows up for you, how does it affect your relationships with loved ones?" or "Are there ways anxiety invites you to relate differently to others in your life?"
- Questions that give the emotion some distance from the person and allow for some inquiry into how the emotion operates in life, like "You've mentioned a couple of times feeling sad. Tell me a little more about sadness. What does sadness look like when it shows up in your life? What does sadness invite you to do in response to it?"
- Imaginative emotional questions like "How would it feel to you if the issue you're concerned about among your coworkers becomes a reality? How do you think that would affect your mood at work?" This may seem like a leading question at first. However, if you're responding to a particular concern of the careseeker, asking them to feel their way into that possibility, it can aid in exploration rather than direct them to certain outcomes.

There are many ways we've been told certain emotions are wrong and shouldn't be felt. But emotions are there for a reason. Some are painful and others pleasurable, but they all carry a message that is important to attend to. When strong emotions are present in a caregiving conversation, become compassionately curious about the messages these emotions convey in the life of a careseeker.

Practice Exercise: Hearing Feelings

Spend some time with a partner who is willing to have an emotion-focused conversation with you for practice purposes. Start with guiding them through a body scan if they're willing to engage in that meditative exercise with you. Have some conversation about what they observed in their body after you're finished.

Then, rather than asking them to talk about a difficult situation with heavy emotions or to make up a scenario about which they really don't have any genuine feelings, ask them to describe something really good that's happened to them in their life recently. Use your reflective listening skills to hear their story and practice asking some emotion-focused questions related to the emotions that show up for them when telling you the story of this good thing that's happened in their life. You can practice these skills with emotions that make us feel good just as well as you can with emotions that cause us pain.

HEARING (WITH) THE BODY

We can hear what another person is communicating not only through the words they speak but also through the language of their body: posture, hand gestures, facial expressions, the proximity of their body to ours. Equally as important, we can use our bodies as listening instruments to hear another person more clearly and compassionately into speech. What we do with our bodies matters in the context of a caring conversation. Here are a few considerations as you develop your embodied practices of care.

Your Own Body in the Practice of Care

The impact on our mental health of eating and sleeping well is strongly documented, and you likely already know this when it comes to your own sense of well-being. When you are in the position to provide caring presence to another, it is important that you've attended to your own body, just as much as to your own emotional well-being. Just as you really do not want to enter a caregiving conversation with someone when you are feeling angry about some issue in your life, you also don't want to enter it when you are tired or hungry. Do what you need to do to take care of your own bodily needs before a caring conversation ensues: take a nap, have a snack, take a walk, drink a glass of water.

Your body is a listening instrument. It is important when you are attentively listening to the stories of careseekers that your body communicates a listening posture. If you are sitting with an individual, sit facing that person or slightly to an angle so that you can see the person and they can see you. However, this posture can vary depending on the norms of a particular cultural context and the genders of the care responder and careseeker. Try not to have anything too large like a desk in between you. Open your posture so that your arms aren't crossed, which can communicate being emotionally or relationally closed off, and try leaning forward a bit toward the person rather than sitting all the way back in your chair the entire time. You might rest your elbows on your thighs to help you achieve just a slightly more forward-leaning posture. You don't have to keep the same posture throughout a conversation, of course, but always attend to what you are communicating with your body about your openness and receptivity toward the person seeking your care.

It is not uncommon to experience various bodily states that hinder your ability to listen attentively. For example, you may start to feel restless in your body or fatigued during a conversation with a careseeker. This may indicate there's something in the person's story that is touching on some part of your own narrative. Remember these moments so that you can reflect further on them later. But in the time of conversation itself, employ your body in helping you address your physical distractions so that you can better attend to the person in your care: shift posture, stretch a set of muscles by tensing them and then relaxing them, take a few deep breaths, or have a drink of water if you have some close by. Attentively listening to another is hard work, not just for our mind but also for the whole of our body.

The Body of Others in the Practice of Care

Noticing facial expressions and body movements can provide you with helpful information in the process of caring conversations. Some embodiments are a bit more obvious in their communication—tears and laughter, for example. Other emotions expressed by our bodies are less obvious, but when we are paying attention, they can come through clearly in a person's facial expression or posture. Largely, even when communicating across cultures, we are usually able to recognize emotions like sadness, anger, fear, joy, and surprise when we see them on the face of another.

If you want to ask about what a person's body is communicating, get curious, not diagnostic. For example, you might notice that in a conversation, when the careseeker begins discussing their relationship with another person—let's call him John—the careseeker changes posture or facial expression but says very little verbally about their feelings about their relationship with John. If that causes you to become curious about what that embodied response is suggesting about their feelings concerning this relationship, you might say something like "I notice that as you've been talking with me about your relationships with John, you often look down at the floor. I tend to interpret that as an expression of sadness, but I'm not sure I'm right about that. What do you think your body is communicating about your feelings concerning this relationship?"

Offering your observations and what you're making of them as a hypothesis is a much gentler and more caring way of engaging a person's embodied communication. Avoid making such an observation as a pronouncement like "I notice your facial expression is one of sadness" or "I can tell you are nervous because your leg is bouncing." These are too presumptive. Just as you are not an expert on another person's life or narrative, you can't be an expert on their embodied communication. Just pay attention to what you are observing and, when it seems helpful, ask compassionate observational questions about what you are seeing and allow careseekers to interpret their bodies for themselves. This approach can open new pathways in the conversation that listening to words alone might gloss over.

MOVEMENT IN THE PRACTICE OF CARE

We often think of a caring conversation taking place in a cozy indoor space—a church office, a parishioner's living room—or perhaps at a hospital bedside. Many caring conversations require the confidentiality that necessitates a private space and a quiet atmosphere. But as we consider our bodies as listening instruments, also consider the ways the body in motion can aid in the context of certain caring conversations.

For instance, walking is demonstrated to have profound effects on our brains. Walking, or rolling in a wheelchair, boosts our abilities to think creatively. Walking or rolling in a wheelchair outside combines the creativity-generating effects of our body's movement with the potential for the larger-than-human world to help engage us in experiences of wonder, which promotes openness and moves us beyond habitual ways of thinking and into creative engagement with the world around us, with all the novel insights possible therein. When possible—especially when a situation calling for care could benefit from more creative and expansive thought—you might invite a careseeker to take a walk with you while you talk. It could be around the block, around the church grounds, or even in an indoor space when necessary.

Short of being able to take a stroll with a careseeker, there are ways of engaging the body in movement in the space of an office or a living room too. In some instances, you might invite a careseeker to try an exercise like the one described in the practice exercise at the end of the chapter. At other times, you might simply ask the careseeker to check in with their body and describe what they feel, as well as what they make of those observations. Remember, don't interpret their bodies for them. Instead, invite their attention and allow them to make interpretations about their observations, all with the intent of helping a richer description of their life and experience come forth.

PHYSICAL TOUCH IN THE PRACTICE OF CARE

When I served as a chaplaincy intern in an urban hospital emergency department, I was called on to visit a young man who came into the emergency room late one Saturday night. The room was dark, and the man was lying in the hospital bed. I sat in a chair beside his bed, and he began to share with me what brought him into the ER that evening, along with a long history of drug use and prostitution and many other experiences that led him to describe himself as "dirty." His story, his affect, his bodily posture, his words all communicated to me that he felt untouchable, unlovable, alone.

When I made visits to hospital rooms back then, I rarely asked if patients wanted to hold hands in prayer. If they made the gesture or asked if we could join hands, I would oblige. But I didn't offer. Except with this man. When he asked me to pray with him, I asked if he would like to join hands, and he gladly accepted.

What made this situation different from so many others in the hospital is that the situation that called for care that late evening was one in which a person felt untouchable because of the life that he lived. And I was a representative of an institution—the church—that had likely helped him come to that damaging conclusion. Asking if he wanted to join hands when we prayed, rather than keeping my distance in the chair or at the end of the bed, was an embodied act of care that communicated a message to this man likely more powerful than any words I spoke to him that evening.

It is important to use touch in the practice of care with intention and caution. Do not presume that another person wants to be touched, even if that is something you feel comfortable doing or have done in similar situations in the past. Always ask permission: "Would you like to join hands in prayer?" "Would it be okay if I hugged you?" And, generally speaking, if what you want to express to the person could be expressed in words rather than through touch, it is best to use words. If the touch is to fulfill a need that *you* have, it is also not likely to be an appropriate use of touch in the context of care, even if there is nothing inherently inappropriate about the touch.

Feeling close with someone in a caregiving situation is very common. You may even describe it as an experience of emotional or spiritual intimacy when someone shares parts of their life and experience with you that evoke strong emotions in them and perhaps even in you. As the care provider, it is up to you to draw appropriate boundaries around touch that seems inappropriate, even if not crossing lines into overtly sexual touch. If a careseeker is searching for physical touch or proximity to you that causes you to feel uncomfortable or wonder if boundaries are being crossed, it is appropriate for you to say something like "I would feel most comfortable if we sat in these two chairs rather than side by side" or "I am more comfortable with a handshake at the end of a conversation than a hug." If you have concerns about how touch is being invited in a caregiving situation, talk them over with a minister, a care team supervisor, or another person in a helping profession.

While boundaries around physical touch are highly important in a caregiving context, keep in mind that appropriate—brief, purposeful, and intentional—touch can be a powerful embodied act of care.

Practice Exercise: Listening to Your Body

Take a moment to notice what is going on in your own body. Sit comfortably in a chair with your feet flat on the floor, your back upright, your hands resting gently in your lap. When you feel comfortable, let your eyes close, or if you'd rather they remain open, let your gaze rest softly on something in the distance. Breathe evenly, focusing on each inhale as your lungs fill with air and each exhale as you release your breath back into the world. Focus your attention on your breathing until you feel calm and centered. Always return to your breath when you begin feeling distracted by thoughts or stimuli in your environment.

As your mind becomes calmer, try focusing your attention on different parts of your body, perhaps starting with your feet. Simply notice how your feet feel resting against the firm ground or floor. As you allow your attention to rest on your feet, describe to yourself how they feel.

Move up your body—your legs, back, hands, shoulders, neck. Notice how each feels in that moment. Describe each to yourself—"my muscles are tight in my legs," "my hands feel relaxed in my lap," "my stomach is growling and feels hungry." Just spend a minute or so noticing how each part of your body feels in the moment, describing those feelings in matter-of-fact and nonjudgmental ways.

If your mind wanders and thoughts encroach on your time of embodied focusing, no worries. Don't fight the thoughts to keep them at bay or judge yourself for getting distracted; just gently return your focus to a part of your body or use some focused breathing to reset your attention.

How did this feel to give some specific attention to your body? What did you notice? What surprised you? What did you learn about your body?

FURTHER READING

Koppel, Michael S. *Body Connections: Body-Based Spiritual Care.* Nashville: Abingdon Press, 2021.

Scheib, Karen D. *Pastoral Care: Telling the Stories of Our Lives.* Nashville: Abingdon Press, 2016.

5

HEARING IDENTITIES AND EMBODIMENTS

The bodies we move around the world in are as much a part of what makes us who we are as our personalities, our spirituality, our relationships, our intellect. The ways that our bodies differ based on gender, race, sexual orientation, age, dis/ability, and so forth shape many of our experiences throughout life. Some of these shaping influences are harmful to us, and others are quite joyous.

For example, on the harmful end of things, race shapes how we experience interactions with the authority figures from school principals to the police in a society imbued with anti-Blackness and structured to protect and privilege whiteness. The ways we experience our gay or lesbian sexual orientation emerging in adolescence may delay our exploration of dating relationships with same-sex peers for fear of school bullying or family rejection, keeping important parts of our lives hidden from others and becoming as a source of fear and anxiety during formative years. If we move through life in a wheelchair, we may be continually confronted with the reality that the physical spaces we need to access were not designed with our bodies in mind.

On the other hand, our diverse embodiments and identities bring very joyful and life-giving experiences to our lives as well. Belonging to a racial, cultural, or ethnic minority may very well bring about experiences of discrimination in society while at the same time ensconcing our lives in a rich, living tapestry of music, food, stories, and ancestral and kinship relations that help us know who we are and who we belong to. All the while, many in the dominant racial, cultural, or ethnic majority may move through life under the mistaken impression that they are somehow cultureless, not knowing where they came from or who they belong to, severed by their own privilege from deep connections to ancestors, to stories, to place, to a people. The queer joys of drag shows and dance scenes have a long history of providing a space for celebration and community when LGBTQIA+ people needed it most, and they continue to offer experiences of liberative delight to queer and trans people. The depth of community formed around a common experience of disability among people who all shared an experience of the world in a particular and unique way that is different from the temporarily able-bodied majority can offer a quality of mutual understanding that many of us may never quite know.

All the ways we differ from one another in embodiment and identity, and the many ways our bodies and identities may differ from the dominant norm, can bring both the difficulties of injustice and violence and the joys of culture and community. Our differences and diversities and divergences from the majority culture do not produce a singular experience. Listening for the ways that our embodiments and identities shape our lived experience and the situations that call for care means listening for multiplicity and honoring the whole of these experiences while guarding against stereotypes and imposed understandings not rooted in the lived experience of the person in front of us.

The ways that our multiply intersecting embodiments and identities shape the practice of spiritual care could fill multiple books (one of them is listed in the Further Reading section). But there are three areas of which spiritual care first responders should be aware: the ways that injustice affects our experience of life in the world based on our particular embodiments or identities, the ways that even subtle and unintentional slights and insults can harm us in big ways, and the limits we place on possibilities of communal care by going no further than a commitment to inclusivity.

TAKING INJUSTICE SERIOUSLY

Sometimes we mistakenly think of spiritual care as a neutral endeavor, as if we are just caring for the individual person before us and forgetting about anything too political in the larger social sphere around us. But this idea is simply a fiction, and maintaining that fiction in our caregiving practice can be harmful. Everything in our lives, from the political policies that affect our rights and protections, to the sociocultural sphere and the narratives that are perpetuated about people based on race or sexual orientation or immigration status, to the individual level at which we make meaning of these things for our life in the world—all of these levels affect our practice of spiritual care for the careseekers we companion.

We can easily think of ways that experiences of injustice and violence become a direct threat to well-being: Michael Brown or Eric Garner or Breonna Taylor or George Floyd or any number of other unarmed Black people murdered by the police when they are walking through their neighborhoods or sitting in their cars or in their own homes. LGBTQIA+ people experiencing school bullying, or workplace discrimination, or family rejection and youth homelessness.[1] The high rates of domestic violence and sexual assault disproportionally affecting women in our society.[2] Even the ways that our politicians and political processes represent the lives of various minority groups can affect the well-being of people on a very individual level in addition to the structural and public policy levels. For example, the Trevor Project's 2021 National Survey on LGBTQ Youth Mental Health found that of the thirty-five thousand LGBTQ youths surveyed, 94 percent reported that recent politics negatively impacted their mental health.[3]

The personal is political, for sure. But the political also becomes personal and affects every aspect of our health and well-being—physical, emotional, relational, and spiritual. As a spiritual care first responder, be attentive to the ways that the large-scale political climate and social narratives about embodiments of race, gender, sexuality, nationality, religion, and dis/ability may be affecting the lives of the careseekers you companion. As pastoral theologian Sonia Waters says, "If you wish to oppress a group of people, you do not need to do so directly. You just need to make them anxious, stressed out, afraid, and physically sick. You need to block a multitude of access points for basic health and socioeconomic stability—some subtle and some systemically obvious—that, over time, box in a person's options for economic and social resources, personal security, and agency."[4] Injustice has major implications for the social structures of our society that determine who lives and who dies—in interactions with the police, through (in)adequate access to health care, in situations of hate crime violence. But large-scale injustices in society also impact the livability of life for the person sitting in front of you in a spiritual care conversation, even when the situation they are facing is not one of life or death.

Here are three guidelines to keep in mind when providing spiritual care with careseekers who embody differences from the dominant majority in your community, culture, or society. First, know that injustice may be affecting the livability of life for the person you are companioning but don't assume that every problem a person faces and asks you to face with them is being experienced in connection to larger concerns of social justice. Careseekers are the experts on their own lives. Listen carefully to what they are saying about the problem they face. However, when it becomes clear that discrimination, injustice, and even violence based on a person's race, gender, sexuality, class, nationality, religion, dis/ability, and so forth is part of the picture for the careseeker, validate that reality. Voice your ability to see the ways injustice or prejudice or structural discrimination impacts the person's life. Having an ally who can see what we see of our lives is validating of our experience in a society permeated by injustice and its persistent denial. Having an accomplice who can stand with us against the forces of injustice is an even greater source of solidarity in the midst of struggles toward justice.

Second, know the time and place to be in caring companionship with someone facing injustices of various kinds. When someone needs you to be in caring companionship with them to talk through whatever they may be facing in their life, they need you to be fully present with them. Even when your passion for justice burns as you recognize the individual, institutional, or social/political prejudices, injustices, or violence they face, use your own spiritually grounding practices to maintain your presence with them in the caring conversation. Return to your foundational skills of attentive and reflective listening, asking helpful questions, drawing on spiritual sources of healing, and attending to the many emotions that may be present in the moment. Though larger social and political realities may be at play, maintain your caring concern for the singularity of the individual careseeker before you. Healing is an integral part of larger movements toward justice.[5] As a spiritual care responder, you are part of the healing ecology in the life of a person faced with social injustices. Agents of healing and care are also agents of justice.

Third, know the time and place to be fully engaged in struggles toward justice. What you learn about the lived realities of people who are facing discrimination, injustice, and violence based on sexuality, gender race, dis/ability, immigration status, or any other marker of human difference should inform how you live out your practice of faith beyond the caregiving relationship. While in the moment of spiritual care, your focus may need to be solely on the individual in front of you. But in your life outside of that moment, seek out ways of being an accomplice in struggles for justice in ways that will affect the lives of people in your community and our larger society. One of the simplest definitions of sin in the Bible is found in the letter of James in the New Testament: "Anyone, then, who knows the right thing to do and fails to do it commits sin" (4:17 NRSVue). Becoming aware of injustices affecting the livability of life for our neighbors requires our faithful response to address the structures upholding those injustices. As theologian M. Shawn Copeland says, "The gospel challenges us not merely to change our lives, but to transform our living. Lived transformation is discipleship, the practice of solidarity with and beside and among those marginalized among us as 'the least.' Theology that rises from the message of the gospel should disturb as well as provoke, encourage as well as console in the furthering of life in the Resurrected Christ . . . this theology can neither ignore nor mitigate the experiences that complexify being human and the real questions these experiences instigate."[6]

When you've become aware of the ways that social injustices affect people's ability to live and flourish, caregivers can't remain silent and apathetic. That awareness should change us, move us, spur us on toward individual and collective action. Help educate others about those realities, form communities that can work on a small slice of those larger social and political concerns, or become active as accomplices in the struggle toward justice by joining a movement or an organization that is tackling the concerns you're most passionate about. These activities are part of what it means for a spiritual care first responder to become involved in cultivating larger communities of compassion and justice that can hold the entirety of our lives in sacred care, in all our embodied diversity.

ATTENDING TO SUBTLE SLIGHTS, INSULTS, AND INVALIDATIONS THAT INJURE

Many of the experiences of injury based on the embodiment of our racial or ethnic identity, our sexuality or gender, our dis/ability or age occur below the threshold of conscious awareness of those who speak or enact them. What many now call *microaggressions* are the subtle ways that we experience invalidating remarks, insulting comments, and aggressive speech targeting some aspect of our embodiment or identity. What makes them micro, however, is that they often occur outside of the conscious awareness of those who perpetrate them, are usually perpetrated unintentionally, and are just ambiguous enough that those experiencing them must wonder if they really heard what they think they heard and whether there was any real intention behind the remark or action.[7] Their near invisibility makes them quite powerful and difficult to confront.

Two misconceptions have arisen as the term *microaggressions* has entered popular speech. *Micro* does not refer to the degree of harm. Instead, it describes the ways that the harm is communicated and experienced, often in ways that are imperceptible to onlookers who do not share the embodiment or identity being targeted. *Micro* refers to the ability of these slights, insults, and injurious communications to fly just under the radar of perception of perpetrators and onlookers. The harm to those targeted, however, can be quite great—especially when considered cumulatively over long periods. In fact, psychologist Derald Wing Sue argues that "aversive events that are ambiguous, nebulous, and uncertain are more likely to be stressful than those which have a discrete and clearly defined and obvious cause."[8] The ambiguity makes them especially difficult to confront and leaves the targeted party with a great deal of psychological distress wondering about the intention of the message they received.

Second, microaggressions are not the same thing as passive-aggressive communication. We can communicate passive aggressively to anyone and usually know that we are doing so when we do. Microaggressions, on the other hand, target someone specifically because of their race, gender, class, sexual orientation, dis/ability, nationality, religious identity, and so forth. They speak to the embodiment of human difference and the multiply intersecting identities with which we move through the world, and they are most often communicated outside the conscious awareness or intention of the perpetrator. We often don't intend the harmful message that is communicated, and we may not even know that we have communicated it in the first place. For the perpetrators, then, microaggressions cut against commitments that we may consciously express—inclusivity, antiracism,

LGBTQIA+ affirmation, equity for women, and so on—and instead express the very messages we would normally repudiate.

This makes microaggressions especially hard to confront. Most often, the perpetrator of a microaggression meets such a confrontation with outright denial such as "Oh, no, I would never say that. You must have misunderstood. I'm not (racist, sexist, homophobic, etc.). Don't be so sensitive." Thus, quite often, those targeted by microaggressions simply don't say anything because the denial and defensiveness becomes even more burdensome to deal with. As a bystander witnessing or overhearing microaggressions or as a care responder hearing about an experience after the fact, it can be very helpful to validate that you heard what they heard, that they're not imagining things. That simple act of validation can ease the psychological stress of the ambiguity of the situation, knowing that someone else also gets what's going on.

It's important to recognize up front that we all communicate microaggressions in ways that we don't intend and of which we often are unaware. Here are some common examples. See if you can discern what the subtle message is in these microaggressions that the speaker may not recognize but that is clear to the recipient:

- To an LGBTQ+ person: "I'm glad our church has you as an example of a gay Christian. You're just so normal. It's easy to accept you."
- To an Asian American: "So where are you from? Ohio? No, I mean where are you really from?"
- To a female pastor after her sermon: "You looked so good up there in the pulpit today. I really like when you wear that outfit to preach."
- To a trans person: "So what kind of surgeries have you had?"
- About a Black political figure: "He just speaks so eloquently."

The examples could go on, and I'm sure at this point you're starting to recognize some that you've heard or experienced or perhaps even spoken. And microaggressions don't have to only be spoken. They can also occur in our environments. For example, a pulpit or communion table that is inaccessible to a person in a wheelchair may communicate that the task of preaching or presiding at Eucharist isn't intended for a person in a wheelchair. The congregation doesn't actually believe that, but we've arranged our space in such a way that the message comes through anyway.

Take seriously the harm that can be caused by microaggressions. The effects often aren't felt after one or two experiences but settle into our bodies after the cumulative experience of multiple microaggressions over a long period of time, often without the sense that responding to them will do any good, and sometimes after our responses have been met with defensiveness, denial, and even retaliation. The stress and anxiety can build over time in ways of which we aren't aware until we're feeling their physical effects. Our communities that proclaim inclusivity and justice-seeking can become places of harm in ways that the majority in the community never sees and the minority feels every time they enter the doors.

Finally, what is most helpful in a caring community's ability to respond in helpful ways when microaggressions arise is simply having some common language and framework for understanding what microaggressions are, how they are communicated, and that we're all likely culpable of inadvertently engaging in microaggressions. Then building communal strategies for bringing microaggressions into greater communal awareness when they occur helps ease the burden of confrontation and the possible harm caused by denial and defensiveness. Finally, modeling ways of responding nondefensively when we are confronted with our slip-ups and inadvertent slights, insults, and invalidations helps us all become more receptive to the corrections we often need when our outward communication doesn't match our deeply held commitments to inclusivity and justice.

MOVING FROM INCLUDING, TO BELONGING, TO HONORING EMBODIMENTS OF DIFFERENCE

Many of the communities we belong to hold a commitment to *inclusivity*. We usually mean by *inclusivity* that we wish for everyone to be able to join us in the community itself—for everyone, whatever race, dis/ability, gender, class, sexuality, or nationality, to feel like they can be included in the happenings of the community. Inclusivity usually means we are committed to practicing hospitality toward those who may be different from the majority within the church or community. The essential question emerging from a posture of inclusivity and hospitality is, How I can make the other feel welcome? It's an important question for a community wishing to expand its circle of inclusion.

While inclusivity and hospitality are important commitments and practices, they can't get us all the way toward where we want to go in our caring practices within communities full of embodiments of difference. *Hospitality* is typically something practiced by those who are at home toward those who are guests or visitors. For many churches, this has meant making space for LGBTQIA+ people to be members or leaders in the congregation, to be married or ordained. It has meant proclaiming that we are a place where people of diverse races can belong. Sometimes it means adding a few other languages to our orders of worship in a few places to make speakers of those languages feel more at home in our services.

But hospitality has its limits. You wouldn't expect to be treated with hospitality in your own home. After all, you're the one who lives there. It's your home, and if anyone is going to practice hospitality, it is going to be you, the host. Continuing to think only of ourselves as a community of hospitality can subtly lead us to a mentality in which there is a core group of us who really belong and are always practicing hospitality toward a group of others who become perpetual guests, while the rest of us are perpetual hosts.

If practices of hospitality are where we stop, it can seem to those of us being included that our presence is always being accommodated but we never really belong. To move from a position of perpetual guest into a sense of being genuinely at home in a community, we shift from practices of inclusivity into practices of *belonging*. The essential question emerging from a commitment to belonging is: What does the other need in order to feel as at home here as I do? It strives for everyone, whatever race, dis/ability, gender, class, sexuality, or nationality, to feel like they can be included in the definition of *us*. A student in one of my classes once made the distinction by saying that *hospitality* means you can sit on the furniture, while *belonging* means you can move the furniture around.

Sometimes these belonging needs are about a richer tapestry of relationships. Beyond chats around the coffee pot after services or a shared meal or two, we become more involved in one another's lives. We know one another more deeply and intimately. We practice greater vulnerability as we let others into the tender places of our own lives. Sometimes these belonging needs are about structural shifts so that those who have been welcomed guests (attending services, showing up for gatherings, etc.) now become more integral in the community's leadership structure, serving on committees and in leadership positions, playing a greater role in the direction and cultivation of the community and its mission. The voices of those different others who have been included at the table through acts of hospitality now become more involved in setting the table. Importantly, when we move into practices of belonging, concerns of justice that affect the lives of others based on embodiments of difference become matters that concern the whole community because we understand our lives as intimately bound up with those who were once other but are now us.

There is another step in the continuum that I'd characterize as *honoring* the differences of others within community. Sometimes, even when we're striving to practice belonging, we reduce the other to some notion of sameness based on the things we have in common, overlooking the embodiments and identities and experiences that make us radically different. Honoring differences is about seeing the gift of the other's embodiments and experiences and identities that open new perspectives for us on the beauty of the world, the complexity of creation, and the ways we have oftentimes unjustly structured society.

The essential question emerging from a commitment to honoring difference is, What does the other have to teach me about myself, our community, the world, or God? By honoring differences, we strive for everyone, whatever race, dis/ability, gender, class, religion, sexuality, or nationality, to be treated with dignity and worth—not just inclusivity and tolerance—and to be viewed as deep wells of sacred wisdom as people created in the image of God. This is a deep valuing of the sacredness of the other's difference, not their sameness. And it requires us, with great humility, to learn how to learn from the differences of others the wisdom that we would not be able to gain without their presence in our lives and communities.

Inclusivity, belonging, and honoring different embodiments and identities may sound like a linear progression from good to better to best. But they are much more cyclical and mutually present commitments and practices. Most of our communities will be engaging in each of these practices to some degree or another simultaneously and directed toward different expressions of human difference. For caregivers, it is helpful to understand how those within your communities are experiencing these commitments and practices and to help the community as a whole to move toward more robust practices of belonging and honoring of difference.

At a time when the US Surgeon General identifies our collective experience of loneliness and isolation as an epidemic, we cannot discount the vital role that community plays in all our lives, contributing to our well-being in fundamental ways, physically, psychologically, relationally, and spiritually.[9] There may be no time in our history when cultivating inclusive communities of deep belonging and honoring human difference among and between us is as important to our collective well-being and survival than this very moment. The relationship between care and justice is critical at a time when communities are fracturing and fragmenting and our collective health is imperiled from political division and the fragmenting of democracy to the collapse of the climate.

Justice and care are two sides of the same coin, or "like peanut butter and jelly," as Shawn Ginwright, professor of Africana studies, says.[10] He continues, "Our movements for justice are fundamentally about how we collectively have concern and empathy for one another. Care is our collective capacity to express concern and empathy for one another. It requires that we act in ways that protect, defend, and advance the dignity of all human beings, animals, and the environment. This gets at the core of what justice is about: the act of caring for the well-being and dignity of others."[11] Care and justice go hand in hand. As you engage in the practice of spiritual care first aid, attend to the communities you are helping to form that hold people in relationships of care and justice. Rich communities of deep belonging holding commitments to the practice of justice will be more sustaining to people over the long haul than individual care responders are able to be.

Practice Exercise: Personal Inventory of Embodiments and Identities

Take an inventory of your own embodiments and identities and think through the ways these position you in your community in relation to others. Here's a guiding template.

It may be helpful, once you're done, to talk this through with others who have completed the exercise too. Learn from one another's experience in ways that increase your empathic capacity to compassionately understand lives and bodies and experiences different from your own.

Consider each of your embodiments and identities such as race, gender, sexuality, class, religion, nationality, dis/ability, language, or other identities.

Consider how each of these embodiments and identities has shaped your life and possibilities in the place(s) you've lived. How have they helped you blend in with the majority and enjoy unearned privileges? How have they marked you as different from the majority and possibly placed a target on you for the experience of individual prejudice or structural injustice?

Sometimes for those of us with embodiments and identities that represent the majority culture, it can be hard to recognize the privileges we've experienced for no other reason than being born in certain skin or a specific country or into a particular body. But try to stick with it and realistically assess your own embodiments and identities.

Are there stories that are related to any of these aspects of your own embodiment that you believe would help others to get what it's like to be you?

Are there things you wish others knew about any particular embodiment or identity you carry that would help them understand the joys and/or challenges of being you?

What are the gifts of your own embodiments and identities and the experiences that come along with them that hold lessons you wish others could learn from?

FURTHER READING

Kujawa-Holbrook, Sheryl A., and Karen B. Montagno. *Injustice and the Care of Souls: Taking Oppression Seriously in Pastoral Care*. 2nd ed. Minneapolis: Fortress, 2023.

NOTES

1 A very helpful resource for understanding school experiences of LGBTQ+ youth is the GLSEN School Climate Survey, updated regularly with new research and accessible at https://www.glsen.org/school-climate-survey.

2 The CDC reports, "Over half of women and almost 1 in 3 men have experienced sexual violence involving physical contact during their lifetimes. One in 4 women and about 1 in 26 men have experienced completed or attempted rape. About 1 in 9 men were made to penetrate someone during his lifetime. Additionally, 1 in 3 women and about 1 in 9 men experienced sexual harassment in a public place." "Fast Facts: Preventing Sexual Violence," Centers for Disease Control and Prevention, accessed December 16, 2023, https://www.cdc.gov/violenceprevention/sexualviolence/fastfact.html#:~:text=Over%20half%20of%20women%20and,penetrate%20someone%20during%20his%20lifetime.

3 "National Survey on LGBTQ Youth Mental Health," Trevor Project, accessed January 30, 2021, https://www.thetrevorproject.org/survey-2021/?section=Introduction.

4 Sonia E. Waters, *Addiction and Pastoral Care* (Grand Rapids, MI: Eerdmans, 2019), 94.

5 A very helpful resource for understanding the role of care and healing in the work of justice is Kelly Hayes and Mariame Kaba, *Let This Radicalize You: Organizing and the Revolution of Reciprocal Care* (Chicago: Haymarket, 2023).

6 M. Shawn Copeland, *Enfleshing Freedom: Body, Race, and Being*, 2nd ed. (Minneapolis: Fortress, 2023), xvi.

7 For more on microaggressions in ministerial contexts, see Cody J. Sanders and Angela M. Yarber, *Microaggressions in Ministry: Confronting the Hidden Violence of Everyday Church* (Louisville, KY: Westminster John Knox Press, 2015).

8 Derald Wing Sue, *Microaggressions in Everyday Life: Race, Gender, and Sexual Orientation* (Hoboken, NJ: John Wiley & Sons, 2010), 106.

9 Office of the US Surgeon General, "Our Epidemic of Loneliness and Isolation: The U.S. Surgeon General's Advisory on the Healing Effects of Social

Connection and Community," 2023, https://www.hhs.gov/sites/default/files/surgeon-general-social-connection-advisory.pdf.

10 Shawn A. Ginwright, *The Four Pivots: Reimagining Justice, Reimagining Ourselves* (Berkeley: North Atlantic Books, 2022), 121.

11 Ginwright, *The Four Pivots*, 121.

PART TWO

THE ART OF HELPING

6

HELPFUL EXPECTATIONS, BOUNDARIES, AND INTRODUCTIONS

No two people necessarily desire the same form of care even if their situations are similar ones. This can be true even if the two people are experiencing the same situation together—even spouses or partners experiencing the death of a child may experience that loss differently. Whether you are a care responder or a careseeker, a painful situation can arise when there are misaligned expectations between the two parties. A careseeker may be expecting to receive something completely different from what a caregiver intends to provide. Yet the two parties in the caregiving relationship may not discover this misalignment of expectations until well into the caregiving process, at which point disappointment and hurt feelings can result.

ALIGNING EXPECTATIONS

A congregant may reach out to you or a care team in the congregation for help getting to and from a medical appointment for a procedure. You might show up at the appointed time, drive the person to the appointment, and return the person home after the appointment. On the way home, the careseeker says, "I really need to stop by the pharmacy and the grocery store for a few items. Could you take me by there on the way?" Or once home, the careseeker may request that you stay for a while to keep them company or help them with a chore.

What the caregiver thought they were committing to is now being stretched beyond what they were actually willing to do. There may be unspoken bitterness over feelings of being taken advantage of. The care recipient may also feel disappointed or angry about not having these needs met because they seemed like such small things to ask.

If that clarity of desires and expectations is not readily supplied, the caregiver should ask for more details to be sure they can provide with the careseeker is requesting. When a connection is initially made between the careseeker and the caregiver, the request of the careseeker should be as fully understood as possible and communicated to the caregiver. For example, "I need to be picked up at my apartment at eight and driven to my doctor downtown, and I need you to wait for me until the procedure is done, approximately an hour, and drive me back to my home."

When a caregiver is reaching out via phone to someone they are concerned about, they might say at the outset of the phone call, "Hi, Joe. I only have about twenty minutes to talk right now, but it was important for me to reach out and see how you're doing." This lets the person know right away that about twenty minutes is the limit for the call so that it doesn't get awkward when the caregiver is desperately trying to find a nice way to get off the call an hour into the conversation.

Talk through and agree on the expectations up front as much as possible. If new or unexpected needs and expectations arise, evaluate them with the careseeker to see if you are still the best person to provide for their care need or whether you might need to ask for some help from others to meet the needs being expressed.

UNDERSTANDING BOUNDARIES

Another area of difficulty can arise when boundaries in the caregiving relationship are breached, even if unintentionally. In the process of providing care for others, you can think of boundaries in four ways. First, there are *boundaries of competence*. These speak to the level of caregiving training and skill one is able to bring to a situation and which situations calling for care may be beyond one's competency to address. For example, in providing caring companionship in a situation of loneliness with an elderly congregant, a caregiver may be well trained in the skills of compassionate listening. This form of caring companionship is likely incredibly buoying to the spirits of the elderly congregant. In the course of visits, however, the caregiver may discover that the congregant is having difficulty caring for herself or preparing regular meals or remembering important details like when to take medications. You may suspect that a form of cognitive impairment has entered the picture for this congregant, but you don't have the knowledge or skills to make this assessment yourself or to know the best steps for accessing the care the congregant may need. This is an example of a boundary of competence. In a situation like this, it is appropriate to seek the advice of someone with knowledge and skills in this area to help you discern the pathway forward.

There are also important *boundaries of time*. This speaks to how much of one's time a caregiver can dedicate to the provision of care in any given situation. You should be as clear with yourself about this as possible before entering caregiving relationships. If you have a short-term caregiving companionship program set up in your faith community, you may publicize the boundaries of time associated with this ministry. For example, the program may intend to pair a lay caregiver with a careseeker for one-on-one conversations over six months, for example. The onus is on you as the caregiver to be clear with yourself about these boundaries of time and then communicate them with clarity and compassion to careseekers.

Then there are *boundaries of relationship*, or how the mutual relationship between caregiver and care receiver is honored. Often in congregational contexts with lay caregivers, the relationship between caregiver and careseeker is a complex one in which there is no rigid boundary between your role as caregiver and other roles you might have with this person. You may also serve on a committee together, sing in the choir together, or engage in social settings with one another. Therefore, a caregiver and careseeker may need to have a conversation at the outset of caring companionship in which it is made clear that when they are working together in other roles, they won't discuss issues that might regularly come up in caregiving conversations. In other situations, you may simply feel that the relationship with another congregant is too complex to add the layer of caregiver-careseeker to the mix. In these cases, it is helpful to have a network of other lay caregivers who can be invited into the situation.

Another important aspect of relational boundaries involves concerns of ethical boundaries that can arise when sexual or romantic feelings develop for a careseeker. Caregiving relationships can form intimate emotional and spiritual bonds between the caregiver and the careseeker.

At times, this form of emotional closeness can develop into what feel like romantic feelings between the caregiver and the careseeker. It is important to be honest with yourself about these feelings when they arise for you. Denial will not help you maintain ethical boundaries with careseekers. Here again, the onus is on the caregiver to be honest with oneself and to maintain clarity with the careseeker about the boundaries of the caring relationship to avoid an unethical breach of those boundaries through engaging in sexual or romantic intimacy with a careseeker. Having someone whom you can talk to about these dynamics when they arise for you (the pastor, another minister, a care team coordinator, etc.) can be very helpful and is highly recommended. At times, ending a caregiving relationship is necessary if relational boundaries become difficult to manage. While difficult, this is a much more helpful and caring decision than the emotional and spiritual pain that can be caused by a breach of relational ethics.

Finally, there are *boundaries of confidentiality*. Confidentiality is the bedrock of good caregiving. When a person shares with a caregiver the struggles and joys of life, the careseeker's trust in the caring relationship is bound up with the assumption that what is shared will be kept confidential and not shared outside of the caregiving relationship. There are, however, times when confidentiality must be broken. You can think about boundaries of confidentiality on three levels.

Complete Confidentiality

Generally, it is helpful in a caregiving relationship for the careseeker to know that what they share with the caregiver will be held in strict confidence and never shared with others. This is the standard level of confidentiality at which most caregiving relationships should operate. But there are situations that arise in which this boundary cannot be maintained.

Breaking Confidentiality with Permission

In some instances, you may find that you really would be helped in your caregiving if you could talk over the problems a careseeker is facing with another person, like the pastor, a spiritual care supervisor, or a caregiving colleague. Primarily, these situations will involve instances in which you may simply need advice about how to address a specific problem or situations involving a conundrum that you need to work through with an experienced professional. In these cases, it would be appropriate to say to the careseeker something like "I think the pastor may have some helpful insight about this situation, and I wonder if it would be okay with you if I talked to her about this situation. I would just like some help in becoming a better caregiver for you."

Other instances in which you may need to ask permission to involve others in the caregiving situation are ones in which you believe that the careseeker may need resources for care or counseling beyond your capacity to provide. These may be either beyond your training or beyond the time you have to dedicate to this person's care, and you need to introduce them to another care professional (more on this below). Or they may be situations in which the person needs physical/material resources that you cannot provide, like help with purchasing groceries or paying a bill.

On occasion, you may also find that a situation you're being asked to address with the careseeker is a difficult one for you personally—either because of your own history with a similar situation or because you are having a hard time empathizing. In these cases, you may believe that someone else is better equipped to take over care or should join you in the caregiving process. If there are no concerns of abuse, violence, self-harm, or suicide that would raise the urgent need to break confidentiality, then all situations like the ones named above should be discussed with the careseeker before you break the confidentiality of the caregiving relationship and involve another party.[1]

When Breaking Confidentiality Is Required

There are situations that cannot be kept confidential due to the potential harm they pose to the careseeker or others. In these situations, confidentiality must be broken to honor the much more important ethical commitment to preserving the life and well-being of others. States also have mandated reporting laws that require helping professionals like clergy to report some of these situations. It is important to know the mandated reporter laws in your state and who is required to report which situations to whom.[2] These situations are when:

- The careseeker has expressed an intention to harm or kill themselves.

- The careseeker shares information about the abuse of a child, the elderly, or the developmentally disabled. Again, in many states, reporting abuse of vulnerable populations is a legal requirement for clergy.
- The careseeker intends to enact violence against another person.

In any of these situations, you must elicit immediate help from the pastor or another qualified professional in dealing with the situation. Chapter 10 more fully addresses these situations.

Questions for Discussion

What aspect of managing expectations and boundaries seems most difficult or uncomfortable for you at this time? How can you imagine managing situations in which those expectations or boundaries become important?

HELPFUL INTRODUCTIONS

When you are providing care as a representative of your congregation or faith community, you are not acting alone. You are acting on behalf of the congregation and with the resources of an entire community behind you. There are professionals—the pastor and possibly other staff ministers—as well as other laypersons who are standing with you in the provision of care. Call on those resources when they are needed.

At times, a person in need of care may benefit from a relationship with someone who has a specific skillset or specialized training or credentials beyond the congregation's own resources. Sometimes this is because the provision of care that you've engaged in with a person is approaching a boundary of time that you or the congregation has set for how long a caring or companioning relationship should last. In other circumstances, a boundary of competence is reached when you realize that a form of care is required that is beyond your skill or experience or your role as a lay caregiver. This is when a referral can become a helpful resource for care.

In the most unhelpful circumstances, referrals can feel like you are simply passing off a person to a professional because the person's situation requires a set of skills, knowledge, or competency you do not possess. But this falls short of the caring companionship that you may hope to offer to others. Pastoral theologian Wayne Oates had a helpful way of framing the art of referral; he called this the "ministry of introduction."[3] As important as any caregiving skill you develop is the ability to connect others to needed resources that can become vital sources of help and healing in situations that call for care. There are three keys to a helpful ministry of introduction.

Refer without Speaking Doom

Ensure that you make an introduction to another caregiver without conveying that the careseeker's situation is just too big for you to handle. Instead, it is helpful to present another helping companion as someone with skills and perspective that may be helpful in this situation or who can companion a careseeker through a longer season than you are able to.

For example, you may encounter a situation that causes you to believe the person's pastor needs to be involved in the caregiving process. You may say something like "I am very appreciative that you've felt comfortable sharing this concern with me. I am honored to be invited to hold this concern with you. I know in some circumstances like this, Pastor Holly has been very helpful, and I wonder if you would consider sharing this concern with her or giving me permission to do so." Think of this ministry of introduction as a privilege, much like you would feel when introducing one of your friends to another friend. Offer the introduction in a way that doesn't intensify the problem but opens greater possibilities for the problem to be meaningfully addressed in compassionate and healing ways.

Referring without Abandoning

Introductions to another caregiver can be made in ways that convey that you are introducing the careseeker to resources that may helpfully add to the caring companionship they receive from you. While the careseeker may need an introduction to another helpful caregiver—the pastor, a therapist, or a community resource, for example—you may still plan to follow up with them with caring support in your role as a lay caregiver or in your role as their pastor if you are referring them to a therapist or other resource. Oates describes the multitude of roles that a spiritual care companion continues to have in a careseeker's life, even after an introduction to another source of support. These include continuing to give emotional support, helping to reinforce the person's trust in the other helping professional, attending to the spiritual needs and faith community involvement of the person, and companioning the person as "a fellow sufferer in the ministry of prayer with and for the person."[4]

No matter how you continue in this person's care, if you are a lay caregiver for your church or the pastor, you will still be a part of the larger congregation alongside them. A referral should not communicate that you no longer wish to continue a relationship, unless there is some way that you are experiencing the caregiving relationship as harmful or inappropriate. Otherwise, continue in your caring companionship while helping the careseeker to enter into a relationship with another helping professional or healing resource that can address the person's needs differently, more deeply, or for a longer duration than you are able to.

Referring while Companioning

During your ministry of introduction, discuss ways that staying in a caring relationship with the careseeker might happen, if that seems appropriate. For example, you're still willing to call the person every few weeks to check in on them, even if another person—for example, a pastor or a therapist—becomes the primary caregiver. Or perhaps you're still willing to meet for conversation about the situation that calls for care, but you need to know that you're not the only person holding those concerns alongside the careseeker. It is important to be clear with the person about these continuing roles of companionship and to be sure both of your expectations are in alignment.

Practice Exercise: Building a Referral Database

Gather a group of caregivers in your congregation, perhaps in consultation with the pastor or another minister or a local counselor or social worker, and discuss together: Which situations of care can you imagine arising in your caregiving ministry that would cause you to engage in the ministry of introduction? Do you already know the people or other community resources you would need to draw on in these situations? If not, do you know how to find them?

With this group of people from the same faith community or the same geographic region, it could be helpful to begin filling out appendix II in this book, which is intended to help you develop a list of helpful organizations and resources in your area that could be of use to careseekers in the future.

FURTHER READING

Lebacqz, Karen, and Joseph D. Driskill. *Ethics and Spiritual Care: A Guide for Pastors, Chaplains, and Spiritual Directors*. Nashville: Abingdon, 2000.

Stevenson-Moessner, Jeanne. *A Primer in Pastoral Care*. Minneapolis: Fortress, 2005.

NOTES

1 See chapter 13 on addressing situations of suicide and chapter 14 on dealing with situations of abuse and violence.

2 See more in chapter 14. For up-to-date laws, search for the mandated reporting laws in your specific state listed on trusted government websites. For a discussion of some intricacies of mandated reporting laws pertaining to clergy, see Child Welfare Information Gateway, "Clergy as Mandatory Reporters of Child Abuse and Neglect," US Department of Health and Human Services, Administration for Children and Families, Children's Bureau, 2023, https://www.childwelfare.gov/resources/clergy-mandatory-reporters-child-abuse-and-neglect/.

3 Wayne E. Oates, *The Christian Pastor*, 3rd ed. rev. (Philadelphia: Westminster, 1982), 261–283.

4 Oates, *The Christian Pastor*, 263.

7

HELPING WITH GOALS AND DESIRES

Many conversations in the practice of spiritual care first aid will be focused on the goals a careseeker holds as important to their life and their sense of fulfillment, meaning, or purpose (e.g., increasing one's social connections to others, making progress on a career trajectory, adding spiritual practices to daily life, overcoming an obstacle in the way of movement toward goals, etc.). Your role as a care responder is not to fix the problem, solve the issue, or give advice on how a person should reach their goal, even if you have dealt with something similar in the past. Instead, listening to a person's goals and desires in an intentional and caring way can help promote movement toward those goals.

Hearing goals and desires is primarily about three things: First is developing a really good understanding of where people are in their lives in relation to a particular area of concern such as a relationship, a spiritual struggle, a career goal, or the like. This is where your ability to listen deeply and attentively and ask helpful questions comes into play. Second is developing a sense of where people wish they were in relation to those goals and desires. The space between those two poles—where a person is and where they'd like to be—is the space where spiritual care can be helpful in moving toward goals and desires. It is a space of movement, exploration, possibility, and sometimes even struggle. Third is developing an understanding of what makes this goal or desire important to the careseeker—that is, coming to know what it would mean in their life if they were able to meet this goal or reach a desired outcome.

WORKING TOWARD GOALS AND ADDRESSING SETBACKS

Oftentimes, a careseeker has a specific goal in mind, and the conversation they seek is about frustrations experienced in working toward that goal.

Once you've listened deeply and attentively to understand where they are in relation to their goal, where they'd like to be, and what it means to them, then some conversation may proceed about the steps they're taking toward their intended goal or desire.

When determining how to make progress toward goals we hold for ourselves, two things are of primary importance: having a big goal, a dream, a desire we're moving toward (this keeps us motivated toward something that holds a lot of potential for our lives) and being able to work in small steps toward that goal, dream, or desire (this gives us practical ways of moving toward the goal and small milestones to celebrate along the way that motivate us further).

One obstacle that sometimes gets in the way of movement toward our goals is not having manageable enough steps to take toward that goal—breaking the big-picture dream down into workable steps—and becoming frustrated by our lack of achievement. When working with a careseeker to establish small tasks to reach larger goals, it can be helpful to think with the careseeker about which small steps seem doable, especially early on. Even small steps may sometimes need to be made smaller—what might be described as *turtle steps*, which are even smaller than baby steps.[1]

When a step along the way toward a goal seems just a bit too large, try cutting it in half to see if it becomes more manageable. If that's still too big, cut it in half again. And again. And again until it becomes manageable for a person to accomplish in the very near future. The aim is getting the step small enough for the person to actually take it. Even if it seems like an infinitesimal step toward the big goals, making those small steps moves us closer toward the goal and gets us unstuck from our immobility in the face of steps that are too large.

Small accomplishments of mini or even micro goals toward a larger goal or dream can help build a sense of confidence in one's ability to make progress toward that end. All the while, however, keep talking about the big-picture goal or dream and its meaning in a person's life because that's the true source of motivation. The turtle-step accomplishments along the way are confidence boosters and practical increments during the journey.

Helpful questions about the meaning of the goal or desire that a careseeker holds allow the careseeker to explore and explain the importance this goal or desire has in the careseeker's life. For example, "If you were able to accomplish X, what difference do you imagine it would make in your life? How would your life be different? As you move toward your desire for X, how do you imagine your life taking shape differently than at present? What would change for you?"

Additionally, therapists John Walter and Jane Peller note the importance of attending to potential setbacks in movements toward goals with care and in ways that don't enhance a feeling of failure. They recommend the helpful question: What might be some signs that you were getting back on track?[2]

This question invites imagination beyond the sense of failure over the setback to picture what getting back on a path toward a goal or desire might look like in the life of a careseeker. Another helpful question Walter and Peller suggest when achieving a goal that seems like a black-or-white issue—such as either "I've succeeded" or "I've failed"—is introducing the notion of progress toward a goal or desire. That question might sound something like: What would be some signs that you were making progress?[3]

Both of these questions allow for some imaginative movement in the conversation to traverse the space between where a careseeker is in relation to a goal or desire and where they wish to be.

MIRACLE QUESTION

The miracle question is an inquiry developed by practitioners of solution-focused brief therapy. We're not training to become therapists, but this particular tool from the method is one that can be helpfully used to understand how a person might imagine their lives if their goal or desire had been reached, even if they don't yet have any clue how to reach it. It's a simple question that evokes imaginative potential. It goes like this: "Let's imagine you go to sleep tonight, and while you are sleeping, a miracle occurs, and your problem is suddenly resolved. When you wake up, what would be different about your life that would indicate to you that the miracle had taken place? What would you notice differently as you get up and move through your day? What would you be thinking, feeling, doing, seeing?"

The aim of this type of imaginative question is to better understand what the careseeker's hopes are in relation to a problem, goal, or desire. It's a *what if?* type of question. It can even involve imagining how others would relate to the problem being miraculously solved or the goal being reached: "Who else would notice that something had changed? What would they be seeing? What would they be noticing about you in the aftermath of this overnight miracle?"

Importantly, the miracle question doesn't solve a problem or miraculously produce the goals or desires being discussed. Instead, it opens some imaginative space to consider what it would look like to move in that in-between space between what is and what could be. The question opens toward possibilities and the many ramifications of those possibilities held in the goals and desires of the careseeker.

SHOULDS AND DARES

Psychologist Jeremy Sutton has developed two additional sets of questions beyond the miracle question that can also be used in helping careseekers assess their goals and desires. First, Sutton offers the *should question.*[4] It has three parts:

- I should: List the thing or things that one feels one should be doing.
- Why? List the reasons one believes one should be doing those things.
- Says who? List the people, institutions, or sources that one feels are telling one to do the thing one feels one must do.

After some exploration of these three questions regarding the "shoulds" one feels, Sutton encourages people to rewrite the *should* statement with the phrase "I could" replacing "I should" in order to create a little more flexibility in addressing the demands we believe others are making on our lives.

This conversation can be helpful in determining whether a goal we have is really our goal or whether it may be someone else's goal for us that isn't central to our sense of call or preferred directions in life. Care responders should be especially attentive to the shoulds placed on people by their religious traditions and community.

Oftentimes, overly moralistic shoulds can come to seem like the demands of one's faith, for example, "I should [date X person, be interested in Y kind of job, do Z with my free time] because something in my faith tradition [my family, my pastor, my church] believes this is the right path for me." The more these external shoulds are placed on us by others in our lives, the more they may come to seem like our goals and desires, and we can become frustrated when our motivation for doing those things seems lacking. In many cases, the goal or desire wasn't ours to begin with, and we may come to find a better path, more faithful to our sense of God's call or the teachings of our tradition if we are able to hold that goal or desire before us for some more careful examination.

Finally, Sutton offers what he terms the *dare question*, phrased as "What would you do if you knew you could not fail?"[5] This question invites a careseeker to explore possibilities related to a goal or desire beyond the limitations they may currently face in moving toward that goal. In the course of conversation that follows, careseekers may find that some of the things they would do if fear of failure were not in the picture are things they could really see themselves doing now and begin taking some courageous steps toward a deeply held goal or desire.

LOVE, LABOR, LEISURE, AND LONGING

If a sense of desire seems vague yet still a bit pressing for a careseeker, it can sometimes be helpful to talk through areas of life in which growth and movement may be desirable yet not yet clearly named. I think about four major areas of life in which growth is often desirable as the 4Ls: love, labor, leisure, and longing. These areas are not a checklist to work down but four areas of life for you, the care responder, to keep in your mind as a mental heuristic to expand your attention toward what you are hearing in the story of a careseeker.

Love

Love encompasses so much of our life's desires. We hold a desire to share love with others—romantic love, the love of deep and abiding friendships, the love of animal companions. We desire to be loved by others. Many of us struggle to love ourselves because of mistakes we have made or messages we have inadvertently internalized from others about our unlovability. And we often desire to experience love at transcendent levels that we might describe as the love of God for us or an encompassing love that embraces the cosmos.

In Martin Luther King Jr.'s book of collected sermons, *Strength to Love*, I am struck by how many of his sermons began with Scriptures on love:

> *Beloved, let us love one another, because love is from God . . . There is no fear in love, but perfect love casts out fear. (1 John 4:7–8, NRSV)*
>
> *You have heard that it was said, "You shall love your neighbor and hate your enemy." But I say to you, Love your enemies and pray for those who persecute you. (Matthew 5:43–45, NRSV)*
>
> *If I speak in the tongues of mortals and of angels, but do not have love, I am a noisy gong or a clanging cymbal . . . and if I hand over my body so that I may boast, but do not have love, I gain nothing. (1 Corinthians 13:1–3, NRSV)*

Love was central to how Martin Luther King Jr. lived and led through the civil rights movement. But King isn't talking about an overly sentimentalized notion of love as a simple feeling we have toward someone or something. King explains, "When I speak of love . . . I am speaking of that force which all of the great religions have seen as the supreme unifying principle of life."[6] Poet and educator bell hooks adds to this description by King, saying, "Love is profoundly political . . . Only love can give us strength to go forward in the midst of heartbreak and misery. Only love can give us the power to reconcile, to redeem, the power to renew weary spirits and save lost souls. The transformative power of love is the foundation of all meaningful social change . . . Love is the heart of the matter. When all else has fallen away, love sustains."[7]

Love was the bridge King used to cross the divide between absolute despair and realistic hope, facing the risk of failure while continuing to strive for a different future and a more just world. Love was the disarming tool of nonviolence King employed to meet his enemies' violence with a soul force that could not be overcome with weapons. Love was the energizing, empowering, animating element in King's life. Amid his own looming depression and in moments of hopelessness and justified despair in the face of persistent injustice, love compelled King forward in the work of justice. Love was the lens that allowed King to see the humanity in the face of others—even his enemies.

In your caring work with others, pay careful attention to those forces that erode the possibilities of love. These forces come in many forms: Sometimes they are outright propagandized accounts of other races, cultures, and religions and politicized messages of hatred toward those who embody a difference from the dominant norm in terms of race, culture, gender or sexual identity, religious commitments, and so forth. Sometimes the forces that erode the possibilities of love hide from our eyes the complex ways that injustice and violence are upheld by institutionalizing prejudice so that even when we witness injustice with our own eyes, we blame the victim for their own oppression and deny that prejudice had anything to do with the situation at all.

Sometimes the forces that erode the possibilities of love are so deeply embedded in the mythos of our nation that we don't even see them at work on our minds and hearts, ensuring we will continue our complicity with an oppressive status quo in ways we don't even recognize as complicit in injustice. And sometimes the forces that erode the possibilities of love are less sociocultural and are, instead, more personal. They come through the messages we've received about ourselves from important figures in our lives—family members; current or former spouses, partners, or significant others; and the communities we've belonged to like churches and schools. Stories have circulated about us as unlovable or as someone needing to work really hard to be loved. These messages can become powerful in the construction of our sense of self over time, and they can teach us erroneous lessons we need to unlearn over time in caring companionship and loving community with others.

Pay careful attention to those forces that erode the possibilities of love and listen carefully for the desires careseekers' hold for increasing those possibilities in their lives: searching for romantic love and companionship, increasing social support networks, strengthening friendships and developing new ones, sharing loving relationship with animal companions and the larger ecological web of life, sensing oneself enfolded in the love of God. All of these are both deeply personal, as we could all attest, and profoundly political, as King and hooks remind us. And they are central to the life of the Divine, as the witness of Scripture so clearly attests.

Labor

By *labor*, I mean those things we put our hands and minds and strength and ingenuity toward that cause us to feel we are making a difference in some way, small or large. I don't necessarily mean a job or our means of employment. Having a way of making a living is, of course, vital. But that activity gets more at our ability to provide for our material needs and those of our loved ones than it does our needs to make meaning from the creativity of our labor.

Sometimes the two can coincide in meaningful ways. Our jobs can be our expressions of making a meaningful difference in the world. At other times, our jobs will be our jobs—making a living for ourselves and our loved ones—and our hobbies, our volunteer activities, our artistic engagements, or the pursuit of our passions will become far more meaningful to our sense of self and contribution to the differences we desire to make in the world.

Even when our labor is not our work, it is a type of work—which is still distinct from leisure. Enjoyable and fulfilling though it may be, it leaves us feeling as though we've really done something that required the best of our strength, our creativity, our intellect, our soulful engagement. One way to think about this area of fulfillment is in the difference between a job and a vocation. *Vocation*, from the Latin word *vocare*, meaning *calling*, bespeaks a summons toward an engagement in which we find meaning and purpose, that which stretches us beyond ourselves.

Here are some questions that may help figure out what those things are for careseekers:

> *What are you doing when you feel most like you're making a difference?*
>
> *What are the activities in your day, your week, your month that, no matter how challenging they are, cause you to feel like you're coming alive when you do them?*

> *What are the things you daydream about doing that would feel intensely meaningful if only you had a little more time to do them?*

Recent retirees are sometimes especially attentive to this dimension of life, especially if their job and their vocation were intimately bound up with one another. It can be an important time in life to ask some of the above questions to discern how one continues to feel engaged in meaningful labors that are no longer tied to employment or that are now possible for the first time because retirement opened the time and space to differently engage one's sense of vocation.

Leisure

We each need something that rejuvenates our spirit, restores our strength, and ushers us into a feeling of rest. There's little that needs to be said about our need to rest. It's even described as a central feature of God's own activity in the creation account of Genesis 2. After the creative labors of bringing about life and beauty and the cosmic community throughout the first six days of creation, God rests on the seventh day.

This is, of course, where our notion of Sabbath comes from. Susannah Heschel, daughter of Rabbi Abraham Joshua Heschel, describes the way that Sabbath was treated in her home: "Observing the Sabbath is not only about refraining from work, but about creating *menuha*, a restfulness that is also a celebration. The Sabbath is a day for body as well as soul."[8] Creating a restfulness that is also a celebration, for body and for soul, is a helpful encapsulation for the gift of Sabbath and our engagement in activities of leisure.

Where does your soul find rest? How do you rest your body? What activities do you engage in not because you have to, not because of your creative labor summons you to, but because you need the rest and celebration that those activities provide you? These are the kinds of questions that help us access our places of deep restfulness and celebration in living. While for many of us, restfulness will look a lot like rest, for others of us, our places of restful leisure will be embodied in very active ways like sports, exercise, dog training, or similar activities that allow our minds and hearts to feel a deep sense of peace.

It is important that spiritual care responders understand that rest, like most things, is distributed unequally. Shawn Ginwright, a professor of education and scholar of trauma and healing among Black youths, describes this as *rest inequality*. "The gap in the quality, duration, and amount of rest we get," including sleep, is shaped by myriad factors such as "income level, housing, employment status, type of work, and race."[9]

In addition to rest itself, leisure more broadly—the pleasurable activities we pursue, the amount of time we have for play and recreation—is shaped by income and race. Whether it is because we work multiple jobs to make ends meet, making leisure difficult to fit into our lives, or because our housing situation is precarious or dangerous, making it hard to ever fully rest, or because we work full time in addition to being a full-time caregiver to our children or elderly parents, many face inequality in access to rest and leisure. Before flippantly prescribing self-care to someone who seems overwhelmed and in need of rest, try to understand their life in its fullness with an eye toward rest inequality. This may help you better strategize with the careseeker manners of incorporating rest and leisure into their lives in ways that are responsive to their lived situation. Remember that the work you do to strive toward racial and economic justice, advocate for better childcare availability in your community, and address concerns of structural inequality is also helping those who need it most to access rest.

Longing

We all need something that draws us out of our bounded sense of self and toward the world beyond us, luring us toward a greater whole. This is the role of what I call *longing* but could also be called *a sense of the transcendent, an enticing into the mystery of being, a call toward relationship with the cosmos*. We were never really meant to be autonomous individuals. We are humans in relationship, forming kinship bonds with one another and the wider ecological web of life, ever attempting to touch the transcendent that exists beyond us through art and poetry and music and prayer, led outside of ourselves and into communion with all that enfolds us in the cosmic communion of creation.

Many will name the orientation of their longings for transcendence and cosmic community with the language of God, the Divine, the Holy, or the Sacred. Others will name this orientation in language much more earthy and seemingly ordinary, focusing on our relationship with the land that sustains our life, our bonds of community that enfold us from birth through death. Because the ways we language our longing is diverse, it takes careful attention to listen carefully for careseekers' longings that draw them beyond their bounded sense of self and into communion with something larger than themselves: human, other-than-human, or Divine. But without this sense of longing, drawing us outward, our lives tend to become very small and egocentric.

Listen for longing. Examples of questions to use might include:

Have you ever felt like you were part of a greater whole? If so, when was it, what were you doing, and who were you with?

What stops you in your tracks and catches you in a sense of awe or wonder?

What are you doing when you most sense a connection to something greater, something beyond, something larger than your individual life?

When longing needs a bit of cultivation, turn toward practices such as the one discussed in chapter 12 that evoke a sense of wonder in the life of careseekers and communities you serve.

One final word of caution: Not every concern that a careseeker brings to you is about reaching a goal or overcoming obstacles to reaching a desire they hold in their life. Sometimes the need is simply to talk through problems for which there is no solution or goal to be reached. At other times, it is to sit with a caring companion in the midst of pain and heartache that can't be easily overcome. Please do not use spiritual care conversational tools for working toward goals and desires in those situations. Reserve these spiritual care first aid techniques for times when there is clearly a goal or desire that a careseeker hopes to reach and enlists your support in doing so.

Practice Exercise: The Miracle Question

Either on your own or in conversation with someone else who is learning these skills alongside you, take the miracle question above and use it to imaginatively engage a goal or desire you hold for yourself. Talk through the question with as much detail and nuance as you can. At the end, see what difference it has made to you to think about having attained that goal or desire and what life is like for you on the other side of it. If you're practicing with another, discuss your experiences with each other.

FURTHER READING

Massey, Denise. *Caring: Six Steps for Effective Pastoral Conversations.* Nashville: Abingdon Press, 2019.

NOTES

1 I first heard this term *turtle steps* from Denise Massey, whose book is recommended at the end of this chapter.

2 John L. Walter and Jane E. Peller, *Recreating Brief Therapy: Preferences and Possibilities* (New York: Norton, 2000), 101. Emphasis in original.

3 Walter and Peller, *Recreating Brief Therapy*, 103. Emphasis in original.

4 Jeremy Sutton, "Should Question," PostivePsychology.com, accessed September 30, 2023, https://positive.b-cdn.net/wp-content/uploads/2021/09/Should-Question.pdf.

5 Jeremy Sutton, "Dare Question," PositivePsychology.com, accessed September 30, 2023, https://positive.b-cdn.net/wp-content/uploads/2021/09/Dare-Question.pdf.

6 Martin Luther King Jr., "The Quest for Peace and Justice," Nobel Lecture, December 11, 1964, http://www.nobelprize.org/nobel_prizes/peace/laureates/1964/king-lecture.html.

7 bell hooks, *Salvation: Black People and Love* (New York: Perennial, 2001), 16–17.

8 Susannah Heschel, "Introduction," in Abraham Joshua Heschel, *The Sabbath* (New York: Farrar, Straus, and Giroux, 1951/2005), xiv.

9 Shawn A. Ginwright, *The Four Pivots: Reimagining Justice, Reimagining Ourselves* (Berkeley: North Atlantic Books, 2022), 223.

8

HELPING THROUGH FEAR, ANXIETY, GRIEF, AND LOSS

Fear is an evolutionary gift to humanity.[1] Without the capacity to experience and respond to fear, we would not have survived as a species. That's why I'd rather not term this a negative emotion. While fear may be uncomfortable, discomfort is not something to simply be avoided. We must cultivate the capacity to listen to these emotions for the messages they carry and attend to them with care so that they don't become overwhelming of our experience of the world.

Emotions like anxiety and worry are also part of the emotional family of fear. Fear and its varying degrees of worry and anxiety are responses to a perceived threat or imminent harm. Fear has a specific objective: to protect us from threat of harm in our immediate environment. Anxiety is usually in response to something a little more ambiguous than a clear and present danger to our well-being. In the brain, fear operates as a subcortical signal to us, occurring outside of the rational thought processes of the neocortex.

There are myriad reasons we feel fear arising in our lives on a day-to-day basis, from fear of something we dread like public speaking to fear of a diagnosis we are waiting to receive to fear related to our own mortality. Collectively, in our present global context, we have no shortage of specific objects of fear arousal, be they the calamitous outcomes of climate collapse that are now at our doorstep or parents sending their Black children out into a world where the police may kill them or a recent pandemic that threatened the life of everyone on the planet. All of these can arouse the feeling of fear while a generalized sense of anxiety likely lingers in the emotional background.

Our specific embodiment and social location influence the fear that we experience. Our economic positions make us more or less susceptible to the immediacy of fear in relation to economic collapse. The stock market dipping may cause some a sense of anxiety, while a sudden layoff, loss of insurance, or impending eviction may stimulate immediate fear in relation to one's well-being.

The racialized body we move about with in the world affects just how relative that fear becomes to us. The threat of police killing is real and is being played out in front of our eyes. A white body may never experience the palpable immediacy of fear from watching the killing of George Floyd on video nor have the memory of that fear brought immediately back to us when we encounter a police officer on the street.

We wake up to the scenes of climate-driven disaster every day—if not in our own backyards, then as portrayed on the news. Climate change poses genuine, immediate, and growing threats to our lives and well-being that are playing out day to day and affect everyone. The threat is no longer in the far future. Our geographic locations have often buffered our feeling the immediacy of these fears that are now becoming more palpable through extreme weather events all over the world.

Fear emotions are relativized by our racial embodiment, our economic situation, even the vulnerability to climate-driven disasters of the geography we call home. Our empathic exploration is required to understand how emotions are triggered differently in our different embodiments in relation to the threats to our well-being that we experience in daily life.

WHEN FEAR BECOMES AN OUTLOOK ON LIFE

Emotions-turned-moods can, over time, morph into a pervasive outlook on life, an orientation toward the world, a temperament or general disposition that shapes one's everyday experience. Fear can, and perhaps has, become a general, unifying perspective on life and is a basic characteristic of our culture in the United States. We experience what philosopher Lars Svendsen terms "the colonization of our life-world by fear" when we come to interpret our environment from a perspective of fear.[2] He goes on to say that "a world you fear is a place where you can never feel completely at home."[3]

In a context that often feels apocalyptic, with life as we know it coming to an end in so many different ways, a world that continually provokes our experience of fear may begin to feel like a world to which we no longer belong. Pervasive moods and outlooks on life structured by anxiety and fear can exert an influence on us that touches all parts of our lives. And some in our social sphere cultivate this pervasive outlook for political gain. We are all too familiar with fear used as political resource, a trump card, a way of undermining the partisan opposition and its leadership. This has become a primary theme in political campaigns at all levels of government and across party lines, instilling fear as a part of our political landscape.

In an era of high connectivity via social media, fear is trafficked through digital emotional contagion. *Emotional contagion* describes the phenomena through which our emotions, either consciously or unconsciously, become more similar to the emotions we perceive in others as we are exposed to their emotions.[4] Digitally, this takes place through the spread of our emotions on the internet, especially through social media. Constant exposure to others' fear, anger, and sadness, whether in person or in the digital realm, can lead us to experience many of the stresses associated with these emotions, even if we caught them from others.[5] Beyond simple memes, deep fakes portend an era in which emotional experiences can be cultivated and curated for cyber warfare that will further increase social or political rifting.[6] When we cannot do anything in relation to the threatening circumstance, we are likely to begin experiencing fear as an overwhelming emotional state.[7]

When fear becomes a general orientation toward life, it erodes trust in other human beings and leads to a decreasing sense of security when we are with others, ultimately contributing to social disintegration; avoidance of those we fear based on racial, religious, or national difference; and an increase of isolation throughout society.[8] Fear as a long-lasting disposition can inculcate a sense of helplessness, giving in to apathy, and immobilization in the face of very real dangers that we've become too fearful to address. Especially within the communities of care that we are cultivating, we must develop the capacity to both hold the real fears that people face related to their well-being and that of their loved ones and also address the fears that are created to divide us from one another, politically, racially, nationally, and likewise.

CARING AMID FEAR

Throughout the biblical text, there are admonitions about fear, almost always inviting those in a frightful situation to lessen their fearful response. Phrases like "be not afraid" show up again and again in the Hebrew Bible and the New Testament. Since fear is an evolutionary gift, we can hear all of those passages in the Bible encouraging us to fear not as messages with a fuller intention behind them. They're not messages that disparage the necessity of fear as an emotion of survival but as admonitions against fear becoming the dominant orientation of one's life. "Do not fear" might be understood as a message like "Do not let the fear you feel consume you. Do not let the fearful experiences of life sever your connection to others and the world around you. Do not let fear immobilize you."

To treat fear with care, we must attend to the ways that some fears are invented for political purposes such as political fear mongering in relation to immigrants, while some fears are felt in direct proportion to critical threats in our surrounding environment such as Black people fearing being harassed, attacked, or killed while taking a jog in a white neighborhood. In both cases—in situations real or imagined—the feelings of threat and danger are stimuli that influence our behavior.

The question when addressing fear is not whether the fear is rational. Remember that fear responses initially occur outside of the rational oversight of the neocortex. Our fear response may even contradict what we rationally think or believe. Fear is an embodied response, and as clinical social worker Resmaa Menakem reminds us, "Our bodies don't care about logic, truth, or cognitive experience. They care about safety and survival. They care about responding to a perceived threat, even when that threat is not real."[9]

To take fear seriously in caregiving, we must be respectful of the fear that another holds and be willing to explore their fears in conversation. Listen with compassion and be willing to be surprised by what you hear. Central questions for caregivers when addressing fear's arousal for individuals or within communities are these:

How do I perceive my well-being, or that of my wider world of concern, being put in danger?

From which harms do we sense the need to protect ourselves and those we love?

How is fear inviting me to respond to others and to the world around me? Does this accord with how I want to be in community with others?

If fear had a voice, what would it be saying to me in those times it arises?

In what ways is fear motivating me toward behavior that seems life-preserving?

In which ways is fear motivating me toward behavior that seems exacerbating of adverse circumstances?

Practice Exercise: Empathic Imagination

In order to exercise your empathic imagination, attempt performing a review of your day imagining yourself in a body different from your own, perhaps a body of a different race or gender, an LGBTQ+ body, a body coming from an entirely different context in the world, speaking another language. But be specific about the body you are placing your imagination within, for example, a Black trans body, a Spanish-speaking immigrant, a Muslim woman wearing a burka.

Slowly let your imagination consider all that you have experienced throughout the day—the people you interacted with, the tasks you performed, the places you traveled, the conversations you had. All of the experiences should be your own. But imagine having those same experiences within the body you're inhabiting in your imagination. What would be different for you? Are there circumstances that you moved through in your day with ease that would have created a context of fear for a person with the body you're imaginatively inhabiting? A circumstance in which you may have been treated with animosity or violence? A place you would have avoided because you were concerned for your safety?

A conversation you had that would have been anxiety-provoking because of your embodiment or language or religion?

Or perhaps you imagined yourself in a body with considerably more privilege in our society than you normally have in your own body. What was different about the experience of your daily routine when you were inhabiting that body? Were fears and anxieties decreased in certain circumstances? Were there places you could imagine yourself going and feeling more at ease? Interactions that turned out differently because of the body you moved around in?

Try this exercise with others and talk about your experience.

HELPING AMID GRIEF AND LOSS

If you are a caring presence in the lives of others, you will likely have the sacred opportunity to accompany others in circumstances of grief. This is a holy time and one full of potential for the caring presence of another to prove sustaining amid the unmooring experience of losing a loved one.

Care in the Immediacy of Death

You may find yourself accompanying careseekers through grief at many stages along the way, sometimes long after a death has occurred and other times in the immediate period after the death of a loved one. This might take place when a person is under the care of hospice and family and friends have gathered at the bedside when the time of death seems imminent or in a hospital room when a patient has taken a turn and the medical staff has called loved ones in. Whether as a family member or friend or as a caring representative of your faith community, if you find yourself at the bedside of one dying, know that you are witnessing and participating in one of life's most profound thresholds, when the veil between immanence and transcendence becomes thin, and you stand on holy ground.

For the past century and a half, our experience with death has become more and more professionalized: people dying away from home in hospitals and the funeral industry taking over care for the dead, which was once the purview of family members.[10] Because of this, families can experience some uncertainty about what to do at the time of death. Loved ones may need a little guidance in knowing how to relate to and interact with one another at the bedside of one who has died or even how to interact with the body of their recently deceased loved one.

It is important that you communicate to those gathered that it is okay to spend time with the body. That it is okay to touch the body. That it is okay to sing songs and pray prayers and anoint the body with water or oil, if that is a meaningful religious ritual for those gathered. While our larger culture has generated a type of fear in relation to dead bodies, time spent with the body of a dead loved one can be a profound and meaningful part of grieving in the initial minutes and hours after death.

Some families may even wish to take care of the body in the home, known as a *home funeral*, by washing the body, having loved ones vigil around the body for a matter of hours or even a few days, filling the space with songs and sacred readings, and shrouding the body before it is cremated or buried.[11] No matter the timeframe a family wishes to spend with the body of their loved one—from an hour to a couple of days—the point is to slow down the often very hurried process that occurs after a death to give loved ones time to say goodbye, to ritualize the threshold of death, and to provide meaningful acts of care for the body of their beloved one. You can help in this process by giving them the permission that many of our institutions fail to give, legitimizing their desire to spend the time they wish at the bedside after a death has occurred.

Care on the Long Journey of Grief

Baptist pastor Lanny Peters says of his experience ministering in the midst of grief, "It's almost become a cliché in our culture that there is this thing called closure that should happen to you and when it does you can move on with your life." He tells a story about a time in his ministry at Oakhurst Baptist Church when he realized that the church had a number of parents who had lost children. Peters says, "Even when they are grown adults, it's not what you expect, for your children to die before you. So one Sunday I declared our church a no closure zone for grief and asked anyone who had lost a child to share if they wished. And almost every one of them did."[12]

You've likely heard a lot about the stages of grief and the eventual goal of reaching a point of acceptance and closure. I want to invite you to put that notion aside for now. There is no linear process of grief and no prescription for how grieving should proceed, nor for how it should resolve. Often, in the days and even weeks after the death of a loved one, a spouse or family receives cards and flowers and phone calls and casseroles. And then, one day, it stops. No more calls, no more cards. Life goes back to its normal pace for everyone else while the family continues in their grief.

It can be helpful for you as a caregiver to check in with grieving loved ones periodically over the course of the first year after a death. Send a card a month or two later to remind them you haven't forgotten the grief they are carrying. Give them a call weeks after the typical calls have stopped. Send a note on the first anniversary of the death to let them know you're still holding them in prayerful thought. These expressions of care will not be painful reminders of their loss, as some often fear. They will be reminders that they are being seen—witnessed—in their grief by someone who cares for them and who is not rushing them toward any false notion of closure. Witnessing another in their pain or grief, without judgment or expectation or unnecessary attempts to rescue, is a sacred practice that requires courage, patience, and compassion.

SAYING HELLO AGAIN

Our relationship with our dead loved ones contains a lot of the stuff of who we are—memories that we only shared with them, things they knew about us that only they knew, the ways we saw ourselves through their eyes that told us important things about who we believe ourselves to be in the world. Burying all of those things with our loved ones can also bury some aspects of our own sense of identity.

Narrative therapist Michael White once wrote that an important task in our grieving is "saying hello again" to our dead loved ones.[13] We can help others do this by asking them intentional questions about their relationship with a dead loved one and how that relationship shapes who they are: their values, their sense of identity, their way of being in the world. These types of questions are often best saved for conversations about a loss after the immediacy of that loss has passed, for example, in the weeks and months after a death, and not at the bedside.

Some examples of questions that can help us say hello again and avoid losing important parts of ourselves that are bound up in our relationships with lost loved ones are:

> *Tell me about what your loved one appreciated about you that you also appreciate about yourself. How did they come to appreciate that attribute about you? Is there a story behind that?*
>
> *Are there places you visited together or stories you shared with one another that bring you comfort to revisit now?*
>
> *If your loved one were seeing you live your life right now, what do you think they would be noticing about you that they would appreciate?*
>
> *What do you know about yourself—your character, your personal attributes, your values—that you came to know through your relationship with your loved one? How did they come to see those things in your life? How are you holding on to that knowledge about yourself in the aftermath of losing your loved one?*
>
> *Where are you and/or what are you doing when the presence of your loved one feels most palpable to you? What is special or significant about those places or activities in relation to your loved one and the relationship you share?*

Except in cases of those who were abusive to us, we all probably long to say hello again to our deceased loved ones so that we don't have to forget those things that are so important to our identities all in the name of closure because a therapist or pastor or well-meaning friend told us that was what we were supposed to experience.

CARE AMID GRIEF'S COMPLEXITIES

Much like the need to contain the timeline of grief through stages or closure, there's also a need we often feel to contain the emotions of grief too—to make our emotions more palatable and socially acceptable to polite company. Just as there is no linear pathway of grief, the emotions we feel in response to a profound loss are often quite unpredictable: calm and peace when we believe we should be broken up and beside ourselves, anger when we thought we'd feel sadness, emotions we never imagined related to grief that come on at completely unexpected times—even long after the death has occurred. Time itself may even seem to stand still in the aftermath of death. Whichever emotions those in your care experience in the aftermath of a death, witness those emotions, help name those emotions in a validating way, and never stand in judgment about what a person in grief is feeling or try to make those feelings fit what you presume someone should be experiencing.

In addition to the complexities of grief's emotions, there are many ways that grief itself—the relationship we hold in relation to the loss—gets complicated. There are many instances of *disenfranchised grief*.[14] These are instances in which the loss we experience is not a type of loss that our social or cultural context regularly supports as a legitimate type of grief. For example, the loss of an early-term pregnancy when no one outside of the couple knew about the pregnancy in the first place and no standard rituals or customs invite the grief into a communally shared context. Or the loss of a beloved pet that feels as profound and significant as the loss of any human companion but is not viewed by one's friends and neighbors as being as significant as losing a human companion. Even the death of a loved one to a cause that seems taboo in one's culture can complicate the grieving process, for example, when a loved one dies by suicide or a drug overdose and the family's community doesn't surround them with compassion and support the way they would if the family member had died of cancer or a car accident.

Ambiguous loss is another common experience that complicates one's ability to grieve.[15] This ambiguity can come in many forms, for example, when a family member goes missing and is presumed dead, but the body is never recovered. The presence of a body has long been an important part of our sense of death's reality. Without one, death can sometimes seem unreal. But other times, ambiguity emerges because our loved one is still with us but is not the loved one we've always known. For example, Alzheimer's and dementia can inalterably change our relationship with a loved one long before death. Memories fade, shared stories become known to only one person in the relationship and forgotten by the other, personalities can change in surprising ways. We may feel like we've lost our loved one, even when they are still with us.

In circumstances of disenfranchised grief, you may become one of the few people in a person's life who knows about the loss or who sees the intensity of the pain caused by the loss. It can be a gift for you to talk openly with that person about their loss, helping to bring their grief out of the shadows and into the light of loving compassion. You may also work with the careseeker to decide who else in their life they would like to invite into compassionate conversation about their grief so that they don't have to hold it alone. But, as always, follow the lead of the careseeker when discussing how to invite others in.

In situations of ambiguous loss, your acknowledgment of the unique and difficult circumstances the careseeker is facing can be validating of their sense of ambiguity. This acknowledgment may help careseekers become gentler with themselves, seeing how ambiguity intensifies and augments their experience of grief in ways they may not have anticipated or ever witnessed in the lives of others. And if you are part of a faith community, finding ways to regularly educate the community as a whole about experiences of disenfranchised grief and ambiguous loss can help the entire collective become more compassionate companions to those within the community undergoing a complex grief journey.

In many cases, grief is not just about the loss of a person but about the loss of a future. Loss can pose a challenge to our sense of what we expected or hoped for in our future—future stories that likely included the lives of our loved one but now must be rewritten in their absence. As someone providing a caring and compassionate presence in the lives of those journeying through the valley of death's shadows, allow those emotional experiences to be what they are. Notice them, witness them, but do not stand in judgment over them. There is no prescription for how one should feel about a death, and there are certainly no linear processes or streamlined stages that we can move people through on their way to acceptance or closure. Your validating witnessing of a person's grief over a loss that society doesn't see as significant or your willingness to stand in the ambiguity of a loss with loved ones while acknowledging the grief that is taking place long before death has occurred will be sustaining in the midst of disenfranchisement, ambiguity, and grief's general unpredictability.

Practice Exercise: Saying Hello Again

Break the hesitancy about speaking of dead loved ones by finding a partner—a friend, a spouse, or perhaps another caregiver in your faith community—who will agree to talk with you about a lost loved one who died in the more distant past. See the sample questions above and experiment with other possibilities for asking questions that invite reflection on the significance of a relationship with a lost loved one that continues to inform one's sense of self in the world. These aren't the types of questions we are trained to ask, and a little practice can help you form rich questions of continued relationship with the dead. Then perhaps you can invite them to ask you a few similar questions about a loved one you've lost but still hold close.

FURTHER READING

Moon, Zachary, ed. *Doing Theology in Pandemics: Facing Viruses, Violence, and Vitriol*. Eugene, OR: Pickwick, 2022.

Weller, Francis. *The Wild Edge of Sorrow: Rituals of Renewal and the Sacred Work of Grief*. Berkeley: North Atlantic Books, 2015.

NOTES

1 Cody J. Sanders, "Feeling Our Way through an Apocalypse," in *Doing Theology in Pandemics: Facing Viruses, Violence, and Vitriol*, ed. Zachary Moon (Eugene, OR: Pickwick, 2022).

2 Lars Svendsen, *A Philosophy of Fear* (London: Reaktion Books, 2008), 7.

3 Svendsen, *A Philosophy of Fear*, 43.

4 Amit Goldenberg and James J. Gross, "Digital Emotional Contagion," *Trends in Cognitive Science* 24, no. 4 (April 2020): 317.

5 Daniel M. Rempala, "Cognitive Strategies for Controlling Emotional Contagion," *Journal of Applied Social Psychology* 43 (2013): 1529.

6 See "Tackling the Misinformation Epidemic with 'In Event of Moon Disaster,'" *MIT News*, July 20, 2020, http://news.mit.edu/2020/mit-tackles-misinformation-in-event-of-moon-disaster-0720.

7 Paul Ekman, *Emotions Revealed: Recognizing Faces and Feelings to Improve Communication and Emotional Life*, rev. ed. (New York: Owl Books, 2003), 156.

8 Svendsen, *A Philosophy of Fear*, 94.

9 Resmaa Menakem, *My Grandmother's Hands: Racialized Trauma and the Pathway to Mending Our Hearts and Bodies* (Las Vegas, NV: Central Recovery Press, 2017), 28.

10 For more on these cultural and religious shifts, see Cody J. Sanders and Mikeal C. Parsons, *Corpse Care: Ethics for Tending the Dead* (Minneapolis: Fortress, 2023).

11 Sometimes this process can be aided by the presence of a home funeral guide. To learn more about home funeral guides and how to find a trained provider, see www.homefuneralalliance.org.

12 Lanny Peters, email message to author, January 27, 2020.

13 Michael White, "Saying Hullo Again: The Incorporation of the Lost Relationship in the Resolution of Grief," *Dulwich Centre Newsletter*, Spring 1988, 29–36.

14 Kenneth J. Doka, *Disenfranchised Grief: Ministry That Breaks the Silence* (Minneapolis: Fortress Press, 2025).

15 Pauline Boss, *The Myth of Closure: Ambiguous Loss in a Time of Pandemic and Change* (New York: Norton, 2022).

9

HELPING AMID ANGER AND SADNESS

Fear and anger are related, interdependent emotions.[1] Both emotions have the primary objective of *survival*.[2] They also have similar biochemical components.[3] Thus, much of what has been explored regarding fear and anxiety is also helpful to our exploration of anger.

It is important to recognize at the outset that in US society, anger is a racialized emotion that is experienced and expressed differently with different consequences depending on one's racial embodiment. As bell hooks contends, "To perpetuate and maintain white supremacy, white folks have colonized black Americans, and a part of that colonizing process has been teaching us to repress our rage, to never make them the targets of any anger we feel about racism."[4] Buddhist Lama Rod Owens attests to this, saying, "As a Black man, I was conditioned to believe my anger was dangerous—if I channeled anger and expressed anger, then I would be punished. I would be killed, I would be put in jail, I would be silenced. I would be erased."[5] To discuss anger in the United States without recognizing this colonization of emotions would be naive and, for BIPOC (Black, Indigenous, and People of Color) communities, potentially dangerous.

For example, months before the 2021 attempted insurrection at the US Capitol, a group comprised primarily of white men armed with semiautomatic weapons showed up at the Michigan State Capitol in early May 2020 to protest the state's shutdown during the coronavirus pandemic. After being denied entry to the House chamber by police, some armed protesters went into the Senate gallery and shouted down at lawmakers below while they were in session.[6] Police took no forceful action against these white protesters of the state's pandemic stay-at-home order. Weeks later when Black Lives Matter protests erupted over the police killing of George

Floyd all over the country, unarmed protesters—many Black—were met with police in riot gear firing rubber bullets and tear gas into the crowds. In both instances, anger was a motivating factor for the protesters. In each instance, that anger was met with a markedly different response by the state.

Psychologist Richard Lazarus proposes a simple description for the provocation of anger in adults: "a demeaning offense against me and mine."[7] Pastoral theologian Andrew Lester adds that the arousal pattern of anger is physical, mental, and emotional and is characterized by a desire to either attack or defend.[8] Our subcortical brain is well primed to arouse anger in relation to physical threats to our well-being such as when confronted by an armed person posing a threat to our family. But the neocortex and its higher-order thought processes come into play when there are more complicated threats to our values, meanings, worldviews, future plans, and personal identity.[9]

In the realm of cultural traditions, values, and identity, it is easy to see how anger becomes a tool of both political and religious mobilization, holding the physiological promise of sustaining high levels of energy among those experiencing the emotional state, as well as the potential to direct that anger against a common enemy in ways that promote communal solidarity.[10] Anger is a key affective tool in modern political campaigns and is stoked so pervasively and consistently by both politicians and news outlets that it holds the risk of taking on a pervasive outlook on life for many people with whom we will practice care.[11]

WHEN ANGER BECOMES AN OUTLOOK ON LIFE

Psychologist Paul Ekman warns that "one of the most dangerous features of anger is that anger calls forth anger, and the cycle can rapidly escalate."[12] As with fear, anger is a highly contagious emotion, spreading faster than other emotions on social media through digital emotional contagion.[13] This points to what philosopher Achille Mbembe calls *microfascism* via digital technology intent on formatting our minds, shaping our desires, and colonizing the unconscious. Through these processes of computational media and digital technology, our symbolic world is reshaped, "blurring distinction between reality and fiction."[14] No matter the fictional status of the stimuli—memes decrying the loss of cultural values, deep fakes portraying political enemies making anger-inducing speeches that were never actually given, or other political propaganda—the emotional response that the stimuli cultivates is all too real. And that emotional reality holds the power to shape our motivations and our community-building practices.

For any caregiver cultivating life within a community of faith, the emotional power of anger and its easy social contagion amid a politically polarized society must become a focus of caring concern. When anger becomes chronic, it can lead to a host of other emotional experiences that can become more pervasive as a mood or even an interpretative orientation toward life in the world. Some of these more complex and long-lasting emotional experiences are resentment, bitterness, hostility, or hatred.[15] Anger developed as an emotional orientation toward life holds the potential to cultivate cynicism, us-versus-them thinking, contempt, and vengefulness. Relationally, these longer-term emotional dispositions are disastrous.

While focused on couples, psychologist John Gottman identifies criticism, contempt, defensiveness, and stonewalling as the four horsemen of the apocalypse for relational communication,[16] which I believe to be true for relationships beyond romantic couples as well. Once these anger-related patterns show up with frequency, it is difficult to recover healthy relationality as parties move increasingly toward irreparable rifts. Clearly, these horsemen are standard features of our political landscape and fundamental to our inability to come together amid a national crisis like the COVID-19 pandemic to institute even the simplest measures to prevent transmission. On a much smaller communal scale, these four horsemen hold the potential to stymie the potential of faith communities to respond meaningfully to the pressing concerns of care and justice as well.

CARING AMID ANGER

Trying to rationally talk one out of being fearful of angry about a stimulus does not take into account the subcortical regions of the brain that are triggered by these stimuli. Neural pathways develop as a result of traumatic experience. Memories that are connected to the hippocampus and the amygdala record, store, and recall painful and traumatic events, and the entire limbic system can be immediately alerted to danger if the brain interprets a new stimulus as similar to a past traumatic event. The body is mobilized for action before our rational brain can begin reinterpreting the situation.[17]

And yet, Lester posits, anger is a *hermeneutical event*, rooted in our naming and describing of events in our environment that construct the meanings we assign to these experiences.[18] This is especially the case when we are dealing with anger-inducing stimuli that touch on cultural values, meanings, worldviews, future plans, and personal identity rather than the immediate threat of bodily harm. Here, it is the consistent inducement of anger stimuli targeting meaning and values that I am most concerned about becoming an orientation toward life that pervades our interpretation of the world and inhibits our ability to cultivate community with others across myriad lines of difference.

In situations of physical trauma, violence, and abuse that have elevated one's activation of fear and anger responses, it is helpful to seek a trauma-informed, somatically aware clinician who can help one work through the ways that the fear- and anger-inducing trauma is lodged in one's body.[19] But for the pervasive fear-shaped orientations toward life that have become common in our sociopolitical landscape, care responders should develop the competency to address fear orientations openly in order to bring them into the light of a caring exploration.

Central questions when beginning to address anger's arousal for individuals or within communities are these:

How do I perceive my values being threatened?

Against which threats do we sense the need to react in order to protect ourselves and those we love?

How is anger inviting me to respond to others and to the world around me? Are these the ways I most wish to respond to others in my life?

If anger had a voice, what would it be saying to me in those times?

In what ways is anger motivating me/us toward behavior that seems life-preserving?

In what ways is anger motivating me or us toward behavior that seems exacerbating of adverse circumstances?

Practice Exercise: Assessing Communal Anger

Practice assessing the communal dimension of anger either by yourself or in conversation with others who belong to the communities you call home. Consider the communities you belong to. What are the sources of anger that arise within the community? They may be interpersonal disagreements about the community's life and direction or larger social or cultural circumstances that people care deeply about. How does anger first present itself in relation to those concerns? Once you identify an early sign of anger's arousal, see if you can take it back another step or two to hone your ability to notice when the emotion of anger is starting to show up.

How is anger treated when it arises? With curiosity or defensiveness? With curious questions or with oppositional statements? Does the heat rise to the level of developing resentments? Are there ways the community has developed to intervene before anger reaches the level of contempt for one another or for others outside of the community?

Knowing what you've now encountered about how anger operates as an emotion, consider in conversation with others which practices you would most like to institute within your community to address anger in constructive ways when it arises. How will you listen to the message of anger and attend to what is perceived as being threatened without allowing anger to develop into a pervasive outlook on life?

HELPING THROUGH SADNESS

It's not difficult to see how sadness is triggered by all that we encounter in the world around us today. With every species lost and habitat destroyed, with threats to democracy pervasive, with the bodies of our BIPOC[20] siblings treated with violence, the emotion of sadness is present to warn us that something or someone important to us and our wider world of concern is being threatened or destroyed.

Sadness is already one of the longer lasting of our emotions. Triggered in a constant and pervasive manner without sufficient care taken to attend to the messages that sadness is communicating to us, this emotion can develop into longer-lasting moods like a sense of despair, a loss of meaning in our lives, numbness, and even extreme fatigue that is hard for us to explain. While a clinically informed diagnosis of depression may, at times, be appropriate for some, the term *depression* is too clinical to describe the emotional experience of sadness we are all prone to in difficult situations in life.[21]

Whereas fear and anger promote engagement and activity in relation to threatening stimuli such as fleeing or fighting, sadness moves us toward resignation rather than toward struggle.[22] Psychologist Richard Lazarus says that the core relational theme of sadness is irrevocable loss that holds a sense of helplessness about any potential for restoration. He suggests that if the loss is not considered irrevocable, then anger, among other emotions, can be activated to direct behavior toward possibilities of restoring the loss.[23] Sadness can also transcend focus on a single encounter or stimulus and merges with the "existential quality of life in reflecting in general relationships with the world."[24] This is the case when sadness becomes a pervasive mood.

On a personal level, sadness can arise in life when we've experienced the loss of a relationship through a breakup or a death. Sadness can emerge from the loss of an important part of our lives from which we derive some personal sense of meaning or identity like the loss of a job, even voluntarily through retirement. Sadness can even arise over the sense of loss over something we never had in the first place, like the loss of a dream, goal, or desire that we realize is unattainable. In many instances, our experiences of sadness merge with what we might also term *grief*.

In any of these scenarios that have brought about a sense of sadness, remember to invite conversation around sadness in ways that do not locate sadness within the person. Instead, invite conversation about what messages a sense of sadness may be carrying for the person. For example, you might say, "It sounds like your retirement has brought about some feelings of sadness over some important things that you've lost in relation to that job. While retirement was desirable, were there other parts of your life that were tied to that job that you feel you're losing alongside the work itself?" This may prompt reflections on important relationships that were formed at the workplace, a sense of identity that the person formed around their vocation, loss related to a sense of purpose or direction that now must be reconceived. These openings may provide multiple avenues for exploration in relation to the careseeker's changing life situation and the types of spiritual care support they may desire in addressing those changes and the questions they raise.

Seeing sadness as an important emotional experience carrying a message for us that needs exploration in caring conversation can help sadness become an honored, regular, but fleeting part of our lives rather than developing into a pervasive mood or outlook on life.

SADNESS ON LARGER SCALES

There are, however, many ways in which sadness sticks with us, not because it has not been appropriately attended to in a caring way but because the source of that sadness and the losses that brought it about are ongoing. This is the case for many who look at the world around them today and see signs of loss among species and ecosystems or the erosion of trusted institutions from denominations to democracy and, despite efforts to address these concerns, are often confronted with the reality that much of what we are losing in these regards is irrevocable. Our contemporary context of pervasive loss requires a broader vocabulary for our emotions related to loss and sadness, as well as forms of support for bringing these emotional experiences into the caring presence of community.

In addressing sadness in relation to climate change and environmental degradation on a planetary scale, Australian environmental philosopher Glenn Albrecht developed a new vocabulary for what he terms *earth emotions*.[25] These are emotional responses that humans have to the current scale and pace of environmental change. Key among these is the emotion of *solastalgia*, described as "the lived experience of distressing, negative environmental change."[26] Albrecht sees solastalgia causing pain, distress, and ongoing loss of solace that is rooted in one's sense of desolation and a pervasive negative environmental change within a landscape or territory where one feels at home. In addition to a sadness-inducing sense of loss, this eco-change can also feel like an anger-inducing attack on one's sense of place in the world—one's home.[27]

On an economic and political level, womanist theologian and ethicist Keri Day names loss of meaning, despair, and helplessness as feelings associated with economic and political systems, arguing that our current political and economic climate "attempts to render us cynical and apathetic about our ability to be different from the calculating, radically self-interested individual that neoliberal capitalism presumes as given."[28] There are clearly important racial considerations in the experience of sadness too. Poet and playwright Claudia Rankine asked a friend what it is like being the mother of a Black son. Rankine's friend replied, "The condition of black life is one of mourning." Liberal white people, Rankine says, can feel temporarily bad about Black suffering, but "no mode of empathy . . . can replicate the daily strain of knowing that as a black person you can be killed for simply being black."[29] While white people may feel sadness in relation to ongoing racial injustice and violence, this weight of sadness, or condition of mourning, is not experienced equally across racial embodiments.

On the levels of racial injustice, environmental degradation, and political and economic systems, sadness-inducing stimuli are constant and systemic. For these reasons, our ability to bring these emotions into communal contexts of care that help us to listen to the message of these emotions and take action in relation to them—both activities of healing in community and actions of justice-seeking resistance in relation to continually mounting losses—is a necessary approach to caring amid sadness in our world today. In contexts that produce invitations toward apathy, helplessness, and resignation, our ability to cultivate collective pathways toward restoration, healing, and justice is a vital practice of care.

LAMENT

Our expressions of grief can move us toward others in response to profound loss. In the face of pervasive and systemic sources of loss and sadness, *lament* is another grief response familiar in the biblical tradition.

Preaching professor Fred Craddock describes well how the practice of lament is connected to all that provokes within us a feeling of gratitude and wonder: "A lament is a voice of love and profound caring, a vision of what could have been and of grief over its loss, of tough hope painfully releasing the object of its hope, of personal responsibility and frustration, of sorrow and anger mixed, of accepted loss but with energy enough to go on."[30]

Grief and lament, especially practiced within community, are ways to stay present with the sadness and potential anger we are experiencing over the loss of what we hold dear and the fear of impending losses.[31] But it is an emotional experience that moves from solitude and passivity induced by pervasive feelings of sadness into expressions of community and activity in response to pain and loss. Lament is an expression of anger and sadness that is intertwined with practices of justice and repair. While grief and lament help us to sit with the discomfort and pain of losses, this doesn't necessitate reliving those painful losses in ways that exacerbate the trauma that may be associated with them.[32] Whereas sadness is a passive emotion, sometimes leading to a sense of helplessness and resignation if it becomes a long-lasting temperament, grief and lament help to work with the messages of sadness in ways that are actively seeking to live in face of a loss, even as we turn our attention toward practice of justice-seeking.[33]

In addition to exploring losses in conversation with caring others, we often need to intentionally mourn and lament in community. Communally oriented grieving invites us to ask with whom we can share in this important work of grief and lament. We have many practices that place us in community for the complex emotional work of grieving losses: funerals and memorials for loved ones lost to death, silent vigils in the wake of tragedy when words are not enough, protests taking on an emotional tenor of grief and lament when we place our bodies alongside one another in the streets to voice a mixture of sorrow and anger that energizes us enough to go on in our striving toward justice. These corporate practices of grief and lament hold potential to shape our active motivation and communal engagement in face of tragic losses that might otherwise serve to pull us apart or invite us into resignation.

TREATING SADNESS WITH CARE

There are no thoughts that are not colored by feelings, no feelings that do not eventually come into the interpretive sway of cognition, and no feeling state that doesn't resonate throughout the whole of one's body. Sadness as a long-lasting temperament can become immobilizing of our bodies, coloring our thoughts and curtailing our activity in the world. The real danger of sadness becoming the emotional valance that colors our outlook, directing our behavior in relation to our environment, is that sadness's orientation is toward resignation rather than toward struggle, of a learned sense of helplessness and despair rather than active engagement with the problems we face together.

Central questions when caregivers begin addressing sadness for individuals or within communities are these:

> *Which important parts of my world feel like they are being lost or irreparably damaged?*
>
> *How does my well-being, or that of my wider world of concern, feel like it is being taken away?*
>
> *From what stimuli do we sense the need to withdraw, and which stimuli feel too overwhelming for us to handle?*
>
> *How is sadness inviting me to respond to others and the world around me? Are these the ways I most want to respond to others in my life?*
>
> *If sadness had a voice, what would it be saying to me in those times?*
>
> *In what ways is sadness motivating me toward behavior that seems life-preserving?*
>
> *In what ways is sadness motivating me toward behavior that seems exacerbating of adverse circumstances?*

Not only can our individual lives become overtaken by the apocalyptic emotions of fear and sadness and anger, but our practice of faith can also become consumed by these powerful emotions and their ability to direct our attention and shape our action. We can get so mired in the constant and pervasive triggering of these important primary emotions that we begin to do the work of ministry out of fear, as if we are constantly under threat. The experience of sadness becomes the pervasive mood of our worshipping life so that celebration never has the opportunity to emerge and energize us. We begin to undertake all of our work of justice from a place of anger, motivated to counter others' agendas rather than to cultivate a way of being in the world. The relational aim of all three emotions is corrosive to communal bonds, should they become pervasive orientations toward life.

Practice Exercise: Listening to Sadness

Pay attention to the ways that sadness has shown up as a visitor in your life in the past week, month, or year. Sometimes sadness can be brief and fleeting—a response to a scene we witness in our daily life or a story we hear from a friend. At other times, it can be pervasive and overwhelming, threatening to stick around much longer than we would like. Spend some time considering the message that any of the instances of sadness that come to mind held or hold for you. Think through some of the questions above in relation to your own experience of sadness so that you can experience the power those questions hold to explore the emotion with more compassion and nuance than we often allow ourselves.

Connect with a friend, perhaps someone else training in spiritual care first aid skills alongside you, to talk through your mutual experience of sadness. Choose an instance that you can describe while the other partner compassionately listens with the reflecting skills you're learning. Orient the conversation toward the losses that are inviting experiences of sadness, whether personal or planetary in scale.

Discuss together how listening to sadness as an emotion with a message shapes your ability to relate to that emotional experience and relay it to others.

FURTHER READING

Owens, Lama Rod. *Love and Rage: The Path of Liberation through Anger*. Berkeley: North Atlantic Books, 2020.

Coleman, Monica A. *Bipolar Faith: A Black Woman's Journey with Depression and Faith*. Minneapolis: Fortress, 2016.

NOTES

1 Cody J. Sanders, "Feeling Our Way through an Apocalypse," in *Doing Theology in Pandemics: Facing Viruses, Violence, and Vitriol*, ed. Zachary Moon (Eugene, OR: Pickwick, 2022).

2 Andrew D. Lester, *The Angry Christian: A Theology for Care and Counseling* (Louisville, KY: Westminster John Knox Press, 2003), 82.

3 William M. Reddy, *The Navigation of Feeling: A Framework for the History of Emotion* (Cambridge, UK: Cambridge University Press, 2001), 12, as cited in Lars Svendsen, *A Philosophy of Fear* (London: Reaktion Books, 2008), 25.

4 bell hooks, *Killing Rage: Ending Racism* (New York: Henry Holt, 1995), 14.

5 Lama Rod Owens, *Love and Rage: The Path of Liberation through Anger* (Berkeley: North Atlantic Books, 2020), 15.

6 Sarah Rahal and Craig Mauger, "Armed Protesters in Michigan Capitol Have Lawmakers Questioning Policy," *Detroit News*, May 2, 2020, https://www.detroitnews.com/story/news/local/michigan/2020/05/02/armed-protesters-michigan-capitol-have-lawmakers-questioning-policy/3071928001/.

7 Richard S. Lazarus, *Emotion and Adaptation* (New York: Oxford, 1991), 222. Emphasis in original.

8 Lester, *The Angry Christian*, 4.

9 Lester, *The Angry Christian*, 79.

10 Robert C. Fuller, *Spirituality in the Flesh: Bodily Sources of Religious Experience* (New York: Oxford, 2008), 31.

11 One of the key shifts in how fear- and anger-inducing campaign elements developed such modern electoral sway is the racially charged attack ad used by George H. W. Bush in 1988 in his campaign against Michael Dukakis featuring the story of a Black man named Willie Horton. See Peter Baker, "Bush Made Willie Horton an Issue in 1988, and the Racial Scars Are Still Fresh," *New York Times*, December 3, 2018, https://www.nytimes.com/2018/12/03/us/politics/bush-willie-horton.html.

12 Paul Ekman, *Emotions Revealed: Recognizing Faces and Feelings to Improve Communication and Emotional Life*, rev. ed. (New York: Owl Books, 2003), 111.

13 Amit Goldenberg and James J. Gross, "Digital Emotional Contagion," *Trends in Cognitive Science* 24, no. 4 (April 2020): 320.

14 Achille Mbembe, *Necropolitics*, trans. Steven Corcoran (Durham, NC: Duke University Press, 2019), 113.
15 Lester, *The Angry Christian*, 5.
16 See Ellie Lisitsa, "The Four Hosemen: Criticism, Contempt, Defensiveness, and Stonewalling," *Gottman Institute*, April 23, 2013, https://www.gottman.com/blog/the-four-horsemen-recognizing-criticism-contempt-defensiveness-and-stonewalling/.
17 Lester, *The Angry Christian*, 78–82.
18 Lester, *The Angry Christian*, 85, 94.
19 This type of therapeutic trauma work is further described in Resmaa Menakem, *My Grandmother's Hands: Racialized Trauma and the Pathway to Mending our Hearts and Bodies* (Las Vegas: Central Recovery Press, 2017); and Bessel van der Kolk, *The Body Keeps the Score: Brain, Mind, and Body in the Healing of Trauma* (New York: Penguin Books, 2014).
20 Black, Indigenous, people of color.
21 While this chapter deals more with the emotion of sadness rather than the clinical diagnosis of depression or, more formally, major depressive disorder, it can be helpful to know the warning signs of depression in order to engage in a potential appropriate ministry of introduction to a therapist. Some signs may include a change in sleep patterns, changes in appetite, a loss of energy or ability to concentrate, a lack of interest in activities that were once meaningful to the person. A helpful website for understanding more about depression can be accessed through the National Alliance on Mental Illness (nami.org).
22 Lazarus, *Emotion and Adaptation*, 247.
23 Lazarus, *Emotion and Adaptation*, 248.
24 Lazarus, *Emotion and Adaptation*, 251.
25 Glenn A. Albrecht, *Earth Emotions: New Words for a New World* (Ithaca, NY: Cornell University Press, 2019).
26 Albrecht, *Earth Emotions*, x.
27 Albrecht, *Earth Emotions*, 38.
28 Keri Day, *Religious Resistance to Neoliberalism: Womanist and Black Feminist Perspectives* (New York: Palgrave Macmillan, 2016), 14, 17.
29 Claudia Rankine, "The Condition of Black Life Is One of Mourning," in *The Fire This Time: A New Generation Speaks about Race*, ed. Jesmyn Ward (New York: Scribner: 2016), 145–146.
30 Fred Craddock, "Luke," in *Interpretation: A Bible Commentary for Teaching and Preaching*, ed. James L. Mays (Louisville, KY: Westminster John Knox Press, 2009), 229.
31 For a helpful faith community resource on practicing lament, see Terra McDaniel, *Hopeful Lament: Tending Our Grief through Spiritual Practices* (Downers Grove, IL: IVP, 2023).

32 Resmaa Menakem provides a similar description of working through the pain and discomfort of trauma, but the same can be true for our sadness over losses that may be less traumatic yet nevertheless distressing. *My Grandmother's Hands*, 14.

33 Lazarus, *Emotion and Adaptation*, 249.

10

HELPING AMID CRISIS AND DISASTER

Crises are often the times when spiritual care first responders are needed most. Unexpected or tragic events sometimes stretch our coping abilities to the limits. Having a caring companion come alongside us to help us through these times can be strengthening and sustaining and can reduce the potential for long-term emotional, physical, and spiritual stress from the crisis. In fact, crisis researchers believe that the support of other people in caring community may be the most important factor in bringing people through crises and trauma in ways that move people toward resilience in the aftermath.[1]

A crisis can mean at least two things: First, it can refer to an event itself. A sudden and unexpected death in a congregation or community due to an accident or injury or violence, a mass causality event in our town from an industrial fire or a train derailment or a mass shooting, a natural disaster like a flood or earthquake or wildfire—we may colloquially refer to all of these as a *crisis in our community*. Second, *crisis* can refer to our response to a distressing event, as in a crisis response. Our individual responses to these events will be different depending on many factors, ranging from our proximity to the event to our perceived sense of threat to us and our loved ones to our abilities to cope with the stress of the event. When it comes to the most severe psychological response to a traumatic event, post-traumatic stress disorder (PTSD), only about 9 percent of people exposed to a traumatic event ever develop PTSD symptoms.[2] Thus, an event that we might deem a crisis doesn't provoke the same crisis response in every individual affected, nor does a crisis event always result in long-term distress for every person. But in every crisis situation, it is important for spiritual care first responders to be attentive to those affected and provide appropriate care to triage and respond to the needs that arise among people in your community of care.

CARES MODEL OF CRISIS SPIRITUAL CARE

Because events that provoke a crisis happen quickly and a person's crisis response to the event is nearly immediate, crisis care should also happen quickly. Don't wait a few days or weeks until the intensity of the situation dies down before mobilizing a caring response. Other forms of care will be needed in later phases of the crisis and its aftermath. But when a communal crisis like a school shooting or a natural disaster occurs, attend to those within your purview of care immediately. If someone in your care experiences a personal-level crisis like the sudden death of a child or a near-miss accident that could have taken the life of a family member, reach out to those affected as soon as you are able.

Since crises are times when both the careseeker and the care responder can be overwhelmed by the suddenness and intensity of the crisis event, it can be helpful for the care responder to have a simple mnemonic model for holding in mind a way of working with people during crisis. Many such devises exist to help care responders and those providing psychological first aid. The mnemonic devise I offer here is rooted in crisis response research but developed in a way that combines a few elements that may be better represented as separate steps if, for example, someone was practicing psychological first aid as a member of their city's disaster management team. The model I offer here also adds a critical area, spiritual appraisal and response, that is integral to the role of the spiritual care first responder.

The mnemonic devise is CARES. It's easy enough to remember. Each step can progress in a linear fashion, though you may also need to cycle back through steps. The five steps are communicating compassionately, assessing the most pressing needs, responding to symptoms of stress and immediate needs, evaluating ongoing care needs, and spiritually appraising crisis response. Let's take each in sequence to develop more fully what the spiritual care first aid crisis responder is doing.

Communicating Compassionately

Your compassionate, less anxious presence and your ability to engage in active, reflective listening are the foundation to quality spiritual care practice. You might think that during the intensity of a crisis, there are other needs that take precedence over the ministry of presence and compassionate deep listening, but this is not the case. Communicating empathy and compassion through a less anxious presence, attending to your own grounding and healing presence with others, and listening attentively and reflectively are vital during crises. These skills will almost never steer you in the wrong direction. Your compassionate communication continues to be vital and foundational to effective crisis care, as well as for most of what takes place in caring relationships more broadly.

When those who are most directly experiencing a crisis are in the state of heightened arousal—experiencing the fight, flight, or freeze response that we often have when facing a stressful or traumatic event—being companioned by someone who is a sturdy, stable, and less anxious presence can lower the levels of distress a careseeker experiences. When a careseeker feels life is out of control or becomes fearful in the face of a crisis, the calmness and self-confidence of a care responder become the first stage of soothing the heightened fear, anxiety, or emotional arousal prompted by a crisis.[3]

One thing that normally communicates empathy and compassion and enhances understanding of another person's situation is asking helpful questions. In the intensity of a crisis, however, too many questions can be overwhelming. There will be plenty of time and a real need for some exploration of interpretations and meaning-making in the aftermath of a crisis. However, in the early stages following a crisis or disaster, empathic presence and compassionate listening are much more helpful. Thus, reflective listening skills are central to compassionate communicating during a crisis.

One difference in the ways we ask questions in crisis care and in other contexts of care is in the use of open-ended versus closed-ended questions. Remember, open-ended questions invite exploration; closed-ended questions invite yes-or-no responses or brief informational answers. Typically, care responders should lean heavily on open-ended questions that provide the careseeker room to explore, make meaning, and take the conversation in directions we might not anticipate. But in the aftermath of a crisis or disaster, our brains are often not thinking as clearly as they would be otherwise, and open-ended questions are usually not very helpful in that state of extreme emotional arousal. In these circumstances, closed-ended questions can slow down the pace of one's hyperarousal and help the person reengage clearer thinking. Examples include the following:

What is your name?

Were you present when the train derailed?

Would you like some water? Food? Something else?

How are you related to the person in the accident?

Psychologists and psychological first aid researchers George Everly and Jeffrey Lating note that a few of the common mistakes that well-intentioned care responders make during crisis response include probing too quickly for emotions and feelings, asking too many questions that feel interrogating, and rushing the careseeker to answer questions.[4] Sometimes these mistakes emerge from our own anxiety and eagerness to help. Keep a close eye on your own anxiety during crisis response. If you feel yourself taking on the anxiety of those around you, return to some of the grounding practices you've developed to keep yourself as calm as possible in the situation. That may seem too you-focused, but your own ability to stay calm and grounded will have a direct impact on those for whom you are caring through a crisis. Remember that you are your most helpful resource for caregiving. Pay close attention to your own grounding and physical-emotional-spiritual well-being so that you can better companion others in their times of greatest need.

Left unattended, your own anxiety and well-intentioned desires to help can often lead to a few unintended and unhelpful responses. One of the most common is offering promises and assurances that you have no legitimate ability to make. Internalize this admonition: no false promises or cheap assurances. Those sound like:

Everything is going to work out, you'll see.
You're strong, and you'll get through this in no time.
God won't give you more than you can handle.
There's a lesson in this for you. God is trying to teach you something.
Things are going to get better.
At least . . .

We've all heard people offer these statements during a time of crisis. They intend to help, and they usually come from a caring person who genuinely wants these things to be true. But you are in no position to make promises or assurances to people who are living through what may be their worst day ever. Let your compassionate, less anxious presence and your grounded ability to companion the other through crisis communicate the care you wish to convey. Your false promises and cheap assurances will not be helpful in the end and may inadvertently trivialize the suffering that the careseeker is experiencing.

Pay very close attention to any need you feel arising to utter the words *at least* during a person's crisis: "At least she didn't suffer." "Your home was destroyed, but at least you got out alive." "You lost one child, but at least your other two survived." While you may be trying to look at the best part of the situation a person is in and highlight that for them, looking on the bright side or searching for the silver lining is not helpful in companioning a person through a crisis or disaster. Strike *at least* from your caring vocabulary. Instead, acknowledge the pain the person is going through. Validate the sense of heartache and loss a person may be feeling, and listen compassionately to what they most need to express in the aftermath of their worst day.

Assess the Most Pressing Needs

Assessing the most pressing needs a person in crisis is facing means understanding the event that has occurred and the ways a person is reacting or responding to it. Hopefully, through your compassionate communication, you are beginning to understand what has happened and how the person has experienced it. At the stage of assessment, which may begin soon into the conversation, you are becoming especially attentive to the most pressing needs they have. Never assume that you know what these needs are, even if you've experienced a similar crisis or have companioned others through similar crises.

It's first important to know that crises are a part of life. All of us are likely to experience crises. They emerge from difficult circumstances and sometimes have profound effects on our lives, but they are nevertheless commonly occurring. When crises arise, people respond with symptoms that may normally raise concerns about their psychological well-being. Remember that many of these symptoms in the face of crises and disasters are to be expected and should not be pathologized.

For example, many people experiencing a profound crisis or living in the aftermath of a disaster may experience confusion; difficulty concentrating; inability to focus on addressing their immediate needs; feelings of overwhelm, fear, sadness, and anger; disruptions in their sleeping or eating patterns; and a range of other distressing experiences.[5] In everyday circumstances, a combination of any of these experiences may raise your internal red flags that something potentially concerning may be going on with this person that needs careful follow-up and referral to a mental health professional or physician. Amid a crisis or in the aftermath of a disaster, however, all of these are common reactions to crisis and should not be taken as signs of mental, spiritual, or emotional unwellness. For the most part, people experiencing these symptoms will typically recover without intensive specialized professional care.

As you proceed in your assessment of a person's most pressing needs, keep in mind six things that are often needed most in the aftermath of crisis or disaster but access to which may be disrupted by the circumstances: food, water, shelter, safety, medical attention or medications, and community connections. You may be able to assess these needs as the conversation proceeds. However, if some areas don't come up in conversation, just ask:

> *When is the last time you've eaten?*
>
> *Do you and your family know where you'll stay tonight?*
>
> *Are there medicines you depend on that you will need to procure?*
>
> *Is there anyone we might call who could be with you during this time? Family or friends?*
>
> *Can I get you a bottle of water?*

Keep in mind that your presence, compassionate care, and ability to witness the pain and loss a person is experiencing are already meeting one need we have in the aftermath of crisis and disaster. Continue your compassionate communication skills throughout your provision of care.

Respond to Symptoms of Stress and Immediate Need

Responding to symptoms of stress and immediate need is the intervention level of spiritual care first aid crisis response. If you are providing spiritual care first aid in the aftermath of a community disaster—a tornado or hurricane or even a human-made disaster like a mass shooting—it is important that you connect with a network of crisis responders if possible so that you can know where community resources are set up in your area: food, clean water, temporary shelter, medical aid, psychological services, and the like. In the initial emergency phase of a disaster, this information is vitally important and likely not very widely known yet. Again, the most pressing needs to meet in the immediacy of a crisis or disaster are food, water, shelter, safety, medical aid or necessary medications, and community connection. Beyond this, however, other responses to symptoms of stress may also be needed.

One important initial response to a disaster or even a personal crisis is empowerment of those who are feeling disempowered by the event. Providing information on what happened is often necessary in early stages when confusion over what has taken place may prevail. Just that little bit of information can help empower a careseeker. Beyond that information, Everly and Lating name other common questions that arise for careseekers during a traumatic event: "How did this happen?" "Why am I reacting this way?" "Why is this bothering me so much?" "What is happening to me?"[6] It can be empowering to a careseeker to have a little information about common responses to crises and disaster. This is called *anticipatory guidance*, helping careseekers understand common psychological, physiological, and spiritual responses to decrease anxiety over those symptoms if they do arise. Such guidance might sound like:

> You might have some difficulty sleeping.
> Be aware that you may be more irritable than usual.
> It's pretty common to replay this incident over and over in your mind.
> People sometimes lose their appetite.
> Don't be surprised if you want to avoid going back to the area where the incident occurred.
> It's fairly common to withdraw and want to be left alone after an experience like this.[7]

This type of anticipatory guidance can be especially reassuring if you notice some of these responses arising or being hinted at while you are listening to a careseeker's story in the aftermath of a traumatic event.

It is sometimes helpful to assist a careseeker in setting short-term goals in the aftermath of crisis. Pastoral theologian Howard Stone suggests that the most useful goals to set during crisis care should be attainable in a matter of weeks.[8] Arranging a funeral, filling out paperwork for disaster assistance, seeking and securing temporary housing, reconnecting with a network of support—all of these may be helpful goals for which careseekers may need your help strategizing to achieve. Pursuing larger, life-altering plans such as getting a divorce, quitting a job, or moving to a new state in the aftermath of a disaster or crisis is not advisable. While it is typically counterproductive to argue with someone about making such plans, it is usually helpful to encourage them to delay such plans until after the emergency phases of the crisis—the first several weeks, at least—have passed. Then they will hopefully be able to access greater cognitive capacity and future-oriented foresight to make any larger plans that may be necessary.

Finally, while it can feel counterintuitive to care responders just wanting to be helpful, never do for a person in crisis what they can do for themselves—with the exception of culturally expected responses like community members delivering food to the home after the death of a loved one, for example. When a person knows they need to make a phone call to their loved ones across town and has the presence of mind to do so, don't take that task away from them and offer to call on their behalf. If someone knows they need to fill out a form and are capable of doing so, let them do it rather than taking that task away from them. It may seem helpful to do everything you can for someone experiencing a crisis or disaster, but doing little things that are within their competency and control can help them regain a small sense of agency and avert feelings of helplessness. Necessary tasks that they can't accomplish alone may require your aid.

Helping someone feel more in control of various aspects of their life when the larger situation seems wildly out of their control is a method of empowerment. A helpful question to enhance a careseeker's perspective of what might be in their control is the simple but empowering query: What have you done in the past to help manage stressful situations?[9]

They may have a repertoire of skills for coping with stress but may not be cognitively capable of accessing them right away. In all likelihood, the person you are accompanying through a crisis or disaster is a person of resourcefulness and resilience who has done hard things before and will be able to do them again. While it is not your job to provide any cheap assurances that they'll get through this and come out on the other side stronger, it can be an empowering move for a careseeker to help a person recognize their own strengths, capabilities, and resourcefulness. They may just need a little help seeing what is already there in their life and story.

Evaluate for Ongoing Care Needs

When you are providing care in the aftermath of a crisis, assume resilience. Most people return to a state of balance on their own without referral to more acute psychotherapeutic care. People are resourceful and resilient in the aftermath of a crisis, and when a person is well embedded within a community of care, resilience is even more likely. Remember that the majority of people will never develop the symptoms of PTSD or have lingering psychological distress or trauma responses to crises and disasters. But occasionally, more support will be needed.

Evaluating for ongoing care needs is the level at which you, as the care responder, should begin thinking about potential referral needs a careseeker may have so that you can engage in the ministry of introduction to another helping professional or resource. Disaster psychologist Gerard Jacobs names five critical areas of assessment in the evaluating of the ongoing care for people recovering from a crisis or disaster.[10]

First, if the symptoms that are considered common responses to crisis and disaster in the early days following the event persist, a referral to a mental health provider may be needed. Sadness, lack of pleasure from favorite activities, difficulty returning to a routine, recurring memories of the traumatic event, trouble concentrating or thinking clearly or making decisions—all of these are common responses to a traumatic event in the early days. But if they persist longer than 4–6 weeks, there is elevated concern for the longer-term well-being of the careseeker, who may need a little more help returning to a state of balance.

This guideline doesn't mean that someone experiencing a crisis or traumatic event should have gotten over it or returned to a presumed state of life as normal in 4–6 weeks. Grief will persist and should not be rushed. But they may need help with some symptoms that limit them in their day-to-day lives. If you are in the position to follow up with a careseeker in the weeks following a crisis or disaster, ask about some of the common symptoms they were experiencing early on to see whether those have subsided or not. If not, engage in a conversation oriented toward the ministry of introduction to a professional care provider who can address some of those concerns.

Second, if a careseeker is having difficulty functioning in their daily life—for example, on the job, at home, or in their schooling—after the 4–6-week timeframe, more support may be needed to reestablish equilibrium in the careseeker's life. It is important that you issue an invitation to allow you to connect them with a helping resource in a nonstigmatizing way. Everly and Lating add that it is often important to engage in encouragement toward seeking further support, not argument. They state, "At this point, it is often helpful to remind them that seeking further assistance may be a means of helping those who depend on them more than a form of direct assistance for them."[11] If they will not accept an invitation to connect with another helping professional, and if no life-threatening situation such as suicidal thoughts is present, then you may simply check in on the careseeker at a later date to issue an invitation again.

Third, Jacobs encourages care responders to be attentive to whether a careseeker continues to be concerned about the symptoms of distress or behaviors they are experiencing in their own life. At earlier stages in the crisis aftermath, any symptoms that trouble the careseeker can be reframed as common responses to a crisis or disaster to help ease the careseeker's anxiety about them. In later stages, if a careseeker continues to be troubled by symptoms they are experiencing—such as inability to sleep or eat, nightmares, or flashbacks—a referral to a mental health provider may be warranted and welcomed.

Fourth, if there is any indication that the careseeker is experiencing suicidal thoughts or may be a danger to others, then referral to a mental health professional becomes necessary. Chapter 13 offers further information about how to conduct a simple suicide assessment and what to do if suicide seems a thinkable option for a careseeker. Absent of suicidality, people's coping strategies in the aftermath of a traumatic event can also prove harmful over the long term. Alcohol and drug use can sometimes be employed as a coping strategy for the lingering stress of a crisis or disaster and may also necessitate further exploration and intervention.

Fifth, Jacobs reminds us to attend to our boundaries of competence. If what we are experiencing in our attempt to help in the aftermath of crisis or trauma seem beyond our skills and abilities to address or requires more time than we have to offer, it is important to engage in the ministry of introduction to connect the careseeker with another helping professional who can address their ongoing needs.[12]

Even if none of these five concerns is present and no formal ongoing support seems needed, it is important to provide an invitation for the person moving through the aftermath of crisis or disaster to reach out to seek longer-term support if it is needed. Not everyone needs a referral to a mental health professional following a crisis. Again, crises are a common part of our lives. We hope they don't happen too frequently in our lives and communities, but they will occur. The presence of a loving and supportive community and the capacity to regain some abilities to cope with the stress and grief that may follow a crisis are the key elements of support that most of us need following a crisis. Some, however, will need further support moving forward from a crisis.

When no formal referral is needed for ongoing support, then simply help the person strategize how they will turn toward community in the aftermath of their crisis. Isolation is one of the most debilitating experiences in crisis or community disaster. This doesn't mean it is unhealthy to be alone sometimes or to seek solace in solitude as many of us need to find rest, peace, and healing. But the inability to connect with others, signs of withdrawal from family and friends, and the unavailability of a caring community when it is needed make recovery from crisis and disaster more difficult. Everly, Strouse, and McCormack state that "interpersonal support when adversity and trauma strike may be the single most powerful factor to foster resilience."[13]

Spiritually Appraising Crisis Response

Everly and Lating say that the "defining moment of psychological traumatization is when some experience violates some deeply held belief or worldview."[14] Those who are called on to intervene in the midst of crises should be attentive in listening for the ways that the potentially traumatic event may have violated a "deeply held core belief that survivors hold about themselves or the world."[15] Experiences of crisis, traumatic losses, and disasters upset our ways of understanding the world, making commonly held sturdy assumptions of safety and security and order suddenly seem precarious and ephemeral. We may question important aspects of our faith or spiritual beliefs during this time such as the justly ordered nature of the world, the presence and protection of God, and even the meaning of our life. Compassionate companionship through these questions can be especially helpful following a crisis or disaster. First, we will look at three dimensions in which our spiritual grounding may be affected by crises and disasters. After this, we will give attention to how care responders can work with spirituality in crisis.

Three Dimensions of Spiritual Appraisal

There are three dimensions of spiritual appraisal that spiritual care first aid responders should be especially attentive to in the aftermath of crisis and disaster: *transcendence*, *togetherness*, and *tethering*. These three dimensions are each interpenetrating, informing the others, and being informed by the others. A secure sense of belonging in one dimension can enhance our sense of belonging in the others. That which severs our belonging in one dimension—toxic theologies, acts of violence, experiences of rejection, or, in our case, life-upending crises or disasters—can erode our sense of connection in other dimensions. Yet one or another dimension may also become a source of healing when the health of our belonging in another dimension is harmed by crisis or disaster.

Transcendence describes our connection to a context of ultimacy, or God. This dimension speaks to the opening outward of the self toward something beyond the self. Our connection, or belonging, in relationship to God can be strained by many questions that arise amid crisis. We can come to question God's presence in our lives when we've experienced an extraordinary tragedy. When many of our deeply held core beliefs are built around a relationship with God and that relationship comes under stress, worldviews that we've relied on come to seem unstable.

Togetherness speaks to our connection to others in expansive human community. The togetherness dimension invites practices of spirituality that help us to look beyond the self toward one another, to stand alongside one another in grief, in solidarity, in gratitude. Togetherness practices invite us to notice who is missing from among us and whose loss needs mourning. Experiencing a crisis or tragedy that we believe others cannot easily understand may call into question whether others can, or will, companion us in the aftermath. Feelings of guilt over surviving a disaster when others in our community, or even our family, did not can strain our experience of relational togetherness and may intersect with stresses in the transcendence dimension over questions about God's providence in the situation.

Tethering orients us toward our intimate and inextricable relationship to the earth, mooring us in relational solidarity with the wider web of life. Natural or human-caused disasters—for example, wildfires, oil spills, or hurricanes—may especially alter a landscape to which we feel a deep sense of relationality or belonging. Often, and to our detriment, we do not address our connection to landscapes or the wider web of life in relational terms. But belonging to the earth's wider web of life is not optional. Relationships bind us in earthy entanglement. When some of those relational bonds are severed either because the landscape is altered by disaster or because we've been displaced by a disaster, feelings of solastalgia—the pain or distress caused by the "loss of solace and the sense of desolation" connected to one's sense of home or relational entanglement with the landscape and its ecological web—can arise.[16]

Working with Spirituality in Crisis

Aside from the ways that our deeply held beliefs and religious or spiritual worldviews can be disrupted, our religious and spiritual lives can be sources of strength in crisis. Pastoral theologian Mary Beth Werdel describes three broad and interrelated ways that religion and spirituality often support people through crises and traumatic experiences. They help engage in meaning-making through suffering, they help cope uniquely with distress, and they can develop and deepen virtues that provide pathways to growth.[17]

Making meaning out of suffering, crisis, loss, and traumatic events is difficult. Many of the biggest questions that emerge in the aftermath of a traumatic event have no clear answer. Why does evil or suffering exist? How could God let this happen? Why me? Many religious and spiritual traditions have within them sources of wisdom and comfort that, while not necessarily answering these big questions, provide a way forward for making meaning out of suffering, discerning the presence of the Divine amid tragedy, and expressing one's most troubling questions directly to God in protest, in lament, in longing. The book of Psalms is replete with these types of prayers, many written in periods of communal suffering.

Religious and spiritual commitments can also be a source of meaning that helps survivors of crises become helpers to others who are going through the crisis right alongside them or victims of future crises. Many who have experienced a particular hardship sense a call emerging from within that experience to help others facing similar experiences. After attending to one's own needs for care and support and healing, being supportive to others can be a source of empowerment and meaning that emerge in the aftermath of crises.

While religion and spirituality can promote recovery, resilience, growth, and flourishing, other aspects of religion and spirituality can contribute negatively to life in the aftermath of crisis or disaster. Theologies that suggest that crises, disasters, and traumatic events are punishment for something one has done or punishment for larger social evils exacerbate suffering in the aftermath of disaster. Unfortunately, these messages are often propagated by religious leaders. As Werdel notes, attending these theologies of retribution featuring a punishing God, there are often images of "a self who is sinful and worthy of abandonment."[18] It is likely no surprise that those who are able to access comforting and supportive aspects of their religious tradition or spiritual practice are more likely to experience helpful meaning-making and even growth after a traumatic event than those whose religious and spiritual perspective is characterized by "punishment, discomfort, and discontent."[19] Several areas of spiritual practice can become helpful in the aftermath of crisis or disaster.

Research suggests that those who have a higher frequency of daily prayer, individually or corporately, as a form of coping with traumatic events also have higher experiences of post-traumatic growth.[20] While prayer should never be forced on anyone, especially as a means of assuaging the care responder's own anxiety about their ability to help, it can be a sustaining spiritual resource in turbulent times, both individually and corporately. It can allow many of our theological questions to come forth in direct speech to God and be held by others in community who may feel similar burdens of spiritual distress.

Feelings of guilt often arise in the aftermath of surviving a crisis or disaster, especially when others did not make it. Werdel reminds us that "self-compassion is not only a form of self-care; it is an expression that recognizes the sacred reality of the self."[21] One can have self-compassion without a religious or spiritual belief or relationship with transcendence to root that self-compassion. However, when a religious or spiritual worldview or practice is present, drawing on one's spiritual sources of sustenance, it can help root self-compassion. For example, reading comforting passages of Scripture that have been meaningful in one's life, recalling and reflecting on past experiences of one's own self as a beloved child of God, or connecting to others in spiritual community can become helpful in sustaining self-compassion. Crises can provoke a feeling of coming unmoored, like the very ground underneath us is giving way, and there's nothing to hold on to. Spiritual practices that facilitate grounding such as attending to the body's hyperarousal through grounding breathing exercises can help return some sense of stability.

Spiritual practices and religious resources should never be forced on others in the aftermath of crisis, nor should disaster-recovery periods become an outlet for evangelism. Before offering any of these types of spiritual practices, assess which spiritual practices, if any, are important to the careseeker. Finally, if you are providing care within a larger community context following a disaster, it can be important to attend to the multifaith needs of your community. For example, explore these types of questions: Are there ways for displaced Jewish or Muslim members of your community to access kosher and halal meals? Are there places where particular members of your community—for example, Muslims—can gather in prayer when necessary? When lives that are shaped by ritual and communal spiritual practice are disrupted by disasters, the loss of that ritual practice and space can be further spiritually unmooring. A return of those ritual and communal spaces, even in temporary and makeshift ways, can return a sense of grounding amid a crisis.

LONGER-TERM COMMUNITY SUPPORT

Beyond the early stages after a crisis or disaster, there are also larger communal concerns that spiritual care providers should be attentive to. This is especially the case for those leading spiritual care efforts within congregational or other community settings. Rabbi Stephen B. Roberts describes the immediate stage following an initial emergency crisis response within a community facing a disaster as the *disillusionment phase* and often the most difficult phase of disaster recovery.[22]

Suicidality is especially important to attend to during the disillusionment phase of a large-scale community disaster. It may seem that the worst parts of the disaster are behind you, but some in your community may be having a difficult time making meaning in the aftermath of the traumatic event, feeling isolated or alone, experiencing a sense of discouragement and hopelessness amid the rebuilding of their lives, or feeling stigmatized as victims.[23] In fact, others may wish for the direct victims of the crisis or disaster to have gotten over it, gotten better, or recovered by now. The fact that their process of recovery, grief, healing, and rebuilding may take some time can be difficult for those for whom this expression of vulnerability is an uncomfortable sign of all of our human frailty, susceptibility, and precarity to unexpected tragedy and disaster.

Many events can trigger painful memories and emotional struggle for people who have lived through a crisis or disaster: anniversaries of the event itself or of relationships with a person who died in the event and even holidays of significance. As Imam Yusuf Hasan and Rev. George Handzo say, for families and communities, events like anniversaries, holidays, reunions, births, and deaths "are the events that keep us connected to this most important community and reinforce our identities as members of a greater whole. Conversely, any event that impedes our ability to connect in these ways isolates us and reduces our sense of being part of a family."[24] It is important for those charged with the spiritual care of a community to be attentive to how a disaster or crisis, on a familial or a communal level, can impact the experience of these events for a family, church, or community and to create a sense of sacredness and possibly the cultivation of ritual to hold these triggering events with care.

Practice Exercise: Preparing for Disaster in Your Context

If you serve as a care responder in a community of faith, either as a pastor or a lay care provider, it can be helpful to scenario-build with the care team or other leadership body in the faith community. Bring a group together in your church or community or even your neighborhood to think through a scenario of communal disaster. If your area is prone to a particular type of natural disaster like hurricanes or wildfires, perhaps choose one of those. Look at news stories or recall when other communities have experienced a similar disaster to the one you are considering. What did other communities experience in the aftermath of this disaster? What were the most pressing needs of the residents? Which local, regional, or national organizations were present trying to help meet those needs? Have you come across stories of churches' involvement in the crisis response in other communities?

After you've made a thorough list of all that you've learned from these news stories or your own prior experience, think about your own local community. Who would be most vulnerable if this type of disaster occurred near you? What needs would people have similar to the stories you read? Which local organizations would be go-to resources for meeting local needs? How could you imagine your own church or faith community being helpful in the midst of such an event? Which skills and abilities exist in your community that would be helpful in this situation? What assets—building, shelter space, commercial kitchen, lawn for organizing resource providers, buses—do you have that could be employed to meet the needs of your community in a disaster?

Now think about yourself—each individual person engaging in this scenario-building exercise. How do you see yourself being most helpful in the midst of a communal crisis or disaster? Which skills do you have that could be helpful to others? Which skills would you like to develop or hone? How do you see yourself as one part of a larger network of care and support? What needs for your own self-care would be most important to keeping you healthy and resilient as you help others recover from a local crisis or disaster?

You can replay this scenario-building exercise with various crises and disasters or by compounding one disaster with another complication, for example, dealing with a local natural disaster like a tornado, flood, or hurricane during a pandemic or during a period of civil unrest. While it may seem daunting to play through these scenarios with others in your community, working through near-future potentials like this increases our sense of potential helpfulness in difficult situations, and we learn things about ourselves as individuals and communities that help us meet needs in our communities now, outside of disaster situations.

FURTHER READING

Ashley, Willard W. C., Sr., and Stephen B. Roberts, eds. *Disaster Spiritual Care: Practical Clergy Responses to Community, Regional and National Tragedy*. 2nd ed. Nashville: Skylight Paths, 2017.

Stone, Howard W. *Crisis Counseling*. 3rd ed. Minneapolis: Fortress, 2009.

NOTES

1 George S. Everly Jr., Douglas A. Strouse, and Dennis K. McCormack, *Stronger: Develop the Resilience You Need to Succeed* (New York: American Management Association, 2015), 153–168.

2 George S. Everly Jr. and Jeffrey M. Lating, *The Johns Hopkins Guide to Psychological First Aid*, 2nd ed. (Baltimore: Johns Hopkins, 2022), 44.

3 Everly and Lating, *The Johns Hopkins Guide*, 106.

4 Everly and Lating, *The Johns Hopkins Guide*, 122.

5 Everly and Lating, *The Johns Hopkins Guide*, 129–131.

6 Everly and Lating, *The Johns Hopkins Guide*, 153.

7 Everly and Lating, *The Johns Hopkins Guide*, 155.

8 Howard W. Stone, *Crisis Counseling*, rev. ed. (Minneapolis: Fortress, 1993), 47.

9 Everly and Lating, *The Johns Hopkins Guide*, 159.

10 Gerard A. Jacobs, *Community-Based Psychological First Aid: A Practical Guide to Helping Individuals and Communities during Difficult Times* (Cambridge, MA: Butterworth-Heinemann, 2016), 36.

11 Everly and Lating, *The Johns Hopkins Guide*, 180.
12 Jacobs, *Community-Based Psychological First Aid*, 36.
13 Everly, Strouse, and McCormack, *Stronger*, as cited in Everly and Lating, *The Johns Hopkins Guide*, 162.
14 Everly, Strouse, and McCormack, *Stronger*, as cited in Everly and Lating, *The Johns Hopkins Guide*, 162.
15 Everly and Lating, *The Johns Hopkins Guide*, 44.
16 Glenn A. Albrecht, *Earth Emotions: New Words for a New World* (Ithaca, NY: Cornell University Press, 2019), 38.
17 Mary Beth Werdel, *The Paradox of Trauma and Growth in Pastoral and Spiritual Care: Night Blooming* (Lanham, MD: Lexington Books, 2024), 56.
18 Werdel, *The Paradox of Trauma*, 62.
19 Werdel, *The Paradox of Trauma*, 62.
20 Werdel, *The Paradox of Trauma*, 62.
21 Werdel, *The Paradox of Trauma*, 66.
22 Stephen B. Roberts, "The Life Cycle of a Disaster," in *Disaster Spiritual Care: Practical Clergy Responses to Community, Regional and National Tragedy*, 2nd ed., ed. Willard W. C. Ashley Sr. and Stephen B. Roberts (Nashville: Skylight Paths, 2017), 30–33.
23 Roberts, "The Life Cycle of a Disaster," 30–31.
24 Yusuf Hasan and George Handzo, "Anniversaries, Holidays, and Other Reminders," in Ashley and Roberts, *Disaster Spiritual Care*, 209–210.

PART THREE

THE ART OF HEALING

11

HEALING THAT IS TRAUMA-AWARE

The entire world entered a multiyear experience of trauma exposure in 2020 when the COVID-19 pandemic suddenly and dramatically reshaped our lives for a period of years, producing millions of deaths worldwide. Many suddenly lost jobs, incomes, health care, the means to care for loved ones, and proximity to the dying in their final hours.

Our planet, every human, and other-than-human inhabitants therein are currently undergoing the collective trauma of a rapidly changing climate affecting everything from the livability of life in certain ecosystems to the availability of life-sustaining sources of food and water to global migration patterns and the intensity and frequency of severe weather events.

Racialized violence in policing and the carceral system institutionalizes trauma-inducing practices on entire populations in the United States, whether one becomes a direct target of that violence or not. Gender-based and sexualized violence creates circumstances in which some must develop hypervigilance over one's safety, creating a state of chronic stress, even if one never experiences the trauma of direct violence.

The experience of trauma is quite commonplace in our world, though we've not always had the language to talk about it as openly as we do now. Trauma typically begins with an event—a car accident, a natural disaster, an experience of interpersonal violence, living through a time of war, for example—and takes shape through one's embodied emotional response and meaning-making in relation to that horrific event.[1] However, clinical social worker and trauma expert Resmaa Menakem teaches that trauma can also be an embodied response to a longer series of smaller wounds rather than one traumatic event. "It can be a response to *anything* that [the body] experiences as too much, too soon, or too fast," Menakem argues.[2] Not all terrible events cause trauma for every person who experiences them. Events that induce a trauma response for some are merely stressful for others. Events can be traumatic, but the ways individuals and communities experience trauma in relation to those events is much more idiosyncratic. In fact, 80 percent of people who experience a traumatic event do not develop long-term symptoms of trauma.[3]

Professional therapists are better positioned to diagnose trauma, although the definition of *trauma* is often quite disputed. Your goal is to practice spiritual care first aid in a *trauma-aware* way. Because nearly everyone can experience adverse events that create the circumstances of distress and, potentially, trauma, our care needs to account for the potential of trauma whether it is evident or not. Practicing spiritual care that is attentive to this reality will help cultivate compassionate companionship amid these circumstances in ways that are helpful to all, whether or not one's experiences rise to the level of the traumatic.

HEARING TRAUMA

Trauma and various levels of crisis and stress arise out of what minister and psychologist Karen McClintock describes as a combination of painful and life-disrupting circumstances outside of our control alongside what happens inside our bodies and "the ways our central nervous system fires up so we can escape pain or death."[4] This embodied trauma response to an external circumstance outside of our control affects our brain's capacity for impulse control and executive functioning and stays with us in our bodies. She continues, "Trauma is initially an external experience with an internal response . . . trauma lingers in our bodies. Trauma then becomes an internal experience with an external response."[5] Our bodies remain ready to respond to the life-threatening situation, even when that situation has long passed. This is an intensely stressful, embodied experience that can linger for a long time. We can't simply reason our way of our trauma just because the original circumstances of the trauma are no longer present.

Psychiatrist Bessel van der Kolk sums up the experience of trauma, saying, "The essence of trauma is that it is overwhelming, unbelievable, and unbearable."[6] If you are invited into someone's story of trauma, you are standing on ground that is both holy and precarious. It takes courage on the part of the caregiver to hear these stories, and the experience may require you to have an outlet for your own care—a spiritual director, supervisor, or therapist with whom you can process your caregiving. This is especially necessary when a careseeker's traumatic experience touches on one of your own.

It is a helpful practice in any circumstance to have your own spiritual care provider or therapist. Being in a caregiving relationship with people working through trauma responses can bring about experiences of secondary traumatic stress or vicarious trauma, especially when we spend significant time listening to a careseeker recount traumatic events in their own life. Be aware of when you need to talk through your caregiving practice with a helping professional who can aid you in processing your trauma exposure.

Oftentimes, the language of trauma may be used by a careseeker for a response to an event that is uncomfortable, maybe even distressing, but that may not seem traumatic in ways that care responders recognize. It is not helpful to dispute the careseeker's language for their experience. Whether or not you believe *trauma* is an accurate term, respond to the careseeker's language in ways that respect and validate their experience of suffering and distress.

Importantly, however, it is likely not helpful for you as the care responder to introduce the language of trauma to describe another's experience. Remember to stick closely to the language used by the careseeker in describing their own circumstance. When a careseeker names an experience as trauma, it can be a way of recognizing the power that an adverse event had in their lives. When a careseeker imposes that language, it can have a limiting effect, escalating what the careseeker may view as an experience over which they have much more control and are exercising resilience and for which they have much more experience-near language to describe.

As you begin to hear the possibilities of trauma in a careseeker's story, adopt a stance of compassionate not-knowing. Allow the careseeker to tell you which parts of their story they most need to tell, but never push for more details or further elaboration of a traumatic narrative. It is, after all, their story. They have the rights to it and can tell you what they need for you to hear. Your primary job as a spiritual care responder is compassionate, less anxious, nonjudgmental listening and companioning presence.

McClintock helpfully outlines three stages when a careseeker might be experiencing trauma following an overwhelming event. Keeping these stages in mind can help guide your care response when you believe trauma might be present. In the earliest stages following a traumatic experience, she notes that a person experiences tremendous suffering and may feel powerless and disconnected. At this stage, interpretation of the traumatic event is not a helpful approach to care. Instead, helping a person determine how to undertake the regular activities of daily life is key.[7] Is the person able to take care of their needs or those of their family? Could they use tangible help like meals or just a call to be sure they've been able to make it out of bed during some intensely difficult times? Could they use support in developing coping strategies through engaging art, music, or nature? Social isolation is a potential reaction to a traumatic stressor. Are they staying connected to loved ones in meaningful ways? Care responders should also be alert to the possibility of suicide becoming a thinkable option. Never hesitate to ask about suicidal thoughts if it seems possible.

Remember that as a spiritual care first responder—whether a minister, a chaplain, or a lay caregiver—you are not a therapist, and there are boundaries of competence that will require you to help some careseekers add professional caregivers like therapists or physicians to their community of care. Be ready to introduce this conversation when you believe there are concerns that might best be addressed in the context of a therapeutic relationship. This is especially important to remember when a careseeker seems to be in an early and intense stage of trauma response to a distressing incident.

Most people in this initial stage of intense trauma response move into a more manageable stage after some time and with some support. At this middle phase, a careseeker gains more control and agency in their daily life, emotions become less unpredictable, and possibilities for a future begin to emerge in their imagination. At this stage, McClintock says that a helpful question for reflection on their experience of trauma becomes "How have you survived other devastating times in your life?"[8] Skills and resources and communities they've relied on in past difficulties could become important again in surviving in the aftermath of a traumatic incident, though they may not yet see these skills and resources as important in the current context until you help them to explore their application to this situation. This is also a stage at which new skills for dealing with anxiety and stress and painful emotions become more helpful.

Finally, when a person moves further into their thriving in the aftermath of a traumatic incident, new identities begin to emerge, more complex meaning may be made of the distressing incident, and lives begin to be put back together again. Whereas the early stage of trauma-responsive care may require a more directive approach to ensure that daily needs are being met, at this later stage, care responders can return to the more compassionate companioning postures through actively and responsively listening, asking helpful questions, and providing supportive presence.[9] Importantly, there is no timeframe attached to these stages. Rather, care responders should be attentive to the signs related to where a careseeker is in dealing with distressing incidents that prompt a trauma response and, thus, align one's care praxis to the needs of each stage.

TRAUMA-SENSITIVE THEOLOGY

Suffering is not a sign of sinfulness. Experiences of distress are not indicators of moral failure. Our pain is not a proving ground for our faith. In our religious and spiritual quests to make sense of suffering, we have often arrived at answers to questions that cause more harm than good when they are propagated in the midst of a person's immediate suffering. Thus, we must be attentive to the messages we convey about suffering, whether from the pulpit, in Bible studies and discussion groups, in formal care responses, or in casual conversation.

Some of the most unhelpful responses to suffering and trauma are causal statements that we make, often without thinking about how they land amid a person's pain. Examples include "This is just a test of your faith," "God won't give you more than you can handle," and "There's a reason for this experience, even if you can't see it." Each of these statements places the blame on the victim for their own suffering and makes God a culprit instigating the person's suffering.

People are often asking much more important questions about their faith and spirituality during times of trauma—questions that pat answers and thin theology can't adequately address. Three categories of questions identified by McClintock are *why me? why evil?* and *why God?*[10] These are helpful categories of questions to keep in mind as you think through how to be most responsive to another's traumatic circumstances. They are not questions you should introduce as a caregiver but questions that many experiencing traumatic circumstances may already be asking.

Questions of *why me* or *why my loved one* may come from a place of feeling singled out by a traumatic event or circumstance, isolated and alone in a situation of tragedy. Sometimes a person's operative theology may suggest that God has singled out a person for punishment or that their own actions could have instigated the adverse event. Many popular streams of theology and contemporary spiritually suggest that living a good life, a faithful life, a spiritual life leads only to good outcomes, leaving no room for the possibility that bad things simply do happen—accidents, natural disasters, violence—and yet that the traumatic experience is pervaded by the sustaining presence of the Divine.

Pastoral theologians Jan Holton and Jill Snodgrass explain another piece of an unhelpful operative theology of our era: "Many of us have been deeply shaped by the notions of humankind's fallen, sinful nature and the idea that were it not for human disobedience, human existence would be perfect, immortal, and, most importantly, free of suffering and distress. This theology makes suffering not just unfortunate but a punishment to be avoided at all costs. It is a de facto theology of distress in which we can easily become perpetually caught between what should be and what is."[11] Additionally, the question of evil is one as old as most sacred traditions. The issue asks questions such as: Why do bad things happen? Why do they happen to good people? Why would a good God allow traumatic events to occur if God could stop them?

Spiritual care first aid can help a careseeker detach moral meaning-making from the experience of suffering and put some distance between the traumatic event and any cosmic or spiritual purposefulness behind it, targeting the individual for harm. A simple statement can be both validating of the experience of suffering that prompts the question and encouraging of the careseeker to voice their own theologies that are in the process of being shaped by the traumatic event. For example, you might offer, "These are big and important questions about suffering and ones that so many have to ask in the course of life. While I don't have an answer to these questions, I'm grateful to explore them alongside you." It will be a healing gift in the long run to have a compassionate conversation partner in the midst of spiritual ferment, even if it doesn't feel productive to you in the short run as you run short on answers.

Why God? questions can often sound like an indictment against God. It may be uncomfortable for you to hear people ask heated questions of God in the midst of their turmoil and pain, such as: Why didn't you do anything? Where were you? How could you? A person's faith may well be put to the test by traumatic circumstances, but that doesn't mean that the traumatic event is a test of their faith. Use your own calming strategies to sustain your spirit enough to maintain a less anxious presence with a person in this type of pain so that you can hear their questions, validate their experience of suffering, and journey with them as far as they wish to go in exploring these deeply personal inquiries.

Remember, questions like "Why, O God?" are the very questions that were on the lips of our ancestors in faithful striving that produced the words of the psalmist, saying, "Why, O Lord, do you stand far off? Why do you hide yourself in times of trouble?" (Psalm 10:1, NRSVue). They are present in the Christian tradition that contains Jesus's own words of felt abandonment by God, "My God, my God, why have you forsaken me?" (Matthew 27:46; Mark 15:34, NRSVue). Generations of faithful religious practitioners and spiritual seekers in every age have asked these same questions of God, growing in spiritual depth, even amid suffering.

Questions are a sign of faithfulness and spiritual deepening, not a lack of faith. Even though you won't have many answers to provide people in the midst of traumatic experience—and you likely won't—validating the source of the questions can be helpful when a person is fearful of losing their grasp on a faith that once felt solid and now feels on shaky ground.

Sit with the questions. Explore their complexity. Resist easy answers.

RESILIENCE, RESISTANCE, AND REPAIR IN TRAUMA-AWARE COMMUNITIES

Holton and Snodgrass helpfully remind us that "humans most often make meaning of distressing events in community, not in isolation."[12] Healing communities with some sensitivity to trauma can be invaluable relational connections to people experiencing the aftermath of distressing events in their lives. Trauma responses can also make community-building difficult, with lingering feelings of distress of unsafety related to a traumatic experience. Communities that wish to be truly responsive to the trauma of their members can become sources of sustenance and strength in the aftermath of terrible experiences.

Growth happens in the aftermath of trauma. But remember, our growth is not the reason the traumatic event occurred. Many call this type of growth *post-traumatic growth*, and others describe something similar with the term *resilience*. Resilience isn't the outcome of trauma, and traumatic events should never be interpreted by communities of faith as experiences that were meant to simply make us stronger. The suffering they produce is real and needs to be witnessed and validated. But resilience is a capacity, individual and communal, that can arise in the aftermath of trauma.

Trauma specialist Elaine Miller-Karas defines resilience as "the ability to identify and use individual and collective strengths to live fully in the present moment and to thrive while managing the tasks of daily living." It implies not just bouncing back from a traumatic stressor but also the potential to create meaning from the event in ways that transforms life and community.[13] Importantly, all interventions aimed to be helpful in the midst of trauma should be gentle and invitational, not forced on people.

Faith communities responsive to trauma may experiment with the use of mindfulness practices in corporate spaces that allow people to attend to breath and decrease our bodies' anxiety. Normalizing being in movement during meetings if the need arises can help those for whom sitting still for a long period increases anxiety responses. Guiding participants in a meeting or a study through a process of scanning their bodies to see where they are holding tension, guiding their attention throughout their body, part by part, can help people be more fully aware of their bodies given that trauma is an embodied experience and not simply a matter of thinking. However, pastoral theologian and trauma scholar Keith Menhinick reminds us that "learning to scan and sit with the body can make some survivors feel unsafe and bring back a rush of memories and sensations. It's normal and something to look out for." In your gentle invitations toward these practices, always remain open to a careseeker declining for these reasons. If you are practicing these body-focused practices in a corporate setting, Menhinick suggests that grounding stations with water and snacks can be helpful for people needing a break.[14]

Importantly, some who have experienced trauma may bring their anger and conflict into relationship with those trying to help.[15] Thus, leaders in the community need to respond with *boundaried compassion* so that the person acting out anger and disruption in relation to their trauma is not retraumatized by a harsh response yet is also not given permission to disrupt the entirety of a community's life. The work of nurturing resilience is hard but worthwhile.

Importantly, McClintock reminds members of faith communities that despite the important care that can be provided for people in the midst of traumatic experiences, at later stages of recovery from trauma, people may decide to leave a supportive faith community because they are desiring to be known by others outside of their trauma experience as they develop new identities as survivors and thrivers in the face of trauma.[16] This can be potentially painful for a faith community that has endeavored to companion that person through difficult days. But viewed in this light, you might take a person's leaving after a journey of recovery from trauma to be a good sign that they're moving into new generative stages of thriving in their life. And you well may be the faith community that others in that place of thriving will find as they put their lives back together again and seek new supportive community. Your trauma-responsive community skills will be just as important to maintain for these new sojourners in faith community.

Some forms of traumatic experience require more from a community of faith than being a source of healing for members who experience traumatic occurrences. *Resistance* is necessary when forms of violence and abuse are inflicted by others rather than in circumstances of distress and pain caused by accident or natural disaster. Racialized violence and attacks against LGBTQIA+ people, for example, are not occurrences that should invite resilience. They should provoke our resistance. Mass shootings occurring in our grocery stores and schools should not make us more resilient in the face of violence. They should make us more resistant to the threat through our action to decrease their occurrence.

Resistance to systemic injustice that creates disparities between communities based on race, class, immigration status, nationality, sexual orientation, or gender identity requires a community to undertake a serious examination of the ways that prejudice works its way into the lives of entire communities, creating circumstances of chronic stress and trauma. Communities serious about being trauma-responsive must not only create circumstances of healing within community for survivors of these types of traumas but must also be about the work of creating change in larger communities so that historic traumas are not continually perpetuated. Strengthening communal capacities for nurturing resilience and supporting communal practices of resistance to systematic injustice and violence are intertwined capacities for trauma-responsive faith communities.

Nonviolence teacher Kazu Haga asks us to imagine what would happen if we institutionalized healing in the same ways that many of our systems and social structures and institutions have institutionalized violence. Haga asks, "What kind of world could we create?"[17] It is that question that should send our theological imaginations reeling with possibilities for the type of world—and the type of local community—that we most wish to live within. What Jewish faith communities call *tikkun olam* (repair of the world) must become as central to our trauma-responsive communities as repair of the individual body-mind-soul of an individual experiencing trauma.

Practice Exercise: Mindfulness

One practice that can be a source of healing and has had a tremendous positive impact on people experiencing trauma and various forms of distress is mindfulness. Mindfulness is about paying attention to the body, to one's feelings, to sensations in a nonjudgmental manner. It is an embodied way of paying attention. You can practice one specific mindfulness exercise that you can use for yourself and, when appropriate, with careseekers who want to develop healing spiritual practices.

First, sit comfortably in a chair. There is no right pose, but sitting comfortably with your back straight against the chair, your feet flat on the floor, and your hands resting gently in your lap can be a helpful place to begin. There's no need to close your eyes, but you can if you wish. Some who are in various stages of trauma response may not wish to close their eyes, and that's perfectly fine. If you're not closing your eyes, simply rest your gaze on some object or point in the foreground.

As you sit in a relaxed posture, begin to simply notice your breath as you inhale and exhale. You don't need to do anything differently with your breath. Simply notice with singular attention each in breath and each out breath. Notice your lungs filling with life-giving air. Notice your body exhaling breath that will nurture other beings.

As you allow your attention to be more fully engrossed in your body's breathing, let go of other experiences, observations, or distractions. Don't fight thoughts if they pop into your mind. Just notice that the thoughts have come. Then, as gently as you can and without judgment, return your attention to your breath.

When you've done this for a few minutes, return your attention to your surroundings. You might increase your capacity for mindfulness by attempting to increase the time you practice this exercise by a minute or so each time.[18]

FURTHER READING

McClintock, Karen A. *Trauma-Informed Pastoral Care: How to Respond When Things Fall Apart*. Minneapolis: Fortress, 2022.

NOTES

1 A distinct but related concept to trauma is that of moral injury. This has become an especially important concept in providing spiritual care for persons returning from military service in wartime. For a helpful introduction to care amid moral injury, see Zachary Moon, *Coming Home: Ministry That Matters with Veterans and Military Families* (St. Louis: Chalice, 2015); Joshua Morris, *Moral Injury among Returning Veterans: From Thank You for Your Service to a Liberative Solidarity* (Lanham, MD: Lexington Books, 2021); and Nancy J. Ramsay and Carrie Doehring, eds., *Military Moral Injury and*

Spiritual Care: A Resource for Religious Leaders and Professional Caregivers (St. Louis: Chalice, 2019).

2 Resmaa Menakem, *My Grandmother's Hands: Racialized Trauma and the Pathway to Mending Our Hearts and Bodies* (Las Vegas, NV: Central Recovery Press, 2017), 14.

3 Karen A. McClintock, *Trauma-Informed Pastoral Care: How to Respond When Things Fall Apart* (Minneapolis: Fortress, 2022), 36.

4 McClintock, *Trauma-Informed Pastoral Care*, 2.

5 McClintock, *Trauma-Informed Pastoral Care*, 2.

6 Bessel van der Kolk, *The Body Keeps the Score: Brian, Mind, and Body in the Healing of Trauma* (New York: Penguin Books, 2014), 197.

7 McClintock, *Trauma-Informed Pastoral Care*, 157.

8 McClintock, *Trauma-Informed Pastoral Care*, 164.

9 McClintock, *Trauma-Informed Pastoral Care*, 167.

10 Karen A. McClintock, *When Trauma Wounds: Pathways to Healing and Hope* (Minneapolis: Fortress, 2019), 133–143.

11 M. Jan Holton and Jill L. Snodgrass, "A Theoretical and Theological Reframing of Trauma," *Pastoral Psychology* 72 (2023): 343.

12 Holton and Snodgrass, "A Theoretical and Theological Reframing," 341.

13 Elaine Miller-Karas, *Building Resilience to Trauma: The Trauma and Community Resiliency Models* (New York: Routledge, 2015), 6.

14 Keith A. Menhinick, email message to author, August 18, 2023.

15 McClintock, *Trauma-Informed Pastoral Care*, 161.

16 McClintock, *Trauma-Informed Pastoral Care*, 165.

17 Kazu Haga, *Healing Resistance: A Radically Different Response to Harm* (Berkeley: Parallax Press, 2020), 39.

18 The US Veterans Administration also has a free Mindfulness Coach app that can be downloaded to a phone or tablet and used to help in the practice of mindfulness. See, "VA Mobile Apps: Mindfulness Coach," US Department of Veterans Affairs, accessed July 5, 2024, https://ptsd.va.gov/PTSD/appvid/mobile/mindfulcoach_app.asp. Apps like this can be helpful reminders and digital coaches for you as you increase your mindfulness practice.

12

HEALING SUPPORT AMID ADDICTION

Experiences of addiction can be one of the most difficult situations of caring praxis for both the careseeker and the caregiver. There are many reasons for this. Addiction is one of the handful of human struggles that has been of interest to religion, which issues spiritual and moral teachings on the subject; the law, which develops policing, jurisprudence, and carceral practices related to substance use; and the medical-psychiatric establishment, which develops medical and biological theories of addiction and its treatment. Addiction touches on sin, crime, and sickness.

Nearly everyone has thoughts, opinions, theologies, or moral judgments about addictions that are rooted in these religious, legal, and medical assumptions. Often, these assumptions are conflicting, resulting in muddled thinking about addictions and approaches to care. There are also various racial, class, gender, and sexual inequities in society that can determine whether one's addiction becomes a matter of legal concern and, thus, punishment or a matter of medical attention and, alternately, treatment.

Take a brief assessment of your own assumptions about addiction, including your own personal experiences that shape your perspective:

- What experiences of addiction—your own or those of people you love—have informed your thoughts and feelings about the subject?
- What has your religious or spiritual tradition taught you about addiction? What is your own operative theology of addiction?
- Where have you encountered legal perspectives on addiction and substance use (e.g., school programs, media, political campaigns)? What were the prevalent messages? How are people

experiencing addiction spoken of in this framework (i.e., with what language)?

- Where have you encountered medical, psychiatric, or psychotherapeutic perspectives on addiction and substance use? What were the prevalent messages? How are people experiencing addiction spoken of in this framework (i.e., with what language)?

You might talk over these questions with a few others who are interested in the subject so that you can begin to see how many of our perspectives on addiction are shaped differently by varying experiences and the differential weight that we give to religious, legal, and medical assessments of the subject.

A MORE COMPASSIONATE (AND COMPLEX) UNDERSTANDING OF ADDICTION

Rather than holding tightly to any one theory of addiction, I invite you to take a stance toward addiction experience shaped by compassion in the face of suffering. Even if you can't personally understand what struggling with an addiction feels like, you can engage your empathic imagination to come alongside the person in caring companionship. Embodying empathy is harder than it sounds. We regularly meet the experience of another with judgment. Empathy requires bracketing our judgments and attempting to really understand the other's point of view and lived experience. Your skills in active listening and asking helpful, compassionately curious questions come in handy here.

Pastoral theologian Sonia Waters describes pervasive experiences of addiction by saying that "they are all behaviors that begin as ritual attempts to survive something unbearable that is happening in our inner or outer world . . . They are not about pleasure, but about pain."[1] When we understand addiction not as a source of pleasure-seeking but, instead, as a strategy to survive pain, our ability to hold a space of compassion with someone in the midst of struggle with addiction can grow.

Despite our many attempts to pinpoint the cause of a person's addiction, Waters says, "It is not just one cause that creates an addiction, but a dynamic tangle of vulnerabilities that catch the individual in the net of addictive behavior and can accelerate the progression of the condition as it grows."[2] This tangle of causes includes the personal, relational, and social. Addictions that develop within this web often help a person to cope with stress and distress and to regulate emotions. They can become such a part of a person's way of being in the world that the notion of simply quitting doesn't quite capture the complex task of disentangling the various parts of one's personal, relational, and social life from the substance use.[3]

With a stance toward care amid addiction that is rooted in compassion in the face of suffering, we must meet our internalized judgmental attitudes with empathy for another's pain. We counter our simplistic theories of addiction's causes or origins with more complex and dynamic perspectives about how addiction develops in a person's life as a means of coping. Compassion, empathy, complexity—let these be your guides as you enter into caring relationships with people facing addiction.

WHAT HELPS AND WHAT DOESN'T

Addiction is likely a situation that calls for care beyond your boundaries of competence. Other professionals and peer-based recovery support like Alcoholics Anonymous and Narcotics Anonymous may be called for to meet the needs of a careseeker. However, you still might be called on as a caring companion for this person on their longer journey of recovery.[4] You may be the first person a careseeker approaches at the outset of that journey. It is important to have some clarity with yourself about your role in this person's support system and to make that role clear with the careseeker. Whether you are accompanying a person in caring companionship at the early stages of contemplating a journey of recovery or very late into the maintenance stage of their recovery, there are a few helpful guidelines for care to have in mind.

First, pastoral theologian and psychologist Carrie Doehring warns caregivers against falling into the taking-sides trap. This trap presents itself when a careseeker is ambivalent about making a change and is caught between two strongly opposing desires. For example, a careseeker may want to abstain from or moderate the use of alcohol or other substances and may also wish to continue use of an addictive substance. Both desires can be present simultaneously. Both can be quite strong.

Falling into the taking-sides trap, you may find yourself arguing for abstinence from substance use and the careseeker arguing for continued use. This, Doehring says, brings the internal conflict between these two desires—use and cessation—into the external relationship between caregiver and careseeker. Instead, it is more helpful to, and respectful of, the careseeker to allow this conflict between strong desires to remain internal and for the caregiver not to take sides. Instead, supportively talk with the careseeker about their ambivalence between use and moderation or abstinence. What reasons do they have for thinking about quitting their substance use? How does continued use seem enticing? What has them thinking about these questions at this moment? How have they thought about these questions differently over time? The caregiver arguing for one side rarely helps the situation, especially when the careseeker is not yet ready to make the decision to attempt quitting.[5] Even when it's difficult not to take sides, the most helpful approach is engaging in active listening, reflecting what you're hearing in the desires of the careseekers—conflicting though those desire may be—and allowing the careseeker to talk out their ambivalence with you as a caring companion.

Second, never get caught up in an argument with a careseeker about whether or not they have a substance abuse problem or addiction. Not only is diagnosis not your responsibility as it is outside of your boundaries of competence as a spiritual care first responder, but this type of struggle between you and a careseeker is also not effective in helping a careseeker come to a decision to make a change. It will, nevertheless, be tempting to argue with a person about whether their substance use is a problem, but it simply doesn't work. And when a careseeker's shame begins to develop or strengthen in relation to the judgmental and argumentative or preachy stance of the caregiver, then we are actively working against a careseeker's chances of making movements toward a process of recovery. A careseeker may not yet be ready to acknowledge a problem with their substance use and begin making small changes in the direction of recovery. In this early stage, it is much more helpful to allow the careseeker to talk with you about their substance use and other aspects of their life without pushing them toward change.

Aside from what doesn't work—and what may actually cause harm in the caregiving relationship—there are approaches to care amid addiction that are actively helpful. First, though, Waters reminds caregivers that the brain of the person who chose to start taking a substance is not the same brain that has to make the decision to stop taking it.[6] The brain changes in relation to the substances we take over time. That means the journey of recovery in the midst of addiction is much more complex than you might initially imagine—more complex than a simple decision to stop once and for all. Hopefully this understanding will help increase your capacity for compassion when providing care for others who are grappling with addiction.

When accompanying someone through addiction and recovery, attend carefully to the values, goals, and strengths of a careseeker. A helpful practice when summarizing what one is hearing in spiritual care conversations with people trying to address addiction and other change-oriented processes is for the summary of the conversation to begin with the problems that were discussed. It should end with the values, goals, strengths, and affirmations that arose, emphasizing signs of change rather than focusing solely on problems.[7]

Support the careseeker in focusing on the next step of recovery rather than the big goal of quitting. For example, talking with the person about what the rest of their day looks like or how they're going to take care of themselves in the immediate hours following your conversation can help to focus on living in the present.[8] For someone further along the journey of recovery, good caring practice can involve celebrating good intentions, acknowledging daily efforts made in recovery, recognizing a person's strengths being put on display, or reminding the person of how far they've come in the journey of recovery, even when there have been setbacks along the way.[9] Small steps in a person's desired direction are extraordinarily important. Don't miss the small efforts in your desire to help a person reach a bigger goal.

Support a careseeker's desired skills for coping with stress. Remember that addiction often begins as a means of coping with stress and dealing with overwhelming emotions. In addition to whichever other services or supports a person may engage, you may help a careseeker as a spiritual care responder by assisting in developing capacities toward a person's emotional regulation, strengthening relationships with others in community, or cultivating spiritual practices that connect one to sources of compassion and courage. Remember that recovery from addiction is not just about quitting a certain behavior. It also involves developing new and adaptive behaviors and building supportive structures to help keep these stress-coping and emotion-regulating skills growing.

Finally, remember that the person is not the problem. The problem is not even the specific object of one's addiction. It is the relationship one has to that object, substance, or behavior. Helping a person see some possibility to relate differently to a problem they are facing can strengthen their capacity for recovery. You can do this by acknowledging the ways you observe or hear their capabilities in facing the problem and in making the changes they desire to make. Affirming small movements you see them making in relation to the problem can increase their sense of self-efficacy and belief in the possibility that their relationship with the problem will not always remain as it is. This is not cheerleading or grasping for ways to compliment the careseeker. It is observing these signs in their lives and in your shared conversation, then noting what you observe in ways that help them see the significance of what you're witnessing. Even if it is as small as noting a person's initiative to reach out for conversation about an issue they're facing, substance use or otherwise, this can be an affirming acknowledgment of small steps toward a preferred direction.

CARE FOR FAMILY, FRIENDS, AND COMMUNITIES

There are times when your care response will be with a person struggling with addiction as well as their family. At other times, your only caring response may be to family or friends affected by a loved one's addiction. In both of these circumstances, there are helpful things to keep in mind as you respond in a caring way to the stress and pain of people whose loved one is experiencing addiction. Keep in mind that the loved ones of a person struggling with addiction are not just biological family or spouses and children but also intimate circles of relationship that extend to friends, chosen family, intimate partners, and a range of other relationships of love and support.

First, remember that recovery is not the responsibility of loved ones. It is the responsibility of the person dealing with the addition to decide to begin a journey of recovery. Much of the encouragement named above for careseekers can also be helpful to loved ones. While close circles have an especially good reason to want to see their loved one enter a process of recovery or embrace sobriety, they can never force their loved one into recovery. They can confront a loved one about their substance use, encourage them to reach out for support, or talk with their loved one about the effect of their substance abuse on the relationship or family. Ultimately, the person facing addiction will have to decide to engage in a journey of recovery.

It can be helpful at times to talk with a family member concerned about a loved one's addiction in ways that help them recognize that the problems they are observing are not an overreaction—that their perspective on the situation is valid if it is affecting their well-being or that of their family. If their loved one's addiction is affecting their relationship with other family members, the family's finances, or the health and safety of others, such as driving under the influence, there may well be a problem that is going unaddressed, even if the loved one facing addiction cannot yet see it. Avoid diagnosing the problem and instead attend carefully to the picture that is developing of the family's life using reflective listening and compassionate questioning as to the careseeker's perspective. However, if there is evidence of harm to children, the elderly, or other vulnerable people, you need to take further action to ensure the safety of the victims of abuse.

Second, help family members and others in close relationships attend to their own emotional and spiritual needs and not exclusively give of themselves to support a loved one facing addiction who is not ready to change. For a family member or friend of a person facing addiction to make healthy, rational, and responsible decisions about their own care or the care of their family, that person needs to attend to their own emotional and spiritual needs. This can be difficult if a lot of their own emotional energy and that of the family or circle is tied up in responding to the loved one facing addiction. Are they getting enough sleep? Enough to eat? Are they able to exercise and take care of their bodies? These areas of self-care are essential, and asking questions like this can help cultivate much-needed attention on the family member's or friend's own care. Additionally, help them attend to which practices, places, and people help connect them to a sense of goodness, to a grounding in their understanding of the sacred, and to self-compassion.

Help alleviate shame through compassionate, nonjudgmental presence. Loved ones may feel alone, they may have no one else they wish to speak with about this concern, and they may even hold a sense of personal or family shame in relation to their loved one's substance use, especially if it is a family secret. Your compassionate presence may be one of the first healing interventions into that sense of secrecy and shame. Thus, do not insinuate in any way that they are at fault for their loved one's substance abuse or lack of willingness to change. They are making the necessary steps to get the support they need as they figure out how best to relate to their loved one's substance use. Appreciatively acknowledge their courage in making even the smallest steps to attend to their own and their family's well-being.

It is also helpful to know a few local resources that support spouses, partners, adult children, and other family members or relations who are living with a loved one facing addiction. For example, Al-Anon family groups (al-anon.org) are for families and friends of people dealing with alcoholism. Additionally, the Substance Abuse and Mental Health Services Administration (SAMHSA, samhsa.gov) has a free and confidential number that family members can access for information and treatment referral at 1-800-662-4357. Become knowledgeable about local and national resources so that you can offer them when the opportunity is right.

Finally, if you are a leader in a local faith community, the ways that you speak publicly about addiction can affect how members of that community approach you or others within the community when addiction becomes an issue. Waters encourages us to attend carefully to our public messages about addiction, saying, "If we begin to preach and teach that addictions are simply solutions that have turned against us—ways of survival that are no longer useful to us—we can lessen the stigma and imagine new ways of solving and surviving our lives together."[10] Whether or not you know it, people in your faith community are struggling with addictions—their own or those of loved ones. Bring your compassionate commitments and more complex understandings of addiction into the public spaces you inhabit so that others will find the room they need to seek the support and companionship they desire in facing addiction in their lives.

Practice Exercise: Entering Recovery in Your Local Context
Imaginatively and empathically put yourself in the place of someone in your town or city who is struggling with a substance addiction—alcohol, for example—and wants help to enter a process of recovery and sobriety. Think about who you would trust with this part of your life and struggle. Who would you turn to for caring companionship? Where would you look for help addressing your addictive behavior? What meetings are available, and how much effort would it take to get to them? Who would you imagine feeling comfortable talking to about your substance use and desire for sobriety? Your pastor? Other congregants at your church? People in your friendship circles? What causes you to feel more or less comfortable speaking with any of these people about substance use? Try to put yourself in the place of a person seeking avenues for recovering in your community and see how easy or difficult it is for you to map out a plan for gaining the support you would need. This will help you in building your capacity to help others in that journey when they most need it.

FURTHER READING

Waters, Sonia E. *Addiction and Pastoral Care*. Grand Rapids, MI: Eerdmans, 2019.

NOTES

1 Sonia E. Waters, *Addiction and Pastoral Care* (Grand Rapids, MI: Eerdmans, 2019), 18.

2 Waters, *Addiction and Pastoral Care*, 5–6.

3 While there can be many other forms of addiction, this chapter focuses on substance use (drug and alcohol). The approaches developed here, however, can be applicable to addictions in other forms as well.

4 For those unfamiliar with the term *recovery*, the National Institute on Drug Abuse defines it as "a process of change through which people improve their health and wellness, live self-directed lives, and strive to reach their full potential. Being *in recovery* is when those positive changes and values become part of a voluntarily adopted lifestyle. While many people in recovery believe that abstinence from all substance use is a cardinal feature of

a recovery lifestyle, others report that handling negative feelings without using substances and living a contributive life are more important parts of their recovery." "Recovery," National Institute on Drug Abuse, accessed July 25, 2023, https://nida.nih.gov/research-topics/recovery.

5 Carrie Doehring, *The Practice of Pastoral Care: A Postmodern Approach*, rev. ed. (Louisville, KY: Westminster John Knox Press, 2015), 67.

6 Waters, *Addiction and Pastoral Care*, 39.

7 Waters, *Addiction and Pastoral Care*, 138.

8 Waters, *Addiction and Pastoral Care*, 76.

9 Waters, *Addiction and Pastoral Care*, 116.

10 Waters, *Addiction and Pastoral Care*, 100.

13

HEALING SUPPORT FOR MENTAL HEALTH AND SUICIDE

There are individuals in each of our communities struggling with mental health concerns, even if you don't know about it. Families we all know, perhaps even our own, care for loved ones whose mental well-being is often on edge, who need support to maintain a sense of emotional well-being and relational connectedness. Churches and other faith communities often become places where people struggling with mental health concerns turn to find respite and support and where their families turn for care as they care for their loved ones with mental health conditions.

The World Health Organization defines mental health as "a state of mental well-being that enables people to cope with the stresses of life, realize their abilities, learn well and work well, and contribute to their community" and as a state that is "integral to our well-being."[1] That is likely a description of mental health we can all identify with—sometimes because we've experienced it in abundance and at other times because we've noticed some central component of that state lacking in our lives. WHO estimates that as of 2019, around 970 million people in the world were living with a mental health condition, anxiety and depression being the most prevalent.

That statistic has likely grown in the years since. "The Mental State of the World Report," conducted for the fourth time in 2023 with 500,000 participants from 71 countries, notes that the COVID-19 pandemic sent global mental health on a precipitous decline with no indications that mental well-being is returning to pre-pandemic levels. People under age 35 experienced the steepest declines during the pandemic, and those levels of mental well-being remain, amplifying a pre-pandemic trend of poorer mental well-being for younger people around the globe.[2] As a global health issue, mental well-being is a concern that every community must address within its communal web of relationships.

Many things affect our mental health. Exposure to adverse circumstances like poverty, violence, disability, and inequality elevates our risk of developing a mental health condition.[3] That means that whatever we do to address concerns of inclusivity, justice, and well-being for those pushed to the margins of society has a direct impact on the ability of people to live with a sense of mental well-being. Alleviating poverty is improving mental health. Advocating for people with disabilities is advocacy for mental well-being. Antiracist work in our communities serves to bolster mental and emotional wellness. Care and justice are intimately bound up together.

At other times, our mental well-being is affected by circumstances taking shape in our lives—job loss, relationships that become tense or end through breakups or death, world events that create distress in our lives. In many of these circumstances, the supportive presence of others through difficult times can get us through to the other side of a dip in our mental well-being. Still other mental health conditions are created by neurochemical imbalances that need the support of psychotropic medications prescribed by a physician to bring our neurochemistry into balance, or they can be caused by more sustained neurological conditions that require some combination of supportive therapies and medications and robust community support throughout one's lifetime.

In every situation in which mental health concern arises, however, the understanding and support one receives from one's loved ones and wider community are vital to establishing, reestablishing, or maintaining well-being. Pastor Emmy Kegler, who has lived with depression since she was a teenager, says, "Mental illness is not a moment but a journey, and to walk it (or walk with someone in it) requires sustenance and endurance."[4] Spiritual care first aid skills are needed to recognize when mental health concerns may be at play in a caregiving relationship, as is the knowledge necessary to begin this journey with a person whose mental well-being is intimately tied to the communal care they receive along the way. Much of the spiritual care we provide to people with mental and emotional health concerns draws on the same basic skillset. In most ways, spiritually and communally caring for someone with a mental health condition will look like the care you provide for anyone in your community.

One note is helpful up front, however: as a spiritual care first responder, whether a pastor or lay leader, it is not your job to diagnose mental health concerns. That is why this chapter doesn't outline how any particular concern takes shape diagnostically. Rather, it outlines common symptoms experienced in relation to various mental health concerns, how you can be a spiritual companion with a person experiencing these concerns, and how your community can be supportive to them and their loved ones. This is your primary role in the life of a careseeker experiencing mental health concerns, and it is a role that is essential to their long-term well-being. It is a vital responsibility.

There are, of course, ways that symptoms show up that move beyond our boundaries of competence to address: certain symptoms like delusions and hallucinations and disorganized thought patterns, situations in which medication may be needed to regulate the biological function of the brain in relation to a mental health concern, and situations of severe suicidal thoughts. In some of these situations, the spiritual care responder needs to engage in the ministry of introduction to connect the person with a professional counselor or a physician. But in most situations when there is a mental or an emotional health concern, the skillfulness you bring to companioning someone through these difficult times—gentleness, compassion, a less anxious presence, skills of deep listening, and connection to community—will be the essential skills needed as a spiritual caregiver, alongside whichever mental health or medical professionals also involved in a careseeker's life.

LONELINESS AND ISOLATION: CULTIVATING VITAL RELATIONAL CONNECTIONS

US Surgeon General Dr. Vivek Murthy issued an advisory in 2023 titled "Our Epidemic of Loneliness and Isolation." The advisory outlines in statistical detail the ways that social connection is a strong social determinant of individual health, community well-being, and a community's resilience when natural disasters strike. A fundamental human need, social connection—our ability to rely on one another—is "crucial to survival."[5] Remarkably, every increase in social connection corresponds with a reduction in risk across multiple health conditions, not only mental and emotional health.[6]

Social connection is vital to our mental well-being. In fact, the longest scientific study of happiness ever conducted is the eighty-four-year-long (and counting) Harvard Study of Adult Development. This study found that the single factor that most determines our health and happiness is good relationships. That goes for physical health, mental health, and even longevity of life.[7] So a statistic like one in four Americans feeling lonely should concern us as we look at the mental health needs of our communities.[8] Just as constructively addressing poverty, racism, and ableism in our communities and wider society also serves to support mental health, so, too, does careful attention to the ways we support social connection and cultivate communal bonds serve to strengthen the bedrock of mental and emotional well-being, which is good relationships.

You don't need a license or degree to listen, to care, to support, or to nourish the well-being of others in your life. In fact, if we only rely on credentialed professionals to provide the care we need in our communities, we'll be incredibly bereft of the relational resources we each need to find healing amid pain and brokenness and to flourish in our lives. This is what an all-hands approach to spiritual care means. It requires all of us knowing that we are integral in the web of relationality that holds each one of us in belovedness and belonging.

In his book on care for people with mental health problems, pastoral theologian John Swinton says, "It is difficult to conceive of something as apparently basic as friendship as a serious form of pastoral care for people encountering such difficulties . . . that such a basic relationship as friendship could be central to the mental health care of people living with severe forms of mental health problems."[9] There are, of course, biological roots to some mental health problems, from the neurochemical imbalances we may experience leading to depression to the breakdown of myelin insulating the nerve cells in the brain linked to Alzheimer's disease. But the one factor, above all, linked to every metric of health is good relationships.

Even mental health concerns that have a biological basis are not exclusively biological. Our relationships, our spirituality, our sense of belonging, our connection to the wider ecological web of life all have a bearing on our mental health and overall well-being. Among all types of problems we face in life, mental health problems often come along with an experience of isolation. At times, family and friends put some distance between themselves and loved ones experiencing mental health concerns because they are unsure how to help or have become weary of the helping journey. At other times, people struggling with mental health in our communities withdraw from the social connections they've enjoyed in times of greater mental well-being. Decreasing isolation for those experiencing mental health concerns through caring companionship is an essential source of healing support. The very best medications and therapies cannot replace communal connection, and medical and therapeutic support have a much better chance of working well for an individual if that person also has the support of a loving community.

As a spiritual care first aid responder, your best resource in companioning someone in distress is the helping relationship you develop with that person. As a leader in a congregation or other type of community, the most significant contribution you will be able to make to the holistic health of members of your community is the cultivation of rich, caring relationships shared across the community you serve. This, at base, is what good attention to mental well-being looks like in a community.

SPIRITUAL CARE AMID ANXIETY

It is important to note that nearly all of us deal with anxiety in some way or another. Living in a world on the edge of climate collapse, amid disruptive political turmoil and multiple wars almost always raging on view in the palm of our hands, with technological acceleration outpacing our ethical abilities to keep up with its usage, and with economic precarity touching so many of our lives so much of the time, it would be untenable to think that we could live without some degree of anxiety entering our experience. Anxiety is not pathological. In fact, it can serve an important purpose in our lives, signaling us that something needs attention.

For most of us, anxiety is situational; it arises in relation to a vague sense of threat we perceive around us, something that is worrying us. When that situation changes, our anxiety usually alleviates. For others of us, anxiety is more generalized. We experience a sense of threat or persistent worry unrelated to anything going on in our lives. Situations change, but our anxiety doesn't. This may alert us to a type of anxiety that needs a little more careful attention. As noted, the mental health of young people is a global health concern, and social psychologist Jonathan Haidt argues, "Anxiety and its associated disorders seem to be the defining mental illness of young people today."[10]

For most, anxiety comes and goes without much to concern our overall mental well-being. For some, anxiety rises to the level of a mental health concern when it encroaches on our ability to live our lives on a day-to-day basis, causing us persistent distress that is intense and prolonged. As psychiatrist Thomas Mackenzie and pastoral theologian Christie Cozad Neuger describe it, anxiety becomes a mental health concern when it affects our functioning in a negative way and most often when it is not attached to a specific event or concern but becomes a "free-floating" sense of uneasiness, tension, restlessness, apprehension, or worry.[11] There are several things we might be on the lookout for that can alert us to the presence of this type of anxiety that may be impinging on one's mental well-being.

One sign that anxiety may be becoming a mental health concern is when patterns of *catastrophic thinking* emerge. These thought patterns heighten the strength of anxiety in a person's life over time, "mobilizing an epidemic of fears that flood one's consciousness" and making the situations we face feel unmanageable and overwhelming.[12]

Experiences of *panic* can also be signs that anxiety has become a mental health concern. These are times when we experience bodily signs of danger—"racing pulse, rapid breathing, tremor, sweating, dilated pupils, sense of danger"—in the absence of an emergency. The brain believes that an emergency is occurring and can put our bodies into high alert within seconds, with episodes of panic lasting half an hour. They come quite unbidden by any actual danger or emergency but appear out of the blue and without warning.[13]

Recall that many people experiencing a profound crisis or living in the aftermath of a disaster may experience confusion; difficulty concentrating; inability to focus on addressing their immediate needs; feelings of overwhelm, fear, sadness, and anger; disruptions in their sleeping or eating; and a range of other distressing experiences. In the presence of a crisis, disaster, or traumatic event, these symptoms are not indicative of a mental health concern. They are to be expected in the midst of crises.

Anxiety triggers our body's response system to possible danger, in contrast to fear, which triggers this system in the presence of danger. As part of our body's response system to danger, anxiety is a deeply embodied experience. It can be felt as tension, tightness, or discomfort in the body; through emotions like dread, worry, and exhaustion; and in our thought patterns through ruminations, catastrophizing, black-and-white thinking, and lack of clarity in our thinking.[14] When there is a danger present, this is a very helpful alert system. When this same anxiety alarm system is on high alert even when there are no possible threats or dangers present, anxiety becomes an unhelpful form of distress.

Remember that not all spiritual care first aid is solution-oriented; rather, it is grounded in a less anxious way of being with others in distress. Mental health advocate and educator Carlene Hill Byron, who has been treated for depression or bipolar disorder since she was nineteen years old, says, "We don't need to know how to move a distressed person to a solution; we can simply sit with that person and seek understanding together with God. We can even be the experience of the ordinary that orients a sufferer to a place of safety in this world."[15] This is a helpful word for care responders. As a less anxious companion with a careseeker experiencing heightened anxiety, your deep listening skills can be a grounding experience amid the body's alert system.

Questions that help the careseeker express what's in their heart and on their mind can invite naming what one is feeling about what is going on in their life or in the world. Avoid assuring the person that they have nothing to worry about or encouragements that they should just give their anxiety to God. When one's bodily alert system signals anxiety, we can't simply reason or pray our way out of it, even though prayer more broadly may be a very helpful spiritual resource amid anxiety. Paying attention to how one is experiencing their body (like a body scan) or even helping someone move their body around a bit (like taking a walk together) can bring greater awareness to how anxiety is being held in the body.

Finally, pastor Emmy Kegler provides caring companions and all who confront anxiety in their lives with a helpful grounding technique known as *5-4-3-2-1*. It's a simple tool: name out loud five things you can see, four things you can feel, three things you can hear, two things you can smell, and one thing you can taste.[16] This type of exercise can help put a person back into closer contact with the experience of their own body and the world around them through simple attention to what their senses are communicating to them about their surroundings.

SPIRITUAL CARE AMID DEPRESSION

Experiences of depression are a regular part of the lives of many within our congregations and community. Spiritual care first aid responders may be among the first to notice some signs of depression and may be the first people with whom a person experiencing symptoms of depression can bring that experience into speech.

Various experiences can indicate that depression may have entered one's life as a mental health concern. Among these experiences are loss of interest in things that once interested us, loss of pleasure in things that once brought us pleasure, significant changes in appetite or sleep, fatigue and loss of energy, feelings of worthlessness or guilt, disruptions in our ability to concentrate or think with our usual clarity, and, potentially, thoughts of suicide.[17] We may experience any of these things in the midst of sadness over a situation in our lives. But when they become elongated over a period of time or they are not related to a particular situation like a personal loss or tragedy, something more may be going on with a careseeker's mental health.

It is important to distinguish the experience of depression from that of grief. Many of the above experiences occurring following a loss (of a loved person or animal, a job, a relationship, one's health, etc.) do not indicate the experience of depression as a mental health concern. Grief and depression may look quite similar. Both require caring companionship, but grief is focused on a particular experience of loss, while depression is more generalized. Grief is likely to result in a long journey through the experience of loss, aided by caring companions, that decreases in intensity over time, although it doesn't necessarily go away. Depression is likely to linger for a longer period, ebbing and flowing in intensity, but may need more care in the form of psychiatric support and/or therapy.

Mania is another experience that sometimes occurs alongside depression in what we often term *bipolar disorder*—that is, experiencing both poles of emotional experience: depression and mania. Times when we feel manic may cause us no alarm because we feel elevated in our mood, like we have all the energy in the world and can conquer any tasks. To our loved ones or spiritual care responders, however, experiences of mania can look quite out of the ordinary as people may take on an inflated sense of self-esteem or grandiosity, experience a decreased need for sleep, exhibit rapid speech and/or racing thoughts, and become easily distracted or overly involved in goal-directed activities.[18] Often, consequences of actions become difficult to consider when one is experiencing mania. Typically, these experiences indicate the need for a care responder to help the careseeker locate an appropriate mental health provider in order to be evaluated for treatment.

It is important to note that for adolescents, a well-documented surge of mental health crises began in the early 2010s. Social psychologist Jonathan Haidt points to a surge of major depressive episodes in US teens (ages 12–17) around 2012 across all races and social classes.[19] Haidt ties this mental health crisis among teens to the introduction of smartphones. More and more time was spent in virtual worlds—for some teens, almost constantly—creating a "profound transformation of human consciousness and relationships" between 2010 and 2015.[20] Attention to the ways social media engagement affects the mental well-being of the communities we serve is an important concern for a comprehensive approach to mental health, not just for teenagers but for people of all ages engaging with social media.[21]

Finally, know that the low energy that sometimes comes along with depression can mean that daily tasks become very difficult. So helping a person experiencing depression to figure out which tasks may be feeling overwhelming at the moment and what support they may need to accomplish these tasks can be an important role for a care responder. This includes the task of making necessary medical appointments. So if a referral seems needed, follow up with what support might be needed in order for the careseeker to connect with a mental health provider or physician so that you can facilitate that important introduction as helpfully as possible.

SPIRITUAL CARE AMID DISRUPTIONS OF THOUGHT

Anxiety and depression—the most common problems we encounter with our mental health—typically affect our feelings or mood, although both also influence our clarity of thought. Other mental health concerns are more squarely experienced in the realm of thought. These often show up as disruptions in our perceptions and interpretations of the world.

The most well-known of these types of mental health concerns, *psychosis*, generally indicates "an impairment in the brain's ability to perceive accurately and interpret the world in a way consistent with how others see things," including symptoms like "delusions (false beliefs) and hallucinations (false perceptions)."[22] Hearing voices that others aren't hearing is one prominent form of hallucination. These symptoms are very disruptive in the life of one experiencing them and distressing for loved ones companioning them.

Swinton says, "One of the major barriers that separate the person with schizophrenia from the rest of society is the fundamental *incomprehensibility* of their condition."[23] It can feel confusing to family, friends, and care responders to engage with a loved one who is experiencing the types of symptoms that are typically labeled as schizophrenia. Thus, the person with schizophrenia symptoms can become stigmatized by others who cannot understand their experience, especially when they live within a society that also stigmatizes them. The stigma often associated with psychotic symptoms, and the stress they create for many friends and family members, can often lead to extreme disruptions in a person's social and communal life. Thus, caring companionship becomes vital amid the crisis created by psychosis and other disruptions of thought.[24]

Occasionally, psychotic symptoms can occur with bipolar disorder and depression too. These symptoms can also be part of another illness such as brain tumors or brain injury or the use of substances. It is vital that observation of disturbances of thought like the ones described above be evaluated by a medical doctor to assess the causes and best course of treatment. This is a circumstance in which your ministry of introduction to another caring professional can become lifesaving.

As a spiritual care first responder, you cannot argue with someone experiencing delusions or hallucinations out of their beliefs or perceptions. Instead of arguing against or agreeing with a careseeker's disturbances of thought, it is best to attempt connecting with that person through empathy.[25] For example, empathize with the stress they are experiencing over their thoughts or perceptions because, even if the stress stems from hallucinations or delusions, it is still felt as very much real in the body.

COUNTERING STIGMA IN COMMUNITY CARE

Mental health advocate and educator Carlene Hill Byron clearly names what most people with mental health concerns desire when reaching out for help to congregations and spiritual care providers: a sense of meaning amid their suffering, a sense that life has a purpose amid their difficulties, recognition of value by God and others in community, a place to belong even when mental health concerns become difficult, and the confidence and hope found in faith.[26] One of the more important concerns to address is the role that stigma plays in making a sense of belonging difficult for people with mental health concerns and their families. Several practices can help reduce the potential for stigma to attach itself to an experience of mental health concerns. Most center on our use of language.

It is common to hear mental health terms used to describe things that aren't mental health concerns—for example, someone who is overly organized being called *OCD*, someone quickly changing moods being described as *bipolar*, or the use of *schizophrenic* to describe experiences that have nothing to do with mental illness simply because they don't make sense to us. These inappropriate uses of language that may describe a concern someone in our community may really be contending with make the experience less speakable within the context of that community by pejoratively using mental health terms, thus attaching a stigma to a mental health concern that many people experience.

Additionally, language often attached to the mental health concerns—for example, *suffering from depression*—elevates the experience of depression in ways the individual may not attach to the experience. While diagnosis is not in your purview as a spiritual care responder, know that even diagnostic language applied to mental health problems is fraught. Some people find it liberating to have a diagnosis to describe an experience they share with many other people, while others reject diagnostic language as inadequately descriptive of their experience. It is usually helpful to stick close to the language that a person uses to describe their own experience rather than applying language—your own or a diagnostic label—to their experience.

In your discussion with careseekers and other spiritual care first responders about mental health concerns, it is important to continue using language that separates the person from the problem. Rather than calling a person *depressed*, or *schizophrenic*, or any other label that gets used as an identifying marker, it is most helpful to speak of people who are experiencing a mental health concern or, better still, to use whatever language the person uses to describe the concerns they're facing. But do not totalize the person's life by making their mental health concern their identity.

Psychiatrist Stephen Olson and pastoral theologian Joretta Marshall helpfully remind us that when someone receives a diagnosis related to a mental health concern, that diagnosis should not become a totalizing label for the person. They say:

> It is important to help the individual, family, and community understand that this is not the only—nor perhaps most important—thing to know about someone. People who live with the disease ought not to be seen by others or understand themselves as defined by the disease; they continue to be children of God who are called by their own name in God's richness and grace . . . Listening carefully, responding nondefensively, resisting the temptation to overinterpret the cause or meaning of someone's illness, supporting healthy religious experiences and understandings of God, and remaining comfortable with questions that have no answers can help people move from feeling helpless and hopeless toward recovery.[27]

The person's life is a lot more than their mental health concern or diagnosis, and our language needs to make room for other parts of their life to be foregrounded and not become totalized by a mental health struggle.

Mental health concerns that occur along the autism spectrum are also vital for a congregation or faith community to address, as are experiences of Alzheimer's and dementia and persons experiencing intellectual disabilities. While these issues may not apply specifically to spiritual care first aid, they are vital concerns for spiritual care for persons in community over the long term, both for spiritual care companions who accompany individuals and families through these mental health conditions and for the communities they're part of.[28] Increasing awareness of the care needs of people with intellectual disabilities, dementia, and neurodiversity and adjusting our community practices accordingly can create the hospitable spaces needed for people seeking a place to experience belonging to God and to others.

Finally, we must destigmatize seeking mental health treatment within our communities of faith. As we attend to barriers to mental health treatment such as lack of insurance or ability to pay, as well as a lack of access to mental health professionals, we must normalize counseling and psychotherapy and encourage people in our communities to seek the support they need amid mental health concerns before those concerns even arise.

Kegler provides a set of helpful questions to ask when you are unsure where to go in conversations centered on helping careseekers access mental health treatment:

- What are you afraid of about trying to get (treatment, medication, therapy, etc.)?
- Are there barriers such as money, time, etc.?
- What solo activities help you feel more grounded?
- What group activities help you feel more grounded?
- When do you feel connected to others? What kind of treatment might help with that?
- What would feeling better look like for you?
- How do you think God wants you to get better?[29]

HELPING IN SITUATIONS OF SUICIDE

It is likely that in the course of your caring ministry, you may be the one to first discover that a person is contemplating suicide, and you will need to help them find appropriate resources in order to stay alive. Here are some general guidelines to prepare for an initial caregiving response in situations of suicidal thinking.

Practice the Question

Don't be afraid to ask a person if they are considering hurting themselves or taking their own life if you have any reason to believe this may be the case. Asking someone directly and without euphemism is important. For example, "After our conversation today, I think it's important that I just ask for some clarity. Are you thinking about the possibility of hurting yourself or killing yourself?"

Practice that question and other variations. Practice them aloud. Practice them in the mirror. Practice them with a friend. It is helpful to have the words on the tip of your tongue so they come out in a clear and caring way.

When asking this type of question, never use fuzzy euphemisms like "Are you thinking of checking out?" or "Are you considering doing something drastic?" Euphemisms like this are unhelpful and subtly communicate your discomfort in discussing the subject of suicide. Clear and direct questions are best and may invite the person to say what they've wanted to share but needed the invitation to express. There may be no one else in a person's life who will ask them this important question.

In many cases, if you don't ask directly when you suspect that suicide may be a thinkable option, the person simply won't share that information with you. Contemplating suicide is difficult to divulge to another person, and sharing that piece of a person's experience with you is a brave act. It also requires bravery on your part to be a courageous listener, to ask clear and direct questions, and to open yourself to hearing what needs to be spoken.

It is important to know that asking a person whether they are thinking about suicide will never put the idea in their head. That's a myth that keeps us from asking what we need to ask. Try to put that worry out of your mind. If you have any reason to ask, then do so.

When the Answer Is Yes

If you discover that someone is contemplating suicide, it is helpful to have basic means of assessing the best practices of care for the situation. Here are three levels of care to have on hand depending on how a person responds to your question about whether suicide is a thinkable option for them.

"Yes, I've Thought about It before but Not Seriously"

In a situation in which the person has thought about suicide in the past or had passing thoughts about it but has never made any plans or developed any intention to actually do it, the danger may be low. You can ask the person again for clarity just to be sure this is what they are saying. For example, "It sounds like you've thought about suicide in the past, but just so I'm understanding correctly, do you have any thoughts about it now? Or any plans to kill yourself?"

If the thoughts of suicide were in the distant past or the person clearly has no plans or intention to complete suicide, an appropriate caring response is to invite that person to allow you to connect them with other caring resources. A first step would be helping the person have a conversation with the pastor or another minister. If you're a layperson in a congregation, the next step may be the pastor or another minister of the church. If you're a professional in ministry, then you may wish to help that person connect with a therapist if one is desired. If they already have a therapist, it can be helpful to ask them if they've spoken with their therapist about their consideration of suicide.

It is also always appropriate to leave a person with a suicide hotline number, even when suicide may not be a serious intention. Always have a number like 988, which is the National Suicide Prevention Lifeline, ready at hand. You might also say to the person, "If anything ever changes for you and you do find that you're thinking about suicide, I hope you will feel free to talk with me about that anytime. Would you call me if that becomes the case?"

"Yes, I've Thought about It but Don't Have Any Plans to Actually Do It"

When a person is more actively thinking about suicide in the present but hasn't made any plans or expressed any intentions to kill themselves, there is a slightly increased level of concern, even if suicide may still not be an imminent threat to the person's life. Even if they hem and haw a bit about whether they have a plan, or they hesitate to answer in much detail, assume this is a situation that needs some extra attention.

An appropriate caring response would be, with a little more insistence, to invite that person to have a conversation with another caring resource like the pastor of the congregation or a therapist. You can offer to go with them to have this conversation if they are nervous going alone. Even if they are not willing to have this conversation, if you are a layperson providing care in a faith community context, this is a situation in which you need to take the initiative to talk to the pastor or minister supervising the lay caregiving program about this person's situation so that appropriate follow-up can be planned.

It's also worth noting that sometimes you may receive a reply that isn't quite clearly a yes but indicates increased concern. Often this could come as a statement about the difficulty of talking about the subject of suicide, for example, "I don't know. It's hard to talk about this." Likely, suicide is a thinkable option for this person, but they're having trouble talking about it. In these cases, it can be validating and invitational for you to acknowledge how difficult it can be to broach the topic of suicide with another person while still issuing the invitation to engage with you on the subject. For example, you might reply, "Yeah, it can be really difficult to talk about suicide with another person. It can feel pretty vulnerable for most people to discuss. But I'd love to get some clarity if possible about whether suicide is a consideration for you right now."

"Yes, I Am Thinking about Killing Myself"

This indicates a more pressing concern that needs immediate attention. Here are a few steps for care that you should commit to memory and use if the situation calls for it.

First, ask for more information: "Do you know how you might kill yourself?" "Is that method available to you now?" The more it seems there is a plan in place and an intent to carry out that plan, the more urgent it is for you to act decisively in the moment. You don't need to be absolutely sure that the threat of suicide is immediate. If what you hear causes you to suspect it is, then action is required on your part. Commitments to confidentiality must be broken in order to preserve life and well-being.[30]

Second, stay with the person. If someone is actively considering taking their own life and has a plan and intention to do so, do not leave them alone. The only exception to this rule is if there is a weapon present, and you do not personally feel safe staying in the room with them. In that case, go somewhere safe nearby and call 911 for help. But if you do not sense your physical safety is threatened, then simply stay with them directly in your sight.

Third, get further help immediately. As long as you are not fearful for your own life, then there are a few options you have to help this person get the care they need:

- Ask the person to let you take them to the local hospital emergency room. Any hospital will know what to do in the case of suicidal thoughts. It doesn't need to be a psychiatric hospital; any hospital will do. Just get the person in the car with you and take them to the local ER, and the medical professionals will perform the appropriate assessments and make necessary plans for intervention and care. If, for any reason, you believe it would be dangerous to drive this person to the hospital, move to another option below.

- If they are unable or unwilling to go with you, call someone who may be able to help them. For example, if they have a therapist, ask them to let you call that person or sit with them while they call their therapist.

- If there is no therapist, you can sit with them as they call or text the National Suicide Prevention Lifeline at 988. Store this number in your phone if you're afraid you'll forget it. If they are not up for making the call, you can call the lifeline and ask for help in dealing with the situation. The lifeline is staffed twenty-four hours a day.

- If there are no other options, calling 911 is appropriate when you believe a person is in imminent danger of dying by suicide. Communicate to the operator that the person you are with is in psychiatric distress and needs an ambulance because they are contemplating suicide. Then stay with the person until help arrives.[31]

As a lay caregiver, it is always appropriate to have a conversation with your pastor or another ministry leader about any situation in which suicide is a possibility. Please exercise the communal nature of care within a congregation and do not try to carry the weight of this situation alone. You may be the first to discover the possibility of suicide for an individual with whom you are practicing care, but you should always avail yourself of helping professionals who can provide the level of care and support that is needed. This is where the first aid metaphor is so helpful. What you do in the initial stages of the situation may not be all that is needed, but your first caring responses can initiate the lifesaving process.

And Still . . .

The hard truth is that often despite great efforts of care and even sophisticated psychiatric support, some will still die by suicide. In other instances, a person's plans to die by suicide may go undiscovered until it is too late to intervene. In each of these situations, the family and friends and faith community of one who has died by suicide need special care. Feelings of guilt can merge with feelings of grief in ways that take time and caring skill to untangle and work through. This can be complex and long-term emotional and spiritual work for a community, and care should involve ministry professionals or therapeutic support from a wider network. Your caring support for and with your fellow congregants will be invaluable throughout these efforts. You will likely be someone whom others can come to for caring conversation in the process of grieving this loss.

Finally, returning to the concern of language and stigma, the typical ways of speaking of a person *committing suicide* are no longer considered an appropriate way to describe death at one's own hands. We commit crimes; thus, this language has a nearly automatic stigmatizing effect. Rather, it is more appropriate in the aftermath of suicide to describe the act as someone *taking their own life*, *ending their life*, or *dying by suicide*. Language matters in caring practice. It can help invite people into caring relationship or it can strain and sever our connection to others. Words can increase the stigmatization of common human experiences or help gradually decrease stigma's power over lives. Your words are a vital tool in spiritual care first aid, so give them careful attention.

Practice Exercise: Practice the Question

Find a friend or fellow congregant who is also trying to become a better caregiver in situations of suicide. Practice with one another using the words to ask someone if they are considering suicide. Try out various phrasings. Repeat the questions to one another until they roll off your tongue without any hesitation. It may feel uncomfortable at first, and after a while it may start to seem like a silly exercise. But having these words on the tip of your tongue when you need them could be lifesaving. It should start to feel like a perfectly normal question to ask. Any discomfort or awkwardness in practice will be more than worth it should you need to use this skill in caring for another.

FURTHER READING

Kegler, Emmy. *All Who Are Weary: Easing the Burden on the Walk with Mental Illness.* Minneapolis: Broadleaf Books, 2021.

Townsend, Loren. *Suicide: Pastoral Responses.* Nashville: Abingdon Press, 2006.

NOTES

1 "Mental Health," World Health Organization, accessed June 4, 2024, https://www.who.int/health-topics/mental-health#tab=tab_1.

2 Global Mind Project, "The Mental State of the World in 2023: Perspective on Internet-Enabled Populations," Sapien Labs, March 4, 2024, https://sapienlabs.org/wp-content/uploads/2024/03/4th-Annual-Mental-State-of-the-World-Report.pdf.

3 "Mental Health."

4 Emily Kegler, *All Who Are Weary: Easing the Burden on the Walk with Mental Illness* (Minneapolis: Broadleaf Books, 2021), xiii.

5 Office of the Surgeon General, *Our Epidemic of Loneliness and Isolation: The U.S. Surgeon General's Advisory on the Healing Effects of Social Connection and Community* (Rockville, MD: US Department of Health and Human Services, 2023), 9, https://www.hhs.gov/sites/default/files/surgeon-general-social-connection-advisory.pdf.

6 Office of the Surgeon General, *Our Epidemic of Loneliness and Isolation*, 8–9.

7 See Robert Waldinger and Marc Schultz, *The Good Life: Lessons from the World's Longest Scientific Study of Happiness* (New York: Simon & Schuster, 2023).

8 Waldinger and Schultz, *The Good Life*, 21.

9 John Swinton, *Resurrecting the Person: Friendship and the Care of People with Mental Health Problems* (Nashville: Abingdon, 2000), 31.

10 Jonathan Haidt, *The Anxious Generation: How the Great Rewiring of Childhood Is Causing an Epidemic of Mental Illness* (New York: Penguin, 2024), 27.

11 Thomas Mackenzie and Christie Cozad Neuger, "Anxiety Disorders," in *Ministry with Persons with Mental Illness and Their Families*, 2nd ed., ed. Robert H. Albers, William H. Meller, and Steven D. Thurber (Minneapolis: Fortress, 2019), 26–27.

12 Mackenzie and Cozad Neuger, "Anxiety Disorders," 26–27.

13 Mackenzie and Cozad Neuger, "Anxiety Disorders," 33.

14 Haidt, *The Anxious Generation*, 28.

15 Carlene Hill Byron, *Not Quite Fine: Mental Health, Faith, and Showing Up for One Another* (Harrisonburg, VA: Herald, 2021), 55.

16 Kegler, *All Who Are Weary*, 79.

17 William H. Meller and Robert H. Albers, "Depression," in *Ministry with Persons with Mental Illness and Their Families*, 2nd ed., ed. Robert H. Albers, William H. Meller, and Steven D. Thurber (Minneapolis: Fortress, 2019), 4.

18 Meller and Albers, "Depression," 5.

19 Haidt, *The Anxious Generation*, 24.

20 Haidt, *The Anxious Generation*, 34.

21 A couple of good places to start are Cal NewPort, *Digital Minimalism: Choosing a Focused Life in a Noisy World* (New York: Penguin, 2019), and Jenny Odell, *How to Do Nothing: Resisting the Attention Economy* (Brooklyn, NY: Melville, 2019).

22 Stephen Olson and Joretta L. Marshall, "Psychotic Disorders," in *Ministry with Persons with Mental Illness and Their Families*, 2nd ed., ed. Robert H. Albers, William H. Meller, and Steven D. Thurber (Minneapolis: Fortress, 2019), 48.

23 Swinton, *Resurrecting the Person*, 95. Italics original.

24 The average onset of symptoms of schizophrenia is between ages 20 and 25 for men and between 25 and 30 for women. Swinton, *Resurrecting the Person*, 68.

25 Olson and Marshall, "Psychotic Disorders," 49.

26 Byron, *Not Quite Fine*, 54.

27 Olson and Marshall, "Psychotic Disorders," 58–59.

28 For further exploration of neurodiversity, developmental challenges, intellectual disabilities, and dementia, see Daniel Aherne, *The Pocket Guide to Neurodiversity* (Philadelphia: Jessica Kingsley, 2023); Mary McDaniel Cali, *Dementia and the Church: Memory, Care, and Inclusion* (Minneapolis: Fortress, 2023); Anna Katherine Shurley, *Pastoral Care and Intellectual Disability: A Person-Centered Approach* (Waco, TX: Baylor University Press, 2017); Hollie M. Holt-Woehl, *They Don't Come with Instructions: Cries, Wisdom, and Hope for Parenting Children with Developmental Challenges* (Minneapolis: Fortress, 2018).

29 Kegler, *All Who Are Weary*, 55.

30 See chapter 6, "Helpful Expectations, Boundaries, and Introductions."

31 It is important to note that there are a multitude of instances in the United States in which 911 has been called to help in the situation of a mental health crisis experienced by a BIPOC person, resulting in a police response in which the person in crisis is killed by the police. If there is any other option other than calling 911, then you should use it. In some cases, however, there simply aren't any other options, and 911 should be used. Investigate the conversations in your local community or region about mobile mental health crisis response teams. If no such services exist in your area, consider getting the conversation started with your local government.

14

HEALING SUPPORT AMID ABUSE AND VIOLENCE

Violence against women is one of the most ubiquitous forms of violence that you will face as a spiritual care responder. Nearly 20 people per minute are physically abused by an intimate partner in the United States, with one in four women experiencing severe intimate partner physical violence, sexual violence, or stalking; one in three women experiencing less severe forms of physical intimate partner violence; and one in five women in the United States experiencing rape in their lifetime.[1] While sexual harassment is most often perpetuated by strangers, sexual assault is most frequently perpetrated by a relative, friend, or romantic partner.[2] Men experience domestic violence and abuse, too, but the harm is disproportionately carried by the bodies, psyches, and souls of women.

The reality of gender-based violence is one of the clearest examples of the need to practice care with the four-level purview of the individual, institutional, sociocultural, and theological realms. Here is an example of how gender-based violence operates at all four levels:

- Individual: Abuse and violence take place on the bodies of individuals through acts like rape and violent assault. At this level, abuse and violence enact physical, emotional, and spiritual harm against the person experiencing it.

- Institutional: Abuse and violence are often enabled or ignored at the institutional level, with churches expressing silence on the matter, empowering perpetrators, ignoring victims, or perpetuating patriarchal theologies in our preaching and teaching and even embedded in our corporate prayers and liturgies.

- Sociocultural and sociopolitical: Abuse and violence are further enabled at the sociocultural and sociopolitical levels through cultural expressions of patriarchy and laws that protect perpetrators rather than victims of gender-based violence. An additional example of laws harming abuse victims involves gun laws in the United States, causing the ubiquity of guns in a domestic violence situation to increase risk of homicide by 500 percent.[3]
- Theological: At the theological level, our long history of patriarchal theology trickles down through the sociocultural, institutional, and individual levels, normalizing violence against women, identifying God with perpetrators instead of victims, making churches complicit in enabling violence, and instilling in victims the notion that their abuse is part of a supposed divine plan.

As a spiritual care first responder, you may be most involved at the individual level of care for those experiencing gender-based violence. However, as a lay leader or pastor of a congregation, you have purview over the policies and practices of your congregation that so often become complicit in violence. This advocacy can also take shape through the ways we engage in interpersonal conversation that challenge inadequate knowledge of and false assumptions about gender-based violence. As a member of a democratic system of government, you have a responsibility to use the power of your vote and your voice to advocate for laws that better protect victims of abuse and violence, and as a congregation, you may discover a collective sense of call to advocate for these laws together in your ministry of care and justice. As a member of a community of faith, reading and interpreting the tradition's sacred texts together is an act that requires tremendous care so that the weight of your religious or spiritual tradition doesn't tip the scales of care and justice in favor of perpetrators of violence but instead shifts the weight of the community into a position of solidarity and care with victims of abuse and violence.

At every level—individual, institutional, sociocultural and -political, and theological—we must practice forms of care that stand in solidarity with those most vulnerable. Let's begin with the individual level of care, developing a posture of deep listening to the stories of abuse.

LISTENING TO ABUSE STORIES

Above all, believe women. When a woman who has experienced abuse or violence chooses to bring you into her world, to share her experience with you as a trusted spiritual care companion, believe her. Too many women in churches and wider society are further victimized by the complicity of church leaders and others who question their story and doubt the damage done in their lives, tacitly siding with their abuser. Pastoral theologian James Poling argues, "Religious leaders must choose whether to collude with the dominant culture as sanctioning agents of abusive power or to be prophetic critics of the way power is distributed and defined."[4] Part of the way power is distributed and defined in relation to gender-based violence is in the power of the story: Who gets to say what happened and be believed by their hearers? Whose story becomes valid in the eyes of the church, the court, the caregiver? So, above all, believe women.

Danielle Tumminio Hansen is a practical theologian giving specific attention to the ways that spiritual care responders listen to the stories of gender-based violence, especially rape. Hansen suggests that those who have experienced gender-based violence like rape "need supportive witnesses in order to restore the safety and agency that the person who raped them took."[5] The role of the spiritual care first aid responder in the midst of gender-based violence should be that of supportive witness, listening not as one who has the answers or any words that can make the pain of violence better but listening with humility, respect, and a posture of openness to the story that the careseeker needs to tell, as difficult as that story may be to hear.

Hansen names several things that care responders are often tempted to do in the face of stories that are difficult to hear: change the subject to something less intense that feels safer to discuss; attempt to control the story or the emotions of the victimized person, often through platitudes like "At least you're growing stronger from this experience"; interpret the vulnerability of the speaker and their story as weak, socially unacceptable, or simply uncomfortable; or even engage in denial in the face of the victimized person's story, especially when the person who has enacted the abuse or violence is a mutual acquaintance of the victimized person and the spiritual care responder.[6]

Listening to stories of abuse that need to be told is one way to begin breaking the social isolation that is so common in situations of abuse and violence. Hansen reminds care responders that they are in a position of power when listening to the stories of abuse. Denial, platitudes, and shifting the focus of the conversation all serve to entrench social isolation in the experience of abuse. Empathic listening, however, serves to enhance the social belonging so necessary for the cultivation of safety and well-being.[7] She states, "Empathy, therefore, functions as an act of solidarity and a form of resistance that seeks a way to dismantle the isolation that victimized individuals often experience both during and after violation . . . [empathy] creates a space for understanding and acceptance."[8]

Developing a less anxious presence and the skills of active, reflective listening and asking helpful questions are part of the process of becoming a helpful listener to stories of abuse and violence. Give special attention in contexts of abuse and violence to limiting your use of why questions, which often feel blaming even when they aren't. For example, "Why were you in the room with this person?" seems to suggest judgment about the victim's presence in the place she was violated. "Tell me more about how you came to be in this room with him" invites the same reflection but in ways that can be responded to with less defensiveness. Do whatever you can to never pose questions that seem to place the blame on the victim of violence. In addition, Hansen names two more areas of listening to stories of abuse that are important to name here: *layered listening* and *narrative trust.*

In brief, layered listening means using the skills of active listening while also listening to your own relation and reaction to the topic of abuse or violence the careseeker is sharing. As Hansen notes, your own ability to listen well requires you to be aware of the ways you are identifying with or disengaging from what is being shared. Your own history of abuse or gender-based violence may come into the picture for you and invite you out of a posture of less anxious presence and active listening. Awareness of your own triggers and biases related to the subject of abuse, your own cultural and theological assumptions, and your social location (e.g., race, gender, sexuality) in relation to the careseeker are all part of the layered listening that Hansen encourages care responders listening to stories of abuse to develop.[9]

Listening from a posture of narrative trust is similar to experience-near listening—sticking closely to the way the careseeker needs to tell their story in the language they need to tell it and not imposing your interpretations or alternative vocabulary onto the careseeker. Hansen says that narrative trust "requires listeners not only to accept the reality of harm but also to accept that harm might not adhere to accepted contours, such that the listener is being asked to extend their own understand of what harm is."[10] Accept the language that the careseeker uses to describe their situation of violation, even if you believe a different vocabulary is more helpful, more liberative, or more accurate. Allow their story to challenge the assumptions and biases you hold and are becoming aware of through layered listening. Be willing to be moved from the feeling of empathy toward a posture of active solidarity alongside those who have been violated by abuse and violence. As simple as it sounds, your ability to listen carefully and caringly to a careseeker's story of abuse holds healing potential if you can cultivate your listening presence in ways that stay with the story that needs to be told, avoiding the imposition of your interpretation and the temptation to run from vulnerability and discomfort when they arise.

TAKING CARE WITH THEOLOGICAL SOURCES

It is unfortunate, but true, that our theology often gets in the way of our caring response to people experiencing gender-based violence and abuse of all kinds. In the worst cases, toxic theologies can provide cover for abusers to perpetuate violence and can invite those violated by abusers to become docile in face of their abusers—all in the name of God. Grace Ji-Sun Kim and Susan Shaw, both ministers and theologians and both also survivors of childhood sexual abuse, describe the central problem at the intersection of gender-based violence and churches' caring response for survivors:

> The church has told us that women and girls are temptresses, that sexual minorities and transgender people are inherently disordered and sinful, that women and children are supposed to submit to the men in power over them, that survivors have to forgive their perpetrators, and that perpetrators don't need to make restitution for their abuse. Many survivors have internalized these ideas to their own detriment . . . For many survivors, holding onto faith is difficult because churches have often taught ideas of God that are thoroughly tied up with experiences of abuse, and the church and individual Christians have often failed to take abuse seriously and do something about it.[11]

This profound word from Kim and Shaw should serve as a warning for representatives of Christian communities, lay or ordained, to take care with theological messages in contexts of abuse and violence.

Perhaps most commonly, our theological problems stem from common images of God that make God an accomplice in abuse and violence, portraying abuse as somehow in God's will, discouraging victims from questioning God's plan for the use of violence in the victim's life, or encouraging submission to male figures (husbands, priests, pastors, etc.) even as they enact abuse. Attending these images of God, our theological messages often foist forgiveness on the victim as an obligation in response to abuse.

Our attention across all levels of care should attend to the complicity of our theological language and symbols in perpetuating abuse and violence. Kim and Shaw note that common images of God as "all-powerful, dominant, unmoved, and unmoving" often align better with the power of dominators and abusers than with those who are violated by them.[12] Speaking as survivors, they say, "We know what it is to be at the mercy of those with power over us, and this image makes God one more relationship with controlling power over our lives. This image justifies power-over and suggests that to be like God is to exercise power-over."[13] Thus, one form of community care in the context of abuse and violence, which touches every faith community, is to attend with care to the images of God we use in worship. In contrast to images of God's power and dominance, images of God as "healing, mothering, relating, providing, and overcoming" and "a God who shares their experiences and . . . who understands their pain and grief" can become healing and supportive amid abuse and violence.[14] These images appear throughout the text of Scripture but are underrepresented or completely missing in the worshipping life of many congregations due to the influence of long histories of patriarchal interpretations of the tradition that we often confuse with Christian faith itself.

Another way our theologies often get in the way of our supportive presence with those violated by abuse and gender-based violence is in our failure as caregivers to grapple with theodicy. That is, having an insufficient perspective about the presence of sin, evil, and violence in the world and God's place in that picture. We wish the world were not the way it is, and we bend our theologies to fit that desire. "God won't give us more than we can handle," "God must have a plan to use this suffering to strengthen you," and a host of other theological platitudes serve to shield us from the realities of suffering and violence we encounter in the lives of careseekers. They erase the incomprehensibility of the innocent suffering violence at the hands of abusers, all the while implicating God's will in the perpetuation of abuse. As Hansen describes it, "For some listeners, hearing about traumatic experiences viscerally causes them to turn away. Unable to acknowledge the extent to which suffering pervades the world, it is easier for them to deny its existence."[15] Our theological desire for God not to let abuse and violence run rampant in society and even in churches invites us to turn away from experiences of abuse, deny the harm that's perpetrated, and fail to adequately care for those violated or hold abusive parties accountable.

Our theologies of sin, suffering, and evil need room to contain abuse and violence that have no purpose, no deeper meaning, and no place in the will of God. Abuse and violence are not assets added to our lives. Our theologies need a richer concept of God's role in suffering such that God is not the all-powerful orchestrator of events—even the ones that cause great harm to us—but, instead, a God who suffers with us, who stands alongside us in solidarity, whose desire for us is well-being and flourishing of life, which do not come by way of lessons learned at the hands of abusers.

A WARNING ABOUT FORGIVENESS

By far, one of the most abusive theological notions in contexts of abuse is that of forgiveness. Both conservative and liberal theological traditions become complicit in the abuse of women and children with our theologies of forgiveness. In more liberal traditions, we downplay the sinfulness of people and uplift the goodness of humanity and God's grace in ways that can make it difficult to preach and teach accountability for perpetrators of violence. In more conservative theological traditions, we may emphasize human sinfulness but overemphasize God's forgiveness and redemption in place of accountability for perpetrators of violence. Pamela Cooper-White, a pastoral psychoanalyst and Episcopal priest, argues that when it comes to addressing male perpetrators, this leads to "a great deal of emotional energy and material resources poured into an effort to help him avoid containment [of the perpetrator's violence]. 'What he needs is counseling . . .' 'What he needs is our understanding and forgiveness . . .' 'What he needs is our love.'"[16]

One of the most spiritually toxic ways that forgiveness is implicated in the perpetuation of abuse and violence is when it is foisted on the one violated as an obligation that they have toward the one who has abused them. In these situations, statements made from pastoral leaders provide cover for the abuser and send the one violated back into violent situations: "You should forgive him like God forgives us all of our sins," "Your relationship won't get better unless you can let this go and forgive," "You'll feel better if you can bring yourself to forgive him."

As a rule, you should simply avoid introducing any talk of forgiveness in your caring conversations with careseekers who have experienced abuse and violence. There may come a time for this sort of conversation, but it should always be on the terms of the careseeker, not yours. And when forgiveness does become a thinkable option for those violated by abuse, it can be helpful to have a caring companion who can tease apart the often-conflated issues that get unhelpfully bound up in our theologies of forgiveness.

For example, forgiveness does not mean forgetting. One's experience of abuse or violence will continue to be part of one's past and may require a great deal of spiritual care, communal support, and professional counseling to address. One thing that must be continually and intentionally remembered is the courage of the victim-survivor in acting on behalf of their own well-being and healing from abuse and violence.[17] Forgiveness may have a role to play in that process of healing for the victim-survivor but not through forgetting the harm done or the courage to resist the continued perpetuation of that harm.

Similarly, forgiveness is not joined to reconciliation. Sometimes forgiveness is a pursuit of someone violated by abuse and violence because they need it, not because their abuser needs it and not because they wish to reenter a relationship with the one who has perpetrated their abuse. Messages of forgiveness often subvert vital messages of accountability for harm done. But when chosen by the victim-survivor, forgiveness can have the effect of releasing the power and control of the abuser over the one abused, but this should never be pushed on the careseeker. It must always be a choice made by the victim-survivor. Shaw speaks of her own need to forgive her abuser.

> I never confronted my abuser, but I did forgive him eventually, for me, not for him. For me forgiveness means I no longer wish someone harm. It doesn't mean I pretend nothing happened. I realize that there was nothing my abuser could ever say that would satisfy me. I didn't want to hear him say, "I'm sorry." It wouldn't have made any difference. And I certainly didn't want to feel pressure to say, "It's ok." It's not ok. It will never be ok. I will always carry the scars of abuse with me. And there was nothing he could do or say that could have made anything better. I forgave him because it helped me let go of some of my rage.[18]

This is a helpful example of the ways forgiveness can, at times, become part of the healing process for careseekers facing histories of abuse and violence. But note that for Shaw, forgiveness was something that occurred on her terms and not in relationship with her abuser. It did not mean forgetting her experience or pretending that the experience was okay. Forgiveness was something that helped Shaw, something that she initiated in her own time.

Importantly, forgiveness may never enter the picture for some careseekers who have experienced abuse or violence. And that's okay. As a care responder, do not push your own theological agenda in your care for others, and take great care with how you speak of theological concern like forgiveness in larger communal spaces like in sermons and public prayers. This is where toxic notions of forgiveness-as-forgetting and forgiveness-as-reconciliation-without-accountability are pushed outside of direct conversations about abuse and violence, which are often later overlaid on our spiritual care work with victim-survivors. When we speak about forgiveness, especially in contexts of abuse, all of the above nuance and complexity should be part of that communal theological exploration. Above all, as Kim and Shaw note, we should take care to stand in solidarity with those most vulnerable in our teaching and preaching on forgiveness by insisting that "without restoration for the victim, forgiveness cannot happen."[19]

ACCOUNTABILITY FOR PERPETRATORS

As Cooper-White says of working with perpetrators, it is "not about monsters . . . but ordinary men who have learned that violence is necessary to their survival . . . that the only way to have the power of choice, action, and self-determination is to exert power over others."[20] Similarly, biblical scholar Susanne Scholtz argues, "People often believe that rapists are crazy, wild maniacs who attack women on the streets in the middle of the night. It seems difficult to accept that most rapists are ordinary men. They are brothers, sons, husbands, boyfriends, cousins, or fathers known and liked by family, friends, and coworkers. It is thus easier for people to blame women for her so-called provocative behavior, her lack of resistance, or her seductive outfits than to face the hostile aggression of ordinary men toward women in their lives."[21] It is vital for you, as a spiritual care responder, not to think of people who perpetrate violence against women as exceptional or monstrous. Otherwise, you will miss the fact that they are men who may never raise your internal alarms—ordinary men who populate your everyday life and sit in the pew alongside you on Sunday morning.

As a spiritual care first aid responder, you will not likely be engaged in long-term care for perpetrators of abuse. Even well-trained pastors will likely come up against their boundaries of competence in spiritually companioning abusers who will require the help of therapists specializing in the treatment of abusers and their families. Pastors undertaking this work with individual offenders alone are breaching the ethical practice of their ministry. However, everyone has the responsibility of cultivating a less abuse-complicit congregation where the safety and well-being of women and children are prioritized, where those violated are not victim-blamed, and where perpetrators are held accountable for their actions rather than enabled and protected.

Absolutely never help a perpetrator of violence against women or children avoid the legal consequences of their actions. You may feel that this is the compassionate thing to do, perhaps even that you or the church can help him more than the legal system can. But by helping a perpetrator avoid legal consequences and the likelihood of therapeutic treatment that will come along with those consequences, you become complicit in the continued abuse of the offender's victims. Cooper-White says, "Something deep in our psyche as Christians derives more joy and satisfaction out of trying to redeem an offender than trying to protect and vindicate a victim."[22] This theological impulse must be subverted when it comes to working with domestic and gender-based abuse and violence. We must instead lean into the rich theology of the Christian tradition that invites us to stand in solidarity with the victims, willing to risk our comfort to enter into painful places with them, committing ourselves not to abandon them in the times they need our most caring companionship, and cultivating an ethic that leads us to stand on the side of those most vulnerable in any situation—especially when that vulnerability is to their further violence at the hands of their abusers.

You may believe that the abuser is a victim too. Perhaps he also has a history of adverse childhood experiences including abuse at the hands of a parent or family member. Indeed, in his study of male perpetrators of abuse and violence, Poling says, "Each man I interviewed had lived a life of terror himself. Most were victims of sexual violence, physical violence, or severe deprivation."[23] That may all be true. But in the instance of his perpetration of abuse and violence, the offender must be held accountable for his actions, and further violence must be contained. Otherwise, we are not only colluding with his ongoing violence but also perpetuating the cycle of victims sometimes becoming perpetrators of violence later in life if we are not intent on stopping the violence occurring in the here and now. This means that when a reportable offense of violence or child abuse is discovered, a clergyperson should report it to the appropriate local authority—law enforcement in cases of domestic violence and child protective services in the case of the abuse of children.

This responsibility raises another boundary of competence for spiritual care providers: you are not a trained investigator. You should never take it on yourself to engage in investigative work on your own such as interviewing the accused abuser or attempting to validate the facts of the story of the victim prior to making a report that ethically must be made. Not only is this not your role, but it can also complicate and potentially taint any case that may emerge from a report in ways that cannot be undone. Leave investigation to child protective services or law enforcement.

When working over the long term with a parishioner who is an offender, it is vital to support that person by connecting them to treatment services with practitioners specializing in domestic violence or child abuse intervention. Following this introduction to specialty services, you may need to provide ongoing supportive pastoral presence encouraging his continued participation in the program or treatment and attending to the spiritual care concerns that may not be part of the professional counseling he is receiving.

REPORTING GENDER-BASED VIOLENCE OR THE ABUSE OF CHILDREN AND VULNERABLE ADULTS

A spiritual care responder's role in reporting is greatly dependent on whether the victim of abuse is a child or vulnerable adult, in which case reporting may be a legal obligation. Pastors and other designated spiritual care providers in a congregation should become familiar with the mandated reporting laws in the state in which they serve. Typically, these laws pertain to the reporting of known abuse of vulnerable populations—primarily children, elderly people, and/or those developmentally disabled.

If someone is designated by a state as a mandated reporter—that is, someone who is compelled by law to report any instances of the abuse of one of the law's named vulnerable populations such as children or elderly persons—and that person does not report instances of abuse that come to their attention, they may be charged with a misdemeanor. Some states require all people to report instances of abuse, neglect, and violence against vulnerable populations, while other states only require reporting from certain named professions like teachers, counselors, health-care professionals, and sometimes clergy.[24]

Concerns of reporting are shaped slightly differently when the victim of abuse is not in the category of a vulnerable population. When it comes to the abuse of nonvulnerable adults (for example, spousal abuse), more nuance is involved in respecting the autonomy and self-determination of the victim. Take the lead of the victim of abuse and violence in reporting those offenses to local authorities and invite maximum involvement from the victim in the process of reporting.[25] Cooper-White helpfully names two general rules for pastors and congregational spiritual care providers:

- The safety and self-determination of the victim in any violent situation must come first.
- Taking steps to report or contain abuse, when it is safe and agreeable to the victim to do so, is actually helping the perpetrator, although he may not see it that way.[26]

Trust the victim's sense of safety when it comes to confronting the perpetrator and do not take actions to confront the perpetrator without the victim's knowledge. Our spiritual care companionship should always serve to empower victims, not diminish their agency.

To reiterate, the exception to this rule is when the one being abused is a child or vulnerable adult who may not have the agency or ability to report their own abuse or to participate in a process of reporting. In instances of child abuse and the abuse of people with developmental disabilities or dependent elders, the onus of reporting this violence rests on the spiritual care provider. Whatever the mandated reporting laws in your state, if our silence allows abuse and violence to continue, then our silence is unethical.

OTHER CONSIDERATIONS FOR CONGREGATIONS

One final word for pastors and lay leaders of congregations: if a known abuser is continuing to be active in your congregation, it is imperative that the safety of victims and potential victims take precedence over the comfort of the abuser. A person who has engaged in domestic violence, for example, should be removed from positions of authority in the congregation, and no arrangements for that person's continued presence in the congregation should be made without the input of the person they have violated (such as the spouse, partner, or loved one) if that person is also in the congregation.

If child abuse, sexual or otherwise, is part of someone's history, a safety plan should be developed with that person and key leaders in the congregation so that they are companioned by an adult when they present in the congregation and are not allowed to engage children in the congregation. The covenant created with this person may indicate that attendance is only allowed at certain church functions such as the Sunday morning worship service and may outline several adults in the church who have agreed to be a partner with that person while they are on church premises so that they aren't left alone with the potential of encountering children in the hallway or restroom, for example.[27] Great care must be taken to provide for the spiritual needs of a person with a history of child abuse while ensuring that this person's involvement in the congregation never takes precedence over the safety of the congregation's children.

Practice Exercise: Hearing the Voices of Victim-Survivors
Gather with a group of others and talk through what you've learned in this chapter. What helped you think more carefully about your work in spiritually supporting careseekers who have experienced abuse and violence? What questions are you left with?

Access online videos of people who have experienced abuse or violence. An example is the story of Windy Cooler accessible on the Quaker Speak website, in which she describes her experience surviving domestic violence within her Quaker community.[28] You can find others by searching YouTube for "stories of domestic violence," "stories of surviving abuse," etc. Watch a couple of those short testimonies together as a group. Discuss what it was like to hear this story from a survivor of abuse. What themes did you notice that resonate with what you've read here? Which initial reactions or responses did you have to hearing these stories? Did any of those reactions surprise you? What concerns did the story raise for you if you were in the position of providing spiritual care first aid for this person? How did this first-person testimony help you better understand situations of abuse and violence? Which practices of care seem most important in responding to the situation described?

FURTHER READING

Kim, Grace Ji-Sun, and Susan M. Shaw. *Surviving God: A New Vision of God through the Eyes of Sexual Abuse Survivors*. Minneapolis: Broadleaf Books, 2024.

NOTES

1 For updated statistics, see ncadv.org/STATISTICS.

2 Sexual harassment includes verbal and cyber harassment and physical harassment like being touched in public. Sexual assault involves being forced to engage in sexual acts against a person's will and without their consent. Stop Street Harassment, "The Facts behind the #MeToo Movement: A National Study on Sexual Harassment and Assault," February 2018, https://www.nsvrc.org/sites/default/files/2021-04/full-report-2018-national-study-on-sexual-harassment-and-assault.pdf.

3 Jacquelyn C. Campbell et al., "Risk Factors for Femicide in Abusive Relationships: Results from a Multisite Case Control Study," *American Journal of Public Health* 93, no. 7 (2003): 1089–1097. As an example of legislation, the Dickey Amendment prevented the CDC's National Center for Injury Prevention and Control and the National Institutes of Health from receiving federal funding for firearm injury prevention research from 1996 until 2022, when it was lifted. See Colin Poitras, "Lifting of Federal Funding Ban Tied to Increase in Gun Violence Research," Yale School of Public Health, February 7, 2024, https://ysph.yale.edu/news-article/lifting-of-federal-funding-ban-tied-to-increase-in-gun-violence-research/#:~:text=(a)%20In%201996%2C%20the,the%20National%20Institutes%20of%20Health.

4 James Newton Poling, *The Abuse of Power: A Theological Problem* (Nashville: Abingdon Press, 1991), 13.

5 Danielle Tumminio Hansen, *Speaking of Rape: The Limits of Language in Sexual Violations* (Minneapolis: Fortress, 2024), 159.

6 Hansen, *Speaking of Rape*, 168–169.

7 Hansen, *Speaking of Rape*, 170–172.

8 Hansen, *Speaking of Rape*, 175.

9 Hansen, *Speaking of Rape*, 176.

10 Hansen, *Speaking of Rape*, 177.

11 Grace Ji-Sun Kim and Susan M. Shaw, *Surviving God: A New Vision of God through the Eyes of Sexual Abuse Survivors* (Minneapolis: Broadleaf Books, 2024), 3.

12 Kim and Shaw, *Surviving God*, 50–51.

13 Kim and Shaw, *Surviving God*, 51.

14 Kim and Shaw, *Surviving God*, 12.

15 Hansen, *Speaking of Rape*, 160.

16 Pamela Cooper-White, *The Cry of Tamar: Violence against Women and the Church's Response* (Minneapolis: Fortress, 1995), 209.

17 I am especially grateful to Staci Stought for strengthening this insight and for her overall feedback on this chapter flowing from her years of work with victim-survivors. Communication with the author, June 7, 2024.

18 Kim and Shaw, *Surviving God*, 59. Italics original.

19 Kim and Shaw, *Surviving God*, 60.

20 Cooper-White, *The Cry of Tamar*, 206.

21 Susanne Scholtz, *Sacred Witness: Rape in the Hebrew Bible* (Minneapolis: Fortress, 2010), 29.

22 Cooper-White, *The Cry of Tamar*, 210.

23 Poling, *The Abuse of Power*, 17.

24 For up-to-date laws, search for the mandated reporting laws in your specific state listed on trusted government websites. For a discussion of some intricacies of mandated reporting laws pertaining to clergy, see Child Welfare Information Gateway, "Clergy as Mandatory Reporters of Child Abuse and Neglect," US Department of Health and Human Services, Administration for Children and Families, Children's Bureau, 2023, https://www.childwelfare.gov/resources/clergy-mandatory-reporters-child-abuse-and-neglect/.

25 Cooper-White, *The Cry of Tamar*, 224.

26 Cooper-White, *The Cry of Tamar*, 225.

27 There are several helpful resources that congregations may access to develop such plans and protocols. See Brotherhood Mutual, "Registered Sex Offenders in Ministry Activities: White Paper," accessed June 3, 2024, https://www.brotherhoodmutual.com/resources/safety-library/publications/tough-issues-registered-sex-offenders-in-ministry-activities/; "Safe Church Policies," Lutheran Social Services of Minnesota, accessed June 3, 2024, https://www.lssmn.org/services/youth/education/cherish-all-children/churches/safe-church-policies; and a cadre of helpful articles archived at "Safety in Meetings," *Friends Journal*, March 2022, https://www.friendsjournal.org/issue-category/2022/safety-in-meetings/.

28 "Healing from Abuse in Quaker Communities," *Quaker Speak*, June 29, 2023, https://quakerspeak.com/video/healing-from-abuse-in-quaker-communities/.

15

HEALING THROUGH SPIRITUAL PRACTICES

The topic of spiritual practices is bigger than spiritual care first aid, yet incorporating healing spiritual practices can be integral to your spiritual care. Spiritual practices can help bring calm to our souls when our worlds are in tumult. They can restore our connections to the goodness of the earth, others, and God when those connections have been eroded by toxic theologies and spiritual abuse. Spiritual practices can aid in the recovery of mental health when it is on edge, bring equilibrium amid crisis and disaster, and help restore one's relationship to spiritual community. A careseeker's engagement with spiritual practices supports the work of healing.[1]

Remember that careseekers come to you with their own spiritual practices and theological beliefs already well in the process of formation. It is important for you to understand and respect where they are on their spiritual path through deep listening and helpful questions to understand what they are already bringing, spiritually and theologically, to the conversation. Pastoral theologian Carrie Doehring reminds care responders, "When care seekers trust that caregivers will respect what is unique about their religious beliefs, values, and spiritual practices, then cocreation of meanings and practices can begin. The more caregivers respect the unique religious and spiritual worlds of care seekers, the more trust will deepen . . . caregivers need to be theologically accountable for not imposing their theologies."[2]

As a caregiver, try not to be prescriptive in your engagement with spiritual practices. Offer any suggestions you may make for the development of new spiritual practices as experiments that can be attempted and embraced if helpful and let go of if not. Don't assume that what works well for you or worked with another careseeker will work well for someone else.

Just as in other parts of our lives, our spiritual lives form uniquely and with wide diversity.

THREE TS OF SACRED BELONGING

I want to introduce a three-dimensional framework for spiritual appraisal that can help you consider how to help careseekers develop spiritual practices that attend to their experiences of belonging to God, to one another, and to the ecological web of life on earth.[3] These dimensions of transcendence, togetherness, and tethering are intimately connected to each other, overlapping at the nexus of our embodied spiritual lives, as pictured in the figure below. Practices that touch on one dimension can help strengthen—or, conversely, harm—our sense of connection and belonging in the other two dimensions.

Helpful and healing spiritual practices should work to increase our sense of belonging in one or more of these dimensions. A robust spiritual life should serve to increase this sense of belonging in all the dimensions and help us to heal the places where toxic theologies, abusive spiritual leaders or communities, adverse experiences, and individual and collective traumas have severed our connection to one or more of these dimensions. As a rule, helpful and healing spirituality binds us in belonging and belovedness to God, to others, and to the earth.

The transcendence dimension speaks to our sense of belonging to a context of ultimacy, or God. A sense of belonging in this dimension opens us outward beyond the self toward a wider awareness of relationality and belonging. *Wonder* often describes the sense of relationality at the dimension of transcendence. Wonder at the vastness of the cosmos and our place within it. Wonder at the history of God's movement in the world and our chapter in that sacred narrative. Here, we come to know our belongingness to something that is beyond us yet can become bound to us. A belonging that bespeaks our belovedness on a grand scale.

In helping a careseeker develop spiritual practices that connect them to a sense of what is of ultimate importance in life, it is necessary to understand what that sense of ultimacy is for the careseeker. Is it a personal sense of God's presence in their day-to-day lives? Is it a vast Otherness that they feel connected to in the sense of a cosmic Divine presence in the world? Perhaps it is a connection to the movement of Spirit in their lives and the world around them. Do they perceive Spirit's movement best in the stillness of

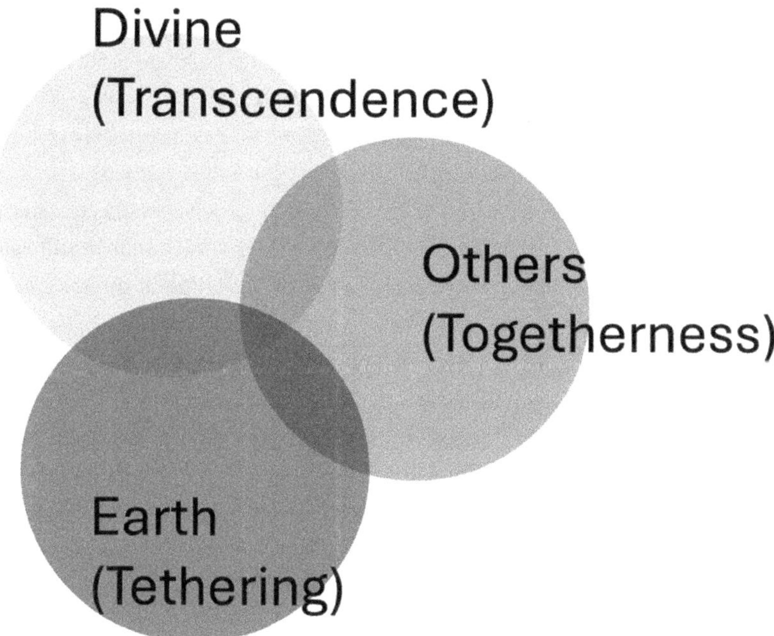

Figure 1: Three Ts of Sacred Belonging to God, to One Another, and to the Web of Life

their heart and mind or in the grandeur of a forest? Understanding a careseeker's relationship to God—or another way that they name what they perceive as ultimate in the world—will help to companion them in developing spiritual practices that connect them in belonging and belovedness to God.

The togetherness dimension speaks of our connection to others in expansive human community. Looking beyond the self and toward one another. Recognizing that we are always selves-in-community, constituted by our relationships in both helpful and harmful ways, brings about both warmth and wounding. Good relationships are a key to our overall health—mental, physical, and spiritual. Some of our spiritual practices should help connect us in belonging to community. Singing together, participating in group meditation and prayer, studying sacred texts together, serving others through acts of hospitality and altruism, reverentially exploring the natural world around us in community—all these can become community-centered spiritual practices that open us toward the transcended dimension while also strengthening the togetherness dimension of our sacred belonging.

Where has a careseeker most clearly experienced belonging within sacred community? In a church at worship in the sanctuary or in an AA meeting in a church basement? Which figures in a careseeker's life have most clearly communicated to them a sense of their own belovedness? What did they do or say that helped them to experience their belovedness? How have communities caused harm or eroded their sense of connection to others or to God? Perhaps in spiritually violent messages about their gender or their sexuality or ostracism over their religious questions and spiritual curiosities?

Spiritual practices do not always need to take place within community, but helpful and healing spiritual practices should always serve to deepen our compassion and connection to others rather than building spiritual silos around us and drawing sharp distinctions between us and them. This is delicate work when a community has been spiritually wounding to a careseeker in the past and may require further help from a pastor or therapist adept in care amid spiritual struggle to more fully engage and work through.

The tethering dimension speaks to our sense of mooring, belonging to the earth's wider web of life in relationships that binds us in earthy entanglement. Webbing speaks not only to our entanglement in the metaphorical web of life but also invokes the stickiness of a spider's web that entangles bodies when we inadvertently walk through it, sticking to our hair, our skin, our clothes in ways that are difficult to escape. While many spiritual teachings and practices have led us to escape the body into the life of the mind or spirit, helpful and healing spiritual practices mend the splits of mind-body-spirit and help us to more deeply sense our belonging to a community that extends beyond the human to the other-than-human web of life—plants, animals, bodies of water, and the landscapes to which we feel a sense of belonging, bespeaking home.

Barbara Holmes, a spiritual teacher and theologian, describes the tethering dimension well by saying, "Human beings are a part of a community of inspirited life. Moreover, the earth, rather than being an inert commodity available for our exploitation, is part of a universe understood to be an organic whole."[4] How have careseekers experienced a wider belonging to the earth community? What have careseekers learned about God through a deep engagement with nature? In what ways have relationships with a particular landscape been healing, bringing solace amid pain, respite amid restlessness, opening wonder amid suffocating self-absorption?

Spiritual practices that increase one's sense of sacred belonging in one or more of these dimensions are helpful toward healing and flourishing. Spiritual practices that sever our connection and sacred belonging in one or more of these dimensions are spiritually toxic. As Doehring helpfully states, "Spiritual practices that foster self-compassion alleviate the punitive judgement, internalized prejudices, and/or spiritual anxiety that cut people off from love—self-love, God's love, relational and communal love."[5] Spiritual practices should connect us with self-compassion, the love of God, love of human community, and our belovedness bound up in the ecological web of life.

HEALING SCRIPTURE AND SACRED READING

Sacred texts hold great power. These texts can be drawn on for comfort and sustenance in times of heartache and pain, when we feel at the end of our rope and our world is coming apart at the seams. Scripture can infuse us with courage and passion when we are summoned to meet the challenges and concerns of our day through acts of justice and peacebuilding. And sacred texts hold the power to harm.

Any sacred source with the power to promote healing and courage and justice also has the potential to enact harm, induce fear, and support injustice. There are no uncomplicated relationships with Scripture. We often pretend an uncomplicated relationship with the Bible is possible, usually by writing off large swaths of Scripture as unimportant and dismissing those who have used the Bible violently as not real Christians. But responsible interpretation demands that we recognize the Bible's power to perform great healing and its power to do great harm. We've witnessed that throughout history, and many of us have experienced it in our own lives.[6]

Pastoral psychotherapist Russell Siler Jones asks the following questions in relation to spirituality more broadly, but they can also be applied to how careseekers are reading and interpreting the sacred texts of their tradition too: "Does a person's spirituality help her make sense of a complicated world? Does it increase her sense of agency? Does it help her treat herself and other people fairly? Does it give her life a sense of purpose and meaning? If so, then let's call it healthy. Does it make her more fearful, more agitated, or more hostile? Does it isolate her from others or from parts of herself? Does it confuse her or weaken her experience of agency? Let's call that harmful."[7]

It is not the role of the spiritual care responder to make diagnostic pronouncements related to the health or harm of a careseeker's spiritual practices. And it is never helpful to try arguing with a careseeker about spiritual beliefs or practices in an attempt to change them. This rarely works, and it puts the careseeker in a posture of defensiveness.

It can be helpful, however, when there are ways that a person's engagement with Scripture seems to be causing harm, severing their connection and sense of belongingness to God, to others, or to the earth, to inquire about how those Scriptures became important to them. You might ask, for example, "Who introduced you to that reading of Scripture?," "How has that passage affected your relationship with God?," or simply, "Can you tell me more about what this Scripture means to you?" These questions can get beyond the text itself to understand how a careseeker is approaching this text and how it is affecting their life.

Scripture can be a difficult source of spiritual practice to recover in ways that are helpful to one's spiritual life for some careseekers. For example, LGBTQ+ people who have spent time in nonaffirming church contexts, people who have belonged to abusive spiritual communities that use Scripture in coercive ways, women who have had Scripture used to diminish their sense of self or call.[8] Though even for those who have had Scripture used against them in harmful ways, there can also exist a longing to recover a relationship to Scripture as a source of sustenance and strength. But tread carefully, attempting to understand how the careseeker wants to relate to Scripture rather than trying to correct their relationship with the biblical text. It is more important to honor the careseeker's experience of harmful encounter with Scripture than it is to defend Scripture itself.

If Scripture is desired as a healing source of spiritual practice, it can be helpful to be able to direct a careseeker to passages that may help sustain them in times of difficulty, for example, directing them to Psalms 13 or another lament in times of grief and mourning. Or when one's sense of belonging to God is in question, passages such as Romans 8:31–39,

1 Corinthians 13, and 1 John 4 that bespeak the expansive nature of love can be sustaining. Scriptures shouldn't be doled out like prescriptions, nor should they be offered in lieu of careful conversation about the spiritual questions and struggles that a careseeker is bringing to you. But used thoughtfully and in response to the desire of the careseeker, sacred texts hold healing potential to companion through times of struggle, connecting us to the Divine with the words of our faith ancestors read time and time again by spiritual sojourners from age to age.

HEALING PRACTICES OF PRAYER AND MEDITATION

Prayer can be employed in helpful ways and in harmful ways in spiritual care. At its worst, prayer can be used in manipulative ways, engaging careseekers in prayer so that we can pray that they will do, think, or feel what we really want them to do, think, or feel in relation to the situation they face, such as "God, I pray that you would lead her to do x, y, or z." Less overtly harmful, but no more helpful, is engaging in prayer as an escape from caring conversation—passing a careseeker off to God because we don't want to sit with them in the unknowing or the pain of the situation that they face. Prayer can be an easy out from a caring conversation when used in that way. When used well, prayer can become a meaningful part of a caring conversation rather than a replacement for it.

At its best, prayer can be a sustaining source of strength, drawing close to God amid a situation that calls for care. Pastor Emmy Kegler says, "In prayer, I seek a mystical companion in the divine force beyond my comprehension that created everything, and the Son of Man born flesh who knows what it is like to despair, to feel alone, to be abandoned."[9] Again, it is important to understand how the careseeker understands and practices prayer. For some, it would be highly unusual if a care responder didn't offer to pray with them during a caring conversation. For others, prayer can feel awkward and even off-putting if offered without conversation or consent.

When a careseeker asks you to pray with them, it can be helpful to ask a simple question like "I would be glad to pray with you. What would be important for us to bring to God in prayer together?" This gives you a better understanding of their relationship with prayer and helps you to keep your own directiveness out of the prayer by focusing on the careseeker's needs, feelings, and desires. This doesn't mean that you might not add your own prayers for them that they haven't named such, as for God's love to surround them or for the Spirit to strengthen them, but your words in prayer will be formed more meaningfully in relation to the careseeker's life if you've talked a bit about their request for prayer before engaging in it.

Alongside prayer, practices of meditation and mindfulness can be helpful sources of spiritual practices for careseekers. Meditation and mindfulness practice has even been incorporated into modern medical practices by many practitioners. The Cleveland Clinic describes it this way: "Meditation is an ancient practice that dates back thousands of years. Despite its age, this practice is common worldwide because it has benefits for brain health and overall well-being."[10] They continue, "Meditation is a practice that involves focusing or clearing your mind using a combination of mental and physical techniques."[11] Some of these involve centering one's attention on the body and physical sensations. Others involve concentrating on a word or phrase or sound to center one's mind and focus. The possibilities for meditation are too extensive to cover in this chapter, but many helpful sources are available to help you develop this resource of caring practice.[12] The practice exercises at the ends of chapters 2, 4, and 11 all offer practices of prayerful meditation that can be helpful to engage with careseekers if appropriate to the situation and desired by the careseeker.

Remember, while you may be excited about how prayer or meditation or mindfulness has helped you or others, a spiritual care situation is not the time to become evangelistic about your favorite spiritual practices. Introduce a practice if you believe it may be helpful. Let the careseeker direct you about whether they are interested in incorporating it into the conversation. And let it go if it seems unhelpful or undesirable to them. You can always teach a workshop or lead a forum in your community to teach new spiritual practices to anyone interested. But in the caregiving situation, let the careseeker direct you to the spiritual practices they are interested in and willing to engage.

A SPIRITUAL ORIENTATION OF WONDER

Pastoral theologian Andrew Lester says, "Our mental processes look for a plot line or a storyline to explain information . . . Each new sensation, stimulus, and interpersonal transaction is shaped by our mental processes into a story, by which our experiences are given their individual distinctiveness as *our* story."[13] The aim of cultivating a spiritual orientation of wonder is to help us subvert the potential for our dominant storyline to be overcome by fear, anger, sadness, and other potentially overwhelming emotional experiences. As mentioned above, wonder is one of the primary ways that we experience belonging in the transcendence dimension, connecting us to something beyond us. A spiritual orientation of wonder serves to open us outward toward the Divine, toward others, and to the wider web of life, shaping our lives and communities toward flourishing and livability, even in a world that feels constantly on the brink of climate collapse, political turmoil, technological acceleration, economic precarity, war, and more.

In a precautionary world where fear becomes a general orientation toward life and future musings are often dominated by dangers rather than possibilities, philosopher Lars Svendsen says that we begin living with "a *telos* that is constantly directed toward catastrophe."[14] We might imagine that a similar telos exists for a life lived from a pervasive outlook colored by anger with its telos, or orientation, of vengeance or a general disposition of sadness with a telos of resignation. Developing a disposition of wonder as a spiritually orienting posture opens us to other orientations in life, moving us outward toward others in the world and toward God.

While wonder doesn't make it onto the list of primary emotions for many modern Western psychologists, a third-century BCE Indian Sanskrit text about the nature of consciousness does name wonder as one of the nine basic emotions. This text links wonder with the ritual act of seeing divinely. Scholar of religion Robert Fuller explains, "Whether occasioned by a temple icon or a sacred place in nature, 'religious seeing' is thought to disclose the life and consciousness that pulsates throughout the whole of creation . . . Religious seeing entails actually participating in the essence and nature of the person or object that elicited this perception (including participating in the essence and nature of the divine ground of this person or object)."[15]

Similarly, Rabbi Abraham Joshua Heschel sees wonder, or what he terms "radical amazement," as a chief characteristic of a religious orientation to the world. He describes this as "perpetual surprise at the fact that there are facts at all."[16] Heschel views wonder as both a form of thinking and a constant attitude that never ceases and must be continually cultivated. Wonder is the origin of one's awareness of the Divine and resistance to the sin of indifference to the sublime, according to Heschel.

Here are some ways Fuller sees wonder operating at the heart of our search for the Divine, as well as in cultivating community with the humans and more-than-humans in our environment: Wonder helps us suspend our habitual ways of looking at the world. Wonder lures us into creative engagement with our surroundings. Wonder induces receptivity and openness and connection to our environment. Wonder prompts us to consider life from new perspectives. Wonder entices us into relational aspects of reality, giving us a vision of our relatedness to the world, to other beings, and to sources of ultimacy, or the Divine.[17]

In addition to a transcendent orientation, philosopher Martha Nussbaum links wonder with the immanent capacity to move beyond self-interest into acts of love, empathy, compassion, and the preservation of life, even when there's no immediate benefit to us personally.[18] This certainly makes wonder a central component of cultivating a caring community. As an emotional orientation informing our ethics, wonder may even serve as a radical antidote to the reduction of all life to its value on an economic scale, of worth to productivity and earning potential, of the web of life to a ledger of natural resources. Wonder can feel like having the whole of your attention caught somewhere between the immanent and the transcendent in deep connection and receptivity to the world around you, awestruck and moved by curiosity and compassion.

Wonder is also an emotional experience that motivates us to "venture outward into increased rapport with the environment,"[19] in contrast to the withdrawal invited by fear and sadness and the hostility and aggression provoked by anger. Wonder promotes long-term communal health and survival by drawing us outward in compassion, curiosity, and connection toward human others, the wider web of life, and the holy.

In an era characterized by rapid change, wonder also aids in the creation of expansive categories of understanding in increasingly novel, uncertain, and even chaotic circumstances. Wonder is, as Fuller argues, "a principal source of humanity's creative adaptation."[20] A community cultivated through wonder becomes ever more curious, creative, compassionate, and connected as emotional experiences of wonder evoke a sense of awe, engagement, and deep interest in the world around us. Each of these wonder-induced characteristics of community can promote problem-solving that subverts the tendency to separate from those on the other side of the fear/anger divide. Each orients us toward possibilities, even in the face of perils. Wonder is a characteristic of human flourishing, without which we may be unable to survive in ways we would deem desirable.

In the biblical text, you can see the centrality of wonder from Genesis to Revelation. You can encounter wonder in the Psalms: "Praise [God], sun and moon . . . all you shining stars. Praise [God], you highest heavens, and you waters above the heavens. . . . Mountains and all hills, fruit trees and all cedars" (Psalm 148, NRSV). You can encounter wonder in the Gospels, most especially in Jesus's parables where he says something akin to, "The kingdom of God is like the tiniest of seeds that you can barely notice that grow into the largest of bushes where birds take shelter and build their nests" (Matthew 13:31–2, paraphrase). Wonder may, indeed, be the most neglected emotional experience by contemporary faith communities and those charged with their cultivation. For all of these reasons, the cultivation of wonder should be a central practice of care within communities.

Many spiritual practices promote a sense of wonder, from singing majestic hymns in a choir or congregation to staring up at the stars in a clear night sky. But, above all, emotional experiences like wonder are embodied. When we cultivate emotional experiences like wonder, we can also do that in ways that engage the fullness of our bodies and senses. Here are some prompts that may help you to engage in your own exploration of wonder in your own life and in the lives of careseekers:

What does wonder taste like?

What does wonder feel like in my body or in a tactile way?

What does wonder look like?

What does wonder smell like?

What does wonder sound like?

What connection to others, human and other-than-human, does wonder invite?

When our lives feel constricted by adverse circumstances, or our religious lives feel like they are closing in on us through a too narrow focus on moralism or teachings that have come to feel constricting, intentionally cultivating wonder through embodied spiritual practices and experiences—from eating a delicious meal to walking in the deep woods—can open us outward in relationship to God (transcendence), to others (togetherness), and to the wider web of life (tethering).

A SPIRITUAL POSTURE OF GRATITUDE

Gratitude holds a strong connection to wonder. Religious writer Dianna Butler Bass defines gratitude at its deepest and most transformative levels as "the emotional response to the surprise of our very existence, to sensing that inner light and realizing the astonishing sacred, social, and scientific events that brought each one of us into being."[21] Gratitude could even be conceived as a response to wonder. But it is not a response inculcated by our dominant cultural influences.

Bass notes the Western historic propensity to define gratitude as a transactional "commodity of exchange," which organizes gratitude around ideals of wealth and power.[22] Theologian Mary Jo Leddy adds to this, "Ingratitude is ingrained in our economic system," having shaped our worldview and imaginations for more than two centuries, shaping the dominant values of our culture in the United States, and rooted in a sense of perpetual dissatisfaction that propels the desires and cravings of consumers.[23]

In contrast to the traditional Western economic-informed definition of gratitude, Bass proposes a spiritual and ethical orientation toward gratitude as a structure of gift and response. Through an ethical lens of gratitude, we begin seeing that everything we need is present in the world. Freely responding to these gifts means cultivating a life of mutual care.[24] She continues, "When we share gifts, we become benefactors toward the well-being of all. Ultimately, the new structure [of gift and response] is a way of being."[25]

Gratitude experienced and expressed outside the commodity model of transactional exchange pairs the emotions we feel in response to life's gifts with ethical responses to those gifts. The implications function on both personal and public/communal levels.[26] Bass argues that gratefulness is "ultimately about connection,"[27] an outward-focusing emotion positioning one toward that which is transcendent—in one's human community, in communion with the more-than-human others in one's ecological setting, or toward the gifts of the Divine. Clearly, gratitude that departs from the commodity-transactional model and enters a gift-and-response mode becomes a countercultural witness against the enclosed self sufficiency, radical independence, and individualism of our economic and political status quo that contribute to our mental and spiritual harm.

"Consumerism works only as long as we are even slightly dissatisfied with what we have," Leddy argues.[28] If we play by the rules of capitalism and consumerism, we are seduced by the belief that a bit more material gain might assuage our dissatisfaction, thus lulling us into complicacy with the status quo and stripping us of impulses toward reform or revolution. Bass adds that in addition to ideals of capitalism, racial privilege also renders white people less capable of experiencing gratitude: "After all, we deserved good things and success. The American dream was ours. God gave it to us. Saying thank you was polite recognition of that fact. Maybe saying thank you too profusely, however, made us feel humiliated that we were not as in control as we thought."[29]

Psychologist of gratitude Robert Emmons describes gratitude as a social emotion. In addition to the physical and psychological benefits such as stronger immune systems, lower blood pressure, and greater experiences of alertness and pleasure, Emmons has also found that gratitude cultivates an individual's sense of generosity, compassion, and forgiveness and leads to decreased feelings of loneliness and isolation, speaking directly to the togetherness dimension. He argues that gratitude is "a relationship-strengthening emotion because it requires us to see how we've been supported and affirmed by other people." In addition to the immanent focus on the support of others and the web of life for our sustenance, gratitude promotes a transcendent focus on "figuring out where that goodness comes from . . . recognizing the sources of this goodness as being outside of ourselves."[30]

During circumstances when the situations we face are ones of very genuine threat to survival, we may need to search for what feels like a gift in our lives, eliciting our openness toward the world and the people around us. Whether cultivating a radical awareness of life's gifts and graces through practices like journaling or through communal ritual like singing, gratitude developed into a pervasive orientation or temperament holds ethical implications. Our ministries of justice-seeking can move away from the motivational resource of anger to take shape as radical responses of gratitude for the gifts of life and our deepest desires to preserve and protect them: the lives of our fellow humans against systems of racism, the lives of our more-than-human companions in the web of life from rampant destruction, and so forth.

There is much in our lives for which we simply cannot be grateful. Gratitude should never be forced on a careseeker, nor should gratitude be confused with looking on the bright side. Some situations are just bad, painful, aversive, and undesirable. That's where grief and lament meet us when we need them most. These moments of pain and difficulty and struggle make each possible experience and expression of gratitude even more important, wherever and whenever gratitude can be cultivated. But for quite a bit else we experience in life, gratitude must give way to grief.

When we notice gratitude showing up in a careseeker's spiritual life, it can be helpful to inquire into it in ways that help to deepen the experience and help the careseeker see the significance of gratitude as a spiritual practice. Pastoral psychotherapist Russell Siler Jones provides these questions to help deepen that inquiry:

- When you're feeling grateful like this, what do you notice happening physically? What does it feel like in your body?
- When you're feeling grateful like this, what thoughts go with this feeling? What do you hear yourself thinking—about God, about yourself, about other people?
- When you're feeling grateful like this, what other moments in your life does it remind you of?[31]

HEALING LANDSCAPES AND MULTISPECIES RELATIONSHIPS

We often treat all that is not human as if it is less than human. Our everyday language betrays this sometimes subtle slight of other-than-human beings in our common categories of *human* and *nonhuman*. I choose the terms *other-than-human* and *more-than-human* because categories of being do not just divide along human and nonhuman lines. The inhabitants of our planetary home are wildly diverse, and according to the biblical witness, they can know the Divine in ways that humans cannot. At very least, they can experience knowing God through different means than humans come to our awareness of God. Thus, beings in the wider ecological web of life can become our spiritual teachers in meaningful ways.

The biblical text is full of expressions of the more-than-human web of life enfolding us as fully imbued with knowledge of the Divine. In response to his companion Zophar's inadequate theologizing about Job's situation, Job encourages his friend toward a more earthy theology: "But ask the animals, and they will teach you, the birds of the air, and they will tell you; ask the plants of the earth, and they will teach you, and the fish of the sea will declare to you" (Job 12:7–8, NRSVue). However, a more literal translation of the Hebrew in verse 8 would be something like this: "*speak to the earth*, and have it teach you" (Job 12: 8, NASB, italics added).

Psalmists and prophets declare the ways that earth and heaven respond to God's presence in the cosmos: "The heavens are telling the glory of God" (Psalm 19:1, NRSVue), "The mountains and the hills before you shall burst into song, and all the trees of the field shall clap their hands" (Isaiah 55:12, NRSVue). The apostle Paul, heady though his theology can be, begins one of his great letters with these words directing readers to the earth's revelation: "Ever since the creation of the world God's eternal power and divine nature, invisible though they are, have been seen and understood through the things God has made" (Romans 1:20, NRSVue).

It is hard to fathom with what language the biblical writers these and numerous other texts could have used to praise the Creator if not with the language of light and waters and clouds and wind and flame. Or with images of thunder and mountains and valleys and springs and streams. Or by drawing into the praise of the Divine the voices of cattle and plants and trees and birds and rocks and sun and moon and sea. For too long, we have excluded the more-than-human ecological web of life from our practice of spirituality. But this sense of rootedness—tethering—of our bodies with the earth is central to a healthy and healing spiritual practice as attested to by both Scripture and science.

Here is a spiritual exercise that can begin to help us and the careseekers we serve to strengthen the tethering dimension of our sacred belonging, connecting us in intimate relationality to the ecological community in spiritual companionship.[32]

> Go outside, wherever you are. Look around to notice what you see. Try to ignore the humans in order to look up, around, and down at what you don't normally notice about the other-than-human around you—trees, grass, birds flying overhead, squirrels running by you. Feel the wind blowing. Notice the sun, moon, or the stars above. See the rocks and soil underfoot.
>
> If you pass by this way often, choose one being in the more-than-human world that surrounds this place and build an intentional relationship in the coming weeks and months. Spend time with this more-than-human being. It may be no more than five minutes a day once or twice a week, but become intentional about this time.
>
> As odd as it may feel at first, talk to this more-than-human part of your life. Communicate with it by touch if you can. Ask questions of this being about the wisdom it holds, about its knowledge of the Divine. Confess what needs confessing. Share the secrets that you need to tell the more-than-human. Express the joys that being in communion with that entity brings to your life. Make your commitments to struggle for the survivability of the earth to this being that exists alongside you in that life space.
>
> The hardest part of this or any relationship is to listen. You may not know how to listen to a tree, rock, or bird yet. But try it and see what you learn about your more-than-human companion, about the world, about relationship, about care, about yourself, and about the Divine.

Climate grief, or eco-grief, will become an even more present part of our experience of climate change and ecological destruction in the coming years.[33] Australian eco-philosopher Glenn Albrecht coined a term that is helpful for spiritual care first responders in this era of ecological devastation. He speaks of our increasing experience of *solastalgia*, which he describes as "the pain or distress caused by the ongoing loss of solace and the sense of desolation connected to the present state of one's home and territory." He says, "It is the existential and lived experience of negative environmental change, manifest as an attack on one's sense of place."[34] Here's a good example of this taking place in ritualized fashion.

In August 2019, Iceland marked the first-ever loss of an entire glacier to climate change with a funeral held on the barren landscape that was once covered in ice, the Ok glacier. They were grieved by the fact that this glacier that had been a part of their community—something they related to daily—was now gone with a grave sense of finality. On that site, at this funerary gathering, they placed a bronze plaque that contains "A Letter to the Future" that reads: "Ok is the first Icelandic glacier to lose its status as a glacier. In the next 200 years all our glaciers are expected to follow the same path. This monument is to acknowledge that we know what is happening and what needs to be done. Only you know if we did it."

In our despair over climate collapse, in the desperation that many of our communities of faith feel to do something that will make a meaningful difference for the survivability of the interwoven tapestry of life on this planet, and even in our most depressed and despondent and dejected states when nothing seems to be making a difference and nothing else seems to matter, we would do well to take the advice of Job, who knew despair and desperation and depression and despondency and dejection more than any other figure in the long communion of saints. And his advice was simple: speak to the earth.

Spiritual practices deepening our relationality with the earth's wider web of life can be healing to our bodies, minds, and spirits in times of distress and despair. These practices hold the potential to heal broken bonds between human and other-than-human, both intimately bound up with the expansive life of God that encompasses the cosmos. Invite the earth to be your ally in spiritual practice in your provision of spiritual care and in your daily life. There are many ways that earth creatures can become our teachers in knowing God more fully and in our own process of becoming better human creatures of the earth.

Practice Exercise: Your Story of Sacred Belonging

As a spiritual care first aid responder, it is helpful to be rooted in your own spiritual practices as you companion others through times of need, crises, deep questions, and explorations of their own spiritual lives. Use this exercise either on your own or with a group of other spiritual care responders to explore and tell the stories of your rootedness in the three Ts of sacred belonging. If you're doing this exercise with a partner or in a group, you can use your deep listening skill and use of beautiful questions to help more of each person's story be told.

Transcendence: My Story of Belonging to God

Tell of a time when you felt especially connected to that which transcends you, a context of ultimacy, or to God. Try to tell this story not in doctrinal language but in narrative detail—a coming to awareness that you were beloved by God. This doesn't need to be your first experience of this sense of belonging. Tell the story that first springs to awareness. What conveyed this connection to you? Where were you? Who was with you? What did you see, hear, feel, taste, smell?

Togetherness: My Story of Belonging to Others

Tell of a time when you felt especially taken by a sense of togetherness—belonging to others, beloved by others. Perhaps even a time when you were taken by surprise by this sense of kinship connection. What did that belonging feel like in an embodied, sensory way—what did it taste like, smell like, look like? What helped cultivate this sense of belonging or kinship?

Tethering: My Story of Belonging to the Earth

Tell of a place in the natural world to which you feel a special bondedness, a place that draws you in, a landscape in which you feel most held or at home, an environment to which you have sense of belonging—present or past, a singular experience or one of continued relationship. Describe its detail and narrate the other inhabitants of the ecological web of life who inhabit(ed) that place alongside you. What did/does it feel like to be in relationship with the earth in this place?

Multiple Rounds of Storytelling

Whether on your own or in conversation with a trusted community, you can take this storytelling exercise further by moving back through the three dimensions for two more rounds of story. On the second round, tell a story of a time when you felt your sense of belongingness to any of the three dimensions severed, cut off, diminished, or otherwise harmed in some way. What were the circumstances of that relational severing? How did a diminishment in your sense of belonging to one dimension affect your sense of belonging to the other dimensions? How did you respond to this diminishment of belonging in one or more of the dimensions?

Finally, on the third round, tell a story about how you experienced healing in your sense of belonging within the dimension in which you experienced that harm. What happened to help promote that healing? Were there things happening in one of the other dimensions that helped bring about a sense of healing in the dimension that was harmed? What did it feel like to experience restoration of sacred belonging in the dimension that was severed?

FURTHER READING

Holmes, Barbara A. *Crisis Contemplation: Healing the Wounded Village*. Albuquerque, NM: CAC Publishing, 2021.

Yetunde, Ayo Pamela. *Casting Indra's Net: Fostering Spiritual Kinship and Community*. Boulder, CO: Shambhala, 2023.

NOTES

1 For texts on spiritual practices more broadly speaking, see Pema Chödrön, *Comfortable with Uncertainty: 108 Teachings on Cultivating Fearlessness and Compassion* (Boston: Shambhala, 2002); M. Robert Mulholland Jr., *Invitation to a Journey: A Road Map for Spiritual Formation* (Downers Grove, IL: InterVarsity, 1993); Cole Arthur Riley, *Black Liturgies: Prayers, Poems, and*

Meditations for Staying Human (New York: Convergent, 2024); and Marjorie J. Thompson, *Soul Feast: An Invitation to the Christian Spiritual Life*, rev. ed. (Louisville, KY: Westminster John Knox Press, 2014).

2 Carrie Doehring, *The Practice of Pastoral Care: A Postmodern Approach*, rev. ed. (Louisville, KY: Westminster John Knox Press, 2015), 1. You may wish to take a moment to review the section on spiritual humility at the end of chapter 3. Keep in mind that there are also other healing spiritual practices spread throughout this book. For example, review the practice exercises at the ends of chapters 2, 4, and 11.

3 This framework was first introduced in chapter 10 in relation to providing spiritual care amid disasters.

4 Barbara A. Holmes, *Crisis Contemplation: Healing the Wounded Village* (Albuquerque, NM: CAC Publishing, 2021), 27.

5 Doehring, *The Practice of Pastoral Care*, 10.

6 A lengthier treatment of this reality can be found at Cody J. Sanders, "How Do I Love the Bible When People Have Used It to Do Such Harm?," Enter the Bible, accessed June 21, 2024, https://enterthebible.org/how-do-i-love-the-bible-when-people-have-used-it-to-do-such-harm.

7 Russell Siler Jones, *Spirit in Session: Working with Your Client's Spirituality (and Your Own) in Psychotherapy* (West Conshohocken, PA: Templeton Press, 2019), Kindle loc. 1994.

8 For more, see Teresa B. Pasquale, *Sacred Wounds: A Path to Healing from Spiritual Trauma* (St. Louis: Chalice, 2015).

9 Emmy Kegler, *All Who Are Weary: Easing the Burden on the Walk with Mental Illness* (Minneapolis: Broadleaf Books, 2021), 32.

10 "Meditation," Cleveland Clinic, accessed June 21, 2024, https://my.clevelandclinic.org/health/articles/17906-meditation.

11 "Meditation."

12 For more, see these classic texts: Thich Nhat Hanh, *The Miracle of Mindfulness: An Introduction to the Practice of Meditation* (Boston: Beacon, 1975); Jon Kabat-Zinn, *Wherever You Go, There You Are: Mindfulness Meditation in Everyday Life* (New York: Hyperion, 1994); Jack Kornfield, *Meditation for Beginners, Six Guided Meditations for Insight, Inner Clarity, and Cultivating a Compassionate Heart* (Boulder, CO: Sounds True, 2004). For more explicitly Christian sources on meditation practice, see James Finley, *Christian Meditation: Experiencing the Presence of God* (New York: Harper Collins, 2004); Thomas Keating, *Invitation to Love: The Way of Christian Contemplation*, rev. ed. (London: Continuum, 2012); Cynthia Bourgeault, *The Heart of Centering Prayer: Nondual Christianity in Theory and Practice* (Boulder, CO: Shambhala, 2016).

13 Andrew D. Lester, *The Angry Christian: A Theology for Care and Counseling* (Louisville, KY: Westminster John Knox Press, 2003), 95.

14 Lars Svendsen, *A Philosophy of Fear* (London: Reaktion Books, 2008), 71.

15 Robert C. Fuller, *Wonder: From Emotion to Spirituality* (Chapel Hill: University of North Carolina Press, 2006), 11.

16 Abraham Joshua Heschel, *God in Search of Man: A Philosophy of Judaism* (New York: Farrar, Straus and Giroux, 1955), 45. I am grateful to my college Dan Smith for making this connection to Heschel's "radical amazement."

17 Fuller, *Wonder*, 12.

18 Martha Nussbaum, *Upheavals of Thought: The Intelligence of Emotions* (Cambridge, UK: Cambridge University Press, 2001), cited in Fuller, *Wonder*, 20.

19 Fuller, *Wonder*, 60.

20 Fuller, *Wonder*, 63.

21 Dianna Butler Bass, *Grateful: The Transformative Power of Giving Thanks* (New York: HarperOne, 2018), 43.

22 Bass, *Grateful*, xxiv.

23 Mary Jo Leddy, *Radical Gratitude* (Maryknoll, NY: Orbis, 2002), 4, 6.

24 Bass, *Grateful*, xxiv.

25 Bass, *Grateful*, xxv.

26 Bass, *Grateful*, xxvi.

27 Bass, *Grateful*, 53.

28 Leddy, *Radical Gratitude*, 23.

29 Bass, *Grateful*, 34.

30 Robert Emmons, "Why Gratitude Is Good," *Greater Good Magazine*, November 16, 2010, https://greatergood.berkeley.edu/article/item/why_gratitude_is_good.

31 Jones, *Spirit in Session*, loc. 2209–20.

32 Many other spiritual practices connecting us to the wider web of life can be found in Lyanda Lynn Haupt, *Rooted: Life at the Crossroads of Science, Nature, and Spirit* (New York: Little, Brown Spark, 2021), and Randy Woodley, *Becoming Rooted: One Hundred Days of Connecting with Sacred Earth* (Minneapolis: Broadleaf Books, 2022).

33 For a helpful treatment of spiritual care for youth amid the climate disaster, see Talitha Amadea Aho, *In Deep Water: Spiritual Care for Youth People in a Climate Crisis* (Minneapolis: Fortress, 2022).

34 Glenn A. Albrecht, *Earth Emotions: New Words for a New World* (Ithaca, NY: Cornell University Press, 2019), 38. This sense of grief is a bit different from the grief we experience at the loss of an animal companion. For those wishing to become better able to provide compassionate care amid the loss of beloved pets, I highly recommend Sarah A. Bowen, *Sacred Sendoffs: An Animal Chaplain's Advice for Surviving Animal Loss, Making Life Meaningful, and Healing the Planet* (Rhinebeck, NY: Monkfish, 2022).

APPENDIX I

ORGANIZING SPIRITUAL CARE FIRST AID IN YOUR COMMUNITY

Spiritual care first aid skills can be meaningfully developed and practiced by individuals. But the power of these skills can be amplified by an organized effort within a community of faith to teach the skills broadly within the life of the community—not just to specialists or people who sign up to join a team of caregivers—as well as by organizing a cadre of people within the community who sense a calling to do more of this work and who are committed to enhancing their skill development and being accountable to the community in their practice of care.

There is no one right way to organize a spiritual care team in your church or community. Stephen Ministries is one popular way that many congregations have chosen to organize care teams within congregations. This ministry offers materials and trainings for organizing, equipping, and supervising a team of congregation members to provide one-to-one care in a Christian context. The training is in depth and extensive and requires a substantial commitment on behalf of the congregation and its designated lay caregivers to undertake this training and implementation. It is a ministry that has been deeply appreciated by many congregations over the decades (learn more at stephenministries.org).

Another helpful approach rooted in a narrative practice of caregiving and developed by two veteran pastoral theologians can be found in *Lay Pastoral Care: A Narrative Approach* by Christie Cozad Neuger and Joretta L. Marshall (Minneapolis: Fortress, 2022). Neuger and Marshall present skills for lay caregivers and provide guidance for congregations in cultivating collaborative learning communities to hone these caring skills. Theirs is a usable guide to developing networks of care that can provide spiritual care within congregational settings. This is an invaluable resource for faith communities wishing to begin lay caregiving teams.

Here, I offer you a menu of options that could be useful for faith communities attempting to bring some organization to the ways that spiritual care first aid is offered within your community. Not all ideas will work for every community, and you may come across ideas that would work if tweaked a bit to fit your own context. Feel free to use this list as a menu of experiments that you may wish to try, or let these ideas spark better ideas for you as you plan an all-hands approach to spiritual care first aid in your community. Each of the possibilities for organizing spiritual care first aid in your community can be added to any other possibility.

NO TEAM, JUST SERVICE

Many faith communities find themselves at their limit for developing new teams and committees. That's an understandable predicament for congregations that are engaged in a wide variety of robust ministries. Any time a group of people forms a community, however, there are care needs that will arise. One of the helpful and practical functions that churches serve in the lives of congregants is the presence of a community that notices when one among them is in need and comes together to help fulfill that need as best they can.

Even if you decide that your faith community isn't quite ready to form a dedicated team of spiritual care first responders, it is possible to organize yourselves in advance to address the many needs that arise within your community. Three key areas comprise frequently occurring needs in most congregations: meals, medical companionship, and prayer partners.

Knowing that these needs frequently arise in most congregations, you can plan ahead by developing a cadre of people who have alerted you—the pastor, volunteer coordinator, or care ministry coordinator—that they are willing and able to help when the need arises. Once or twice a year, at least, have a sign-up list for your congregation outlining these three areas of service, knowing that anyone signing up on that list isn't singing up to be on a team. They are just indicating their willingness to be called on when needed for one specific form of care, likely just a couple of times a year if the list is robust enough. Here are some sample ways of describing these areas of service:

- Culinary compassion: From time to time, folks in the congregation experience brief periods when it is difficult to prepare meals for themselves, for example, during a sickness or after a surgery or through a particularly acute mental health crisis. In these times, it can be a meaningful gesture of compassion to bring someone a meal or to go grocery shopping for them when they are unable to go for themselves. If you would be willing to be called on by [the pastor, the care coordinator, etc.] from time to time to provide a meal for someone or to pick up someone's groceries when they are unable to leave the house, please sign up for this cadre of culinary compassion providers.
- Medical accompaniment: When going in for a medical appointment or procedure, it can sometimes be comforting to have a friend by your side. Sometimes it's just the need for a ride to an appointment when one doesn't have a car or doesn't drive. Occasionally, it's the compassion of a companion during an anxiety-inducing appointment that is desired. At other times, it's necessary to have some accompaniment when one is undergoing mild anesthesia and needs someone to help them get home. If you would be willing to accompany others to a medical appointment on occasion, please sign up to be on this list of caregivers. Please note whether you are able to drive when needed or if you are only able to accompany people to medical appointments when driving isn't necessary. Either way, we would love to have you as a part of this network of support!
- Prayer companions: Sometimes what one needs most is to know that someone else knows what's going on in their life. When a congregant is going through a particularly difficult period or a time of waiting and unknowing, it can be helpful to have someone who simply knows what's going on and commits to hold that person in prayer. That's all. And that can be a lot! There's no obligation to meet together or to provide lengthy

> conversation. The only expectation for those in this network of caregivers is that if you are contacted by [the pastor, the care coordinator, etc.] to be a prayer companion for someone and you say yes, you speak with this person to understand what is going on, and then you commit to praying for them in the coming days. That can be a genuine gift.

You may think of other needs that regularly arise within your faith community that you would like to add to this list. Just keep in mind that if you are not forming a team or a dedicated group of people who are going to hone their spiritual caregiving skills and have regular consultation with one another and, perhaps, with a pastor or other ministry leader, then keep the care tasks you add to this list simple and able to be provided in a one-off fashion with no long-term commitments to a caring companionship with a careseeker.

Finally, one or two key point persons are needed to make this approach to caring support work. This might be the pastor or another minister in the congregation, or it may be a layperson who senses a call to coordinate care. These point people should not volunteer to provide all the caring support the congregation needs. That defeats the purpose of an all-hands approach and can be a recipe for burnout.

Rather, the point person(s) should simply be the list keepers and communication generators of the cadre of caring support. When a care need is made known to the pastor or other care ministry point person, that person can send a request to the appropriate list—meals, medical accompaniment, prayer companionship—to inquire about availability to meet the need in question and then simply connect the person volunteering to meet the care need with the person seeking caring support. It's a simple and lean approach to care within a faith community but one that can have a significant impact on the lives of those in the community facing difficulties.

DEVELOPING A TEAM OF TRAINED SPIRITUAL CARE FIRST AID RESPONDERS

You may choose to name this cohort differently—a care team, caring companions, or something similar—but the purpose would be to support the work of spiritual care within the congregation or community when needs arise among individuals and families. This book, the Neuger and Marshall text, and Stephen Ministries are ideal training tools for such a care team. Here are a few considerations that your faith community needs to work through to make such an idea a reality:

- Purpose: The purpose of this type of care team should be well defined. The purpose of the cohort of care responders should be clear to the congregation or community, and the role of the care responders should be clear to anyone serving on the team. A clearly defined purpose and scope of practice are an important consideration of boundaries for care responders.

  For example, a purpose advertised to the congregation or community might be to provide an intentional one-on-one caring relationship with a layperson especially trained to be a caring, less anxious presence with a person in the congregation who requests this type of relationship during a time of difficulty. This is not a counseling relationship but a partnership of spiritual companionship between peers for short-term caring conversations in times of difficulty, discernment, or spiritual need.

- Leader, Facilitator, or Point Person: Either a pastor or minister in the congregation or one or two people on the care team may be designated as the coordinator of the spiritual care cohort. The coordinator's role and responsibility would include seeking out suitable training opportunities for the cohort to engage in on a periodic basis to keep up their care-responding skills as well as being the contact person for the companioning program.

- Supervision or Consultation: This is another important role that may be fulfilled by the leader or facilitator if that person is highly trained in spiritual care, or this role may be fulfilled by an outside resource that the team brings in as a periodic consultant. For example, an external consultant may be a local therapist, a hospital chaplain or chaplaincy educator, a pastoral care professor at a local seminary, or a retired pastor who has specialized skills in pastoral care. It is helpful for the congregation's care team and its facilitator(s) to have someone they can call on with training in pastoral care or counseling who can talk the team and/or one of its members through any sticky situation that may arise. This consultant may also be someone who can provide periodic training updates for the team. An external consultant should be compensated for periodic consultancy services or any team training or supervision that is provided.

- Process: After an initial contact, the coordinator may speak with the congregant needing care to hear their hopes for a companioning relationship and to ask about people in the cohort whom the congregant may most wish to be paired with or wish not to be paired with. Once agreeing on a few suitable individuals, the coordinator would approach these companions to check their availability and connect the congregant with the companion selected. Finally, a determination needs to be made about the time constraints of the companioning relationship so that the one-on-one meetings aren't presumed to go on forever into the future.
- Training: The spiritual care team cohort should engage in regular training in the basics of a caregiving relationship: active listening, asking helpful questions, assessing for the presence of a mental health concerns or intentions to harm oneself or someone else, etc. These skills could be honed through in-house workshops by workshop leaders from the congregation with professional skills in these areas; they could be provided by the pastor or another minister, or training could be provided by seeking out external trainers (including any person who has been contracted to provide supervision and consultation). Several churches in a geographic area or denominational network may also wish to jointly hold training sessions like this.

Ideally, if the team is using this book as a training resource, each chapter should be read together and discussed using the questions and practice exercises at the end of each chapter. If the team meets monthly for educational conversations and training, one chapter could be read each month, providing for a fifteen-month training schedule for the team, or a few of the chapters could be combined for a twelve-month schedule. After this, the book could be started again as a refresher for continuing team members and to bring new members up to date on training. The team could also select any of the resources listed at the end of each chapter in the Further Reading section to use as training materials after this book is completed.

AS-NEEDED CARING CIRCLES

Some communities may find it difficult to maintain a team of spiritual care responders who can engage in one-on-one care. Yet needs arise that call for special expressions of care beyond those which can be provided by the pastor or staff ministers. These situations may be long-term illnesses, especially traumatic losses, periods when a mental health concern becomes especially difficult, or any number of other concerns that may arise in life. During these times, the pastor or other congregational leader and the person experiencing the situation would invite a small cadre of 3–4 people to form a time-limited ad hoc care circle to serve as an extension of the congregation's care. These as-needed care circles are time-limited and focused on a specific special situation that calls for care.

Ideally, people who make up these time-limited as-needed care circle would have some basic training in spiritual care skills such as reading this book or one like it. Or, at the very least, people called on to engage in this type of ad hoc care would be those whom the pastor or other ministry leader knows to be capable of providing a less anxious, nondirective presence with others in need of care, who can companion the careseeker with compassion and maintain the boundaries of this time-limited, ad hoc approach to caring companionship.

Here are a few guidelines for how such a team might operate in the provision of care:

- The person for whom the ad hoc care circle was created should be seen as the director of the care that is offered. That is to say, this person is the center of the care circle and knows best what type of care they most need, whether an occasional check-in via email, phone call, in-person visit, occasional meal, ride to a medical appointment, and so forth. An initial conversation between the circle members and the careseeker should open conversation about the nature and type of care needed. There should also be occasional check-ins about whether the type of care is best meeting the needs of the care receiver and adjustments made as a result of these conversations. In other words, the care receiver is not the object of the circle's care but is at the circle's center—the one around whom members gather in compassion.

- The ad hoc care circle is a time-limited commitment in response to a unique situation calling for special care. After the first three months, the care receiver, care circle, and pastor or care ministry coordinator should consult about next steps to determine:
    - Whether a care circle is still needed to address the initial situation. For example, in situations of long-term health concerns like cancer treatment, a care circle may companion the careseeker through the duration of their treatment. In other situations like a congregant experiencing a traumatic loss of a child or an especially difficult bout of depression, three months may be the duration of this type of care circle with a check-in at the end of that period to see if continued companionship is needed or desired.
    - Whether the care circle, if it continues, needs a shift in make-up of team members. Some circle members may wish to step away after the first agreed-on timeframe has ended. If so, another person may need to be brought into the circle if further companionship is needed.
    - What other resource of the congregation might be needed if the situation is ongoing. During a long-term illness, many needs may arise for the careseeker and their family. Examples include meals, financial assistance, or navigating the health-care system. Any of these may be beyond the capacity or desire of the care circle to provide themselves. Thus, other resources within the congregation and beyond may need to be garnered to help expand the care provided for the

careseeker. As always, be attentive to the needs for referral to professional care resources if needed.

- The members of the care circle operate as a team. They are each people whom the careseeker trusts to enter into this caregiving relationship. They are not individuals each offering parallel care but a team collaborating to cultivate a caring response to the situation the careseeker is addressing. Thus, the circle members should covenant with the careseeker and pastor or care ministry coordinator to keep confidential their knowledge of the careseeker's situation and what is shared among the careseeker, pastor, and the circle members, unless the careseeker instructs otherwise, for example, when certain details are requested to be shared in community prayers. But as a covenanted care circle, each of the members should be free to share among themselves information pertinent to the care of the careseeker in order to build better collaborative approaches to care and should be free to consult with the pastor or care ministry coordinator about ongoing care needs. As always, keep in mind the periodic need for referral when situations arise that are beyond the care circle's capacity.
- The pastor or other minister providing care in this situation should be a continued resource to both the care circle members and the careseeker throughout the duration of the care circle. While the pastor or other minister may not be a consistent member of the care circle, they continue to serve in their pastoral role with the careseeker and as a consultant to the care circle.

AS-NEEDED DISCERNMENT CIRCLES

There are instances when a congregant or community member faces a question for discernment to make a difficult decision or determine a new life course. Sometimes these concerns arise out of ongoing decision-making about an educational or vocational pathway that is unfolding. Other times, these concerns arise out of an attempt to make meaning of a new stage or phase in life.

While many of these conversations are helpfully addressed in one-to-one pastoral conversations, bringing others into the discernment process may be a helpful next step. When bringing other community members into the process, care must be taken to ensure that those who are invited into the discernment circle are clear about how to listen deeply, provide a less anxious caring presence, and ask helpful, nondirective, open-ended questions. This is absolutely not an advice-giving circle.

Discernment circles are intended to include 3–4 people of the wider church or faith community. The person engaging in the discernment process should have a say in whom they wish to invite into this process alongside them. The duration of these discernment circles should be established up front, likely meeting 1–3 times for an hour or an hour and a half per meeting or two hours for a single meeting.

The following process and guidelines will be followed to establish an intentional discernment conversation for a congregant wishing to engage in a discernment circle.

Process for Organizing Discernment Circle Conversations

- The pastor or coordinator will reach out to the invited discernment circle members, sharing a brief bit of information about the congregant and their situation of discernment, outline the guidelines, and answer any questions that may arise.
- The pastor or coordinator puts the congregant and the other circle members into contact with one another to set up a time and place for the conversation for a minimum of a 2-hour window of time if this is a one-time conversation or shorter periods of 1–1.5 hours if the circle is meeting two or three times.
- The pastor or coordinator may or may not be a part of the intentional discernment group.

Guidelines for Conversations

- Begin with a moment of centering—a time of silence to bring one's full self and centered attention into the room; a brief prayer offered by one of the circle members; or any other centering ritual that is decided on by the group.

- The pace of the conversation should be gentle and guided by the focal person. Periodically, the group should check and ask questions like "Are we talking about the things you most wanted to talk about in this conversation?" or "Are we going at a comfortable pace in our dialogue?"

- The focal person should have some uninterrupted time at the outset of the conversation to describe their situation and their questions of discernment.

- The primary mode of conversation should be open-ended questions. Avoid advice or leading questions. Allow your genuine compassionate curiosity about the focal person and their emerging pathway to guide circle members in asking helpful questions.

- The focal person can decide which questions they wish to address in the group. Some questions they may wish to record for later reflection. Still others they may wish to sit with in silence for a few minutes before moving on. Be comfortable with brief periods of silence.

- When the group's agreed-on time is coming to an end, leave space for spoken gratitude, such as:

  What made you, whether you're the focal person or a group member, grateful about being a part of this conversation?

  What did you, as a group member, come to appreciate or admire about the focal person and the way that they are approaching this process of discernment?

  What did you, as the focal person, appreciate about this process that you want to name aloud?

- After the intentional discernment conversation has ended, allow any further conversation to be initiated by the focal

> person. It will be natural, as members of the same congregation, to reach out to the focal person with concern. That's okay. Just let those be general inquiries into their well-being and not specifically about the topic of discernment unless invited by the focal person to discuss that matter further.

Such discernment practice might emerge into something that isn't organized on an ad hoc basis but develops into a regular group that meets periodically for people who desire to talk about their sense of calling, their vocational and educational pathways, or career decisions with others in faithful community. These groups may be modeled on the Quaker practice of the clearness committee, which holds many of the same values and practices but with a more robust framework honed within Quaker communities.[1]

NOTES

1 See Parker J. Palmer, "The Clearness Committee: A Communal Approach to Discernment," Center for Courage and Renewal, accessed June 25, 2024, https://couragerenewal.org/wp-content/uploads/2022/06/Parker-Palmer_Clearness-Committee.pdf.

APPENDIX II

HELPFUL ORGANIZATIONS AND RESOURCES

Part of becoming a skillful caregiver is knowing where to search for resources when you encounter a care need that you're unsure how to adequately address on your own. You do not need to be an expert on every situation that calls for care. You should have a list of local professional caregivers and both local and national resources with which you can consult and to which you can refer in the ministry of introduction.

This appendix offers sources of exploration and continuing education to cultivate your caregiving skills. It also invites you to fill in local resources in your community that may become helpful to others during your caregiving practice in congregation and community. Please take time to research these local organizations and resources and record information about them for easy access when a need arises.

AGING

US Health and Human Services Aging Resources Listed by State

www.hhs.gov/aging/state-resources/index.html

AARP Fraud Watch Network

Provides up-to-date information on scams and fraud targeting elders.

www.aarp.org/money/scams-fraud

American Bar Association Reporting Elder Abuse (State-by-State Resources)

www.americanbar.org/groups/senior_lawyers/resources/reporting-elder-abuse/

Consumer Financial Protection Bureau

www.consumerfinance.gov

Provides helpful resources on fair treatment and protection on financial concerns, including concerns related to:

Help for Agents under a Power of Attorney:
https://files.consumerfinance.gov/f/201310_cfpb_lay_fiduciary_guides_agents.pdf

Help for Guardians:
https://files.consumerfinance.gov/f/201310_cfpb_lay_fiduciary_guides_guardians.pdf

Help for Trustees:
https://files.consumerfinance.gov/f/201310_cfpb_lay_fiduciary_guides_trustees.pdf

Eldercare Locator

www.eldercare.acl.gov/Public/Index.aspx

National Center on Elder Abuse

Provides resources on training, policy, and best practices on preventing and responding to elder abuse.

www.ncea.acl.gov

Preventing Elder Abuse, Assault, and Theft

www.seniorliving.org/research/preventing-elder-abuse/

Local Council or City/County/State Agency on Aging / Senior Services

Address:
Phone:
Website:
Services Provided:

Local Elder Abuse Reporting Agency

Contact Information:

CHILD ABUSE AND DOMESTIC VIOLENCE

Faith Trust Institute (for education and training in communities of faith)

www.faithtrustinstitute.org

DomesticShelters.org (domestic violence shelter locator by zip code)

Note that the address/location of domestic violence shelters are often not provided on a website to protect clients who may be staying there and fleeing violent situations.

www.domesticshelters.org

National Domestic Violence Hotline:

Operates 24 hours a day, 7 days a week, 365 days a year. The National Domestic Violence Hotline provides tools and support to help survivors of domestic violence. Trained advocates offer free, confidential support; crisis intervention information; education; and referral services in over 200 languages.

1-800-799-SAFE (7233)

www.thehotline.org

Prevent Child Abuse America (National Organization with State Chapters)

Information and resources for the prevention of child abuse

www.preventchildabuse.org

Safe Church Policy Resources

Lutheran Social Services of MN:

www.lssmn.org/services/youth/education/cherish-all-children/churches/safe-church-policies

Safe Church Resources (Mennonite Church USA):

www.mennoniteusa.org/ministry/church-vitality/safe-church/safe-church-resources/

Thrive Safer Churches Abuse Prevention (Christian Reformed Church):

https://www.crcna.org/SafeChurch/abuse-prevention

Your Denomination's Resource Page:

Zero Abuse Project

Education, training, advocacy, and victim support addressing child sexual abuse.

www.zeroabuseproject.org

Local Domestic Violence Shelter

Contact Information:

Local Child Protection Services

Contact Information:

CAREGIVING SKILLS CONTINUING EDUCATION

Mental Health First Aid (for trainings and resources on mental health and substance abuse)

mentalhealthfirstaid.org

Psychological First Aid Online Course (American Red Cross)
www.redcross.org/take-a-class/coronavirus-information/psychological-first-aid-online-course
Stephen Ministries (training for congregations and lay caregivers)
stephenministries.org

DEATH

Conservation Burial Alliance (information on burial that supports preservation and restoration of land)
www.conservationburialalliance.org/
Death Café (information on a simple method to gather people to discuss death)
deathcafe.com
Green Burial Council (information on places where families can practice green or natural burial)
greenburialcouncil.org
National Home Funeral Alliance (information on how families can provide death care in their own homes for their loved ones)
homefuneralalliance.org
The Order of the Good Death (for articles and death-positivity resources)
orderofthegooddeath.com
Local Funeral Director I Trust to Recommend:
Name of Funeral Home:
Name of Funeral Director(s):
Location:
Phone:
Website:

FOOD ASSISTANCE

Feeding America Find Your Local Food Bank
www.feedingamerica.org/find-your-local-foodbank
FoodPantries.org (find food pantries by city and state)
www.foodpantries.org/
Find Food Pantries (US Department of Housing and Urban Development)
www.hud.gov/findshelter/foodpantries

Supplemental Nutrition Assistance Program (SNAP)
www.fns.usda.gov/snap/supplemental-nutrition-assistance-program
Local Food Pantry
Address:
Days/Hours:
Phone:
Website:
Local Free Meal Program
Address:
Days/Hours:
Phone:
Website:

LGBTQ+ RESOURCES

Denominational LGBTQ+ Resource Organizations (with church locators)
Affirmation (Mormon): affirmation.org
Association of Welcoming and Affirming Baptists: awab.org
DignityUSA (Catholic): dignityusa.org
Metropolitan Community Churches: visitmccchurch.com
More Light Presbyterians: mlp.org
Open and Affirming Coalition (UCC): openandaffirming.org
Reconciling Ministries (United Methodist): rmnetwork.org
Reconciling Works (Lutheran): reconcilingworks.org
Q Christian (multiple denominations): qchristian.org
Other:
Other:
Other:
Family Acceptance Project (resources for helping families embrace LGBTQ+ members)
https://familyproject.sfsu.edu
National Resource Center on LGBTQ+ Aging (SAGE)
www.lgbtagingcenter.org
PFLAG (network of meetings for parents, families, and allies supporting LGBTQ+ people)
pflag.org

PFLAG Meeting Nearest My Community (locate via above website)

Address:

Contact Information:

Trevor Project Resources for Supporting LGBTQ+ Youth

www.thetrevorproject.org/resources/

MENTAL HEALTH AND COUNSELING RESOURCES

Find a Therapist (Psychology Today)

Site provides listing of licensed therapists searchable by city or zip code with a brief description of the provider's training, credentials, and practice. Always further investigate potential referral sources on your own before adding them to your referral source list.

www.psychologytoday.com/us/therapists

National Alliance on Mental Illness (NAMI) (resources for mental health support)

www.nami.org

National Institute of Mental Health (NIMH) (resources for mental health information)

www.nimh.nih.gov

Local Crisis Mental Health Center:

Address:

Phone:

Website:

Services Provided:

Local Counselor I Trust as a Referral Source:

Address:

Phone:

Website:

Specialty Areas (e.g., couples, families, LGBTQ+, etc.):

Local Counselor I Trust as a Referral Source:

Address:

Phone:

Website:

Specialty Areas (e.g., couples, families, LGBTQ+, etc.):

HOMELESS SERVICES AND SHELTERS

Covenant House (largest privately funded childcare agency in the United States; shelters and services)

www.covenanthouse.org

Find Shelter Locator (US Department of Housing and Urban Development)

This site can be used to locate shelters, food pantries, health clinics, and clothing distribution centers in your area, as well as information on rental assistance, housing vouchers, and other services.

www.hud.gov/findshelter

Homeless Shelters Directory (nationwide director of shelters and services)

www.homelessshelterdirectory.org

National Center for Homeless Education

nche.ed.gov

Shelter/Resources Finder: www.nche.ed.gov/shelter/

ShelterListings.org (searchable list of housing resources by city and state)

www.shelterlistings.org

Local City/County/State Shelter Locator

Website:

Local Homeless Shelter

Phone:

Address:

Populations Serviced (e.g., adults only, youth only, families, etc.):

Type of Entry (e.g., first-come-first-served, lottery system, referral system, etc.):

Local Homeless Shelter

Phone:

Address:

Populations Serviced (e.g., adults only, youth only, families, etc.):

Type of Entry (e.g., first-come-first-served, lottery system, referral system, etc.):

SPIRITUAL DIRECTORS

Spiritual Directors International

Helpful in finding a trained spiritual director or spiritual companion offering services in various regions of the world.

www.sdicompanions.org

Local Spiritual Director

Name:

Phone:

Address:

Fee:

SPIRITUALITY RESOURCES

Prayer Resources (The Upper Room)

www.upperroom.org/resources/category/prayer

Spirituality and Practice Alphabet of Spiritual Literacy

Exploration of spiritual practices from multiple religious and spiritual traditions.

www.spiritualityandpractice.com/practices/alphabet/

SUBSTANCE ABUSE RESOURCES

Substance Abuse and Mental Health Services Administration (SAMHSA)'s National Helpline: 1-800-662-HELP (4357)

SAMHSA's National Helpline is a free, confidential, 24/7, 365-day-a-year treatment referral and information service (in English and Spanish) for individuals and families facing mental and/or substance use disorders.

Al-Anon Meeting Finder (Family and Friends of Alcoholics)

www.al-anon.org

Alcoholics Anonymous Meeting Finder

www.aa.org

Narcotics Anonymous Meeting Finder

www.na.org

Online Alcoholics Anonymous Meeting Finder

www.aa-intergroup.org/meetings/

Online/Phone Narcotics Anonymous Meeting Finder

www.virtual-na.org/

Local Substance Abuse Treatment Center:

Address:

Phone:

Local 12-Step Meetings:

1. Meeting Type (AA, NA, Al-Anon, etc.):
Day/Time:
Address:
2. Meeting Type (AA, NA, Al-Anon, etc.):
Day/Time:
Address:
3. Meeting Type (AA, NA, Al-Anon, etc.):
Day/Time:
Address:

SUICIDE

National Suicide Prevention Lifeline

Lifeline: 988
Website: 988lifeline.org

When people call, text, or chat 988, they will be connected to trained counselors who are part of the existing Lifeline network. These trained counselors will listen, understand how their problems are affecting them, and provide support. Dialing or texting the 988 number will connect callers throughout the United States to call centers in their state and offer state-specific resources.

Crisis Text Line (free, 24/7 support for those in crisis)

Website: CrisisTextLine.org
English Support: Text HOME to 741741
Spanish Support: text AYUDA to 741741
Support for young persons of color: text STEVE to 741741

Trans Lifeline (transgender specific)—not a 24-hour service

Website: translifeline.org
US Lifeline: 877-565-8860
Canada Lifeline: 877-330-6366

Trevor Project (LGBTQ-specific)

Lifeline: 866-488-7386 (also available via chat and text)
Website: thetrevorproject.org

Suicide Prevention Resource Center (for information and resources on suicide)

sprc.org

Local/State Suicide Prevention Lifeline or Resources

Phone:

Website:

LIST OTHER RESOURCES IMPORTANT TO YOUR CARING MINISTRY